D0322084

LRC Stoke Park
GUILDFORD COLLEGE

A Guide to Practitioner Research in Education

Education at SAGE

SAGE is a leading international publisher of journals, books, and electronic media for academic, educational, and professional markets.

Our education publishing includes:

- accessible and comprehensive texts for aspiring education professionals and practitioners looking to further their careers through continuing professional development

- inspirational advice and guidance for the classroom

- authoritative state of the art reference from the leading authors in the field

Find out more at: **www.sagepub.co.uk/education**

A Guide to Practitioner Research in Education

Ian Menter, Dely Elliot, Moira Hulme,
Jon Lewin and Kevin Lowden

Los Angeles | London | New Delhi
Singapore | Washington DC

370.72
MEN
186663

RESEARCHSKILLS

© Ian Menter, Dely Elliot, Moira Hulme, Jon Lewin
and Kevin Lowden 2011

Apart from any fair dealing for the purposes of research or
private study, or criticism or review, as permitted under the
Copyright, Designs and Patents Act, 1988, this publication
may be reproduced, stored or transmitted in any form, or
by any means, only with the prior permission in writing of
the publishers, or in the case of reprographic reproduction, in
accordance with the terms of licences issued by the Copyright
Licensing Agency. Enquiries concerning reproduction outside
those terms should be sent to the publishers.

SAGE Publications Ltd
1 Oliver's Yard
55 City Road
London EC1Y 1SP

SAGE Publications Inc.
2455 Teller Road
Thousand Oaks, California 91320

SAGE Publications India Pvt Ltd
B 1/I 1 Mohan Cooperative Industrial Area
Mathura Road
New Delhi 110 044

SAGE Publications Asia-Pacific Pte Ltd
33 Pekin Street #02-01
Far East Square
Singapore 048763

Library of Congress Control Number: 2010931092

British Library Cataloguing in Publication data

A catalogue record for this book is available from the British Library

ISBN 978-1-84920-184-1
ISBN 978-1-84920-185-8 (pbk)

Typeset by C&M Digitals (P) Ltd, Chennai, India
Printed in Great Britain by MPG Books Group, Bodmin, Cornwall
Printed on paper from sustainable resources

MIX
Paper from
responsible sources
FSC® C018575

Contents

WITHDRAWN

About the authors

The team of authors are all within the School of Education at the University of Glasgow and have significant experience of working with practitioner researchers in education. Two of the team (Hulme and Menter) are based within the Pedagogy, Policy and Practice group in the School and the others (Elliot, Lewin and Lowden) are or were located within the SCRE Centre. The SCRE Centre was formed in 2001 following a merger between the Scottish Council for Research in Education and the University of Glasgow Faculty of Education. The SCRE team have a long and distinguished track record in supporting teacher researchers in Scotland. The authors worked together on a major national action research project funded by The Scottish Government over 3-4 years, entitled *Research to Support Schools of Ambition*. Their other relevant experiences are indicated in the individual thumbnail sketches below.

Dely Lazarte Elliot

Dely is one of the researchers at the SCRE Centre, School of Education, University of Glasgow. She is part of the MSc Psychological Studies team, lecturing in Educational Psychology and supervising postgraduate students at both Master's and PhD levels. Dely's first degree was from the University of Santo Tomas (Manila). She started her career in Thailand as a kindergarten and primary teacher, subsequently lecturing and doing an MSc at Assumption University (Bangkok) before pursuing a PhD at the University of Nottingham. Dely has been involved in a number of research projects at both national and international levels and has had considerable experience delivering research methods workshops to school and college practitioners and mentoring them as they undertake small-scale and/or action research (e.g. Focus on Learning, Schools of Ambition).

Moira Hulme

Moira is a lecturer in Educational Research at the University of Glasgow. She was Project Coordinator of *Research to Support Schools of Ambition* (2006–10). This post builds on previous experience as a lecturer and teacher educator supporting pre- and in-service teachers-as-researchers at universities in England and Scotland. She has authored a number of publications in the area of teacher education and development and currently leads a range of Practitioner Enquiry and Decision Making courses at the University of Glasgow, where she is co-Director of the Chartered Teacher programme.

Jon Lewin

Jon is the Information Officer in the Research Office at the College of Social Sciences, University of Glasgow. He has worked in the area of information provision and dissemination for about 15 years, and has a particular interest in the use of new and traditional technologies to increase participation in, and disseminate, research to a range of audiences. His work at SCRE includes the development and maintenance of databases, and the design of and support for a number of web-based initiatives to promote participation in SCRE research. He is also involved in design and editorial support of all SCRE's published output, including the SCRE website, research reports and briefing papers for practitioners. He has a particular interest in information design and its impact on the communicability of research findings. In addition, he provides a wide range of information services for the research staff of SCRE, and handles information enquiries from the public and the media relating to all aspects of educational research.

Kevin Lowden

Kevin is currently a Research Fellow at the SCRE Centre at the School of Education, University of Glasgow. Since joining SCRE in 1987, he has been involved with and led a wide range of national and international research and evaluation projects. While the focus of the research has varied over time to include: lifelong learning and skills; health education; promoting opportunities for disadvantaged groups and school transformation, a common aim has been to produce findings that inform policy and practice in education. Most recently he has worked with other colleagues in the School of Education to research and support major school transformation initiatives (e.g. the Scottish Government's Schools of Ambition programme and the Hunter Foundation's 2020 programme). These projects included supporting practitioners to develop their professional skills in research and evaluation and enhancing the capacity of their schools to self-evaluate. His chapters in this book reflect this wealth of research and mentoring experience.

Ian Menter

Ian is Professor of Teacher Education and formerly Deputy Dean of the Faculty of Education, University of Glasgow. He worked as a primary school teacher in Bristol for nine years before entering higher education, holding posts at the University of Gloucestershire, the University of the West of England, London Metropolitan University (Head of the School of Education) and the University of the West of Scotland (Dean of the Faculty of Education and Media). He has been President of the Scottish Educational Research Association and an elected member of the Executive Council of the British Educational Research Association, is a Special Professor at the University of Nottingham and an Academician of the Academy of Social Sciences.

Foreword

Teachers, lecturers and a range of other education practitioners are increasingly being encouraged to develop their professionalism through adopting an enquiring approach to their work. For example, newly qualified teachers in England are now getting the opportunity to study for a Master's in Teaching and Learning (MTL). Experienced teachers in Scotland can now follow a programme to become a Chartered Teacher and a similar scheme has been piloted in Wales. Students who are studying to become schoolteachers or lecturers are increasingly being given the opportunity to undertake small-scale research as part of their programmes of study.

This book has been written in order to provide a straightforward introduction to practitioner research that may be of value both to experienced teachers and to students in training as they begin to engage with enquiry into their own practice. The approach taken in this book was based on a series of short texts that were produced by the former Scottish Council for Research in Education (SCRE). These texts each focused on one particular aspect of small-scale research, such as questionnaires, literature review or interviews. The purpose of the present book is to bring together in a single and accessible volume a wider range of up-to-date advice for practitioner researchers.

The emphasis throughout has been on keeping the approach simple and manageable for practitioners who are new to research and are working or studying full-time. We have sought to be rigorous however and to ensure that we are encouraging high-quality research work. Where you may wish to go further with more ambitious techniques or concepts we have sought to provide guidance on where you may look.

The book has been written by a large team and while we each took the lead in different sections or on different aspects of the book, we have all shared the fundamental commitment to providing clear and focused advice for our readers. We have been greatly assisted in this by our two colleagues, John Hall and Stuart Hall, who played a significant part in laying down the original plans for the book and whose ideas have fed into our writing.

The writing team is based in the School of Education at the University of Glasgow and includes colleagues who have worked in the former SCRE – now the SCRE Centre – which had a long tradition of supporting teacher research across Scotland. In the recent past the team members have all collaborated on supporting teacher research, especially in a project entitled 'Research to Support Schools of Ambition'. At the time of completing this book, this project has recently come to a close. We have drawn heavily on the experience of that work and would like to thank all of the headteachers, teachers, students and others who have contributed to it as well as those with whom we have worked on a range of other similar projects over many years.

We also wish to thank Helen Fairlie, formerly of SAGE, our publishers, whose initial encouragement led to the development of this book. Finally, thanks to Marianne Lagrange and Monira Begum at SAGE for their patient and enthusiastic support as we have struggled (not always successfully!) to meet deadlines.

Ian Menter, Dely Elliot, Moira Hulme, Jon Lewin and Kevin Lowden
University of Glasgow

Acknowledgements

Department for Education and Employment (DfEE) (2000) *Best Practice Research Scholarships: Guidance Notes for Teacher Applications*. Nottingham: DfES Publications.

Baumfield, V. (2009) 'Practitioner inquiry: evaluating learning and teaching?' Paper presented at the Professional Practice Lecture Series, 6th August, Glasgow.

Figure 6.4: EndNote ® © 2010, Thomson Reuters.

Part 1

What is Research and Why Do It?

1

What is Research?

In this chapter we discuss what is meant by research, particularly in education. We examine the idea of 'practitioner research' and what it might mean for teachers, lecturers and other education professionals. This chapter introduces you to some of the key terms that will be used later in the book and gives you a sense of how best to make use of the book for your own setting.

Research, education and practitioner research

The word 'research' carries many meanings and can produce strong reactions.

'Research is just a load of theory.'
'I'd like to research this properly but I really don't have the time.'
'I'm an experienced teacher and I know what works in my classroom – I don't think research can do anything for me.'

These are some of the statements we have heard over many years of working with teachers, statements – even though they may sound negative – which have always led to very fruitful discussions.

In this book, where we set out to provide support, encouragement, advice and even inspiration to education practitioners in developing a research dimension to their work, we are hoping to dispel some of the more worrying misrepresentations of research and its application in educational settings.

It is certainly true that research can be defined in many different ways – each dictionary offers a different slant on the term.

A detailed study of a subject, especially in order to discover (new) information or reach a (new) understanding. *Cambridge Advanced Learner's On-line Dictionary*

Endeavour to discover new or collate old facts etc. by scientific study of a subject, course of critical investigation. *Oxford English Dictionary*

Careful, systematic, patient study and investigation in some field of knowledge, undertaken to discover or establish facts or principles. *yourdictionary.com*

In fact, there is very little agreement between these three – two emphasise finding something new, but the third indicates it can be about 'establishing' facts, that are perhaps already known, that is, confirming knowledge rather than discovering something original. Just one mentions scientific study. Between them they suggest the purpose is to find, variously: information, understanding; facts; facts or principles.

When we have asked teachers or student teachers to say what they think the word 'research' means, they do often mention words like investigation, data, surveys or theory. The way in which we wish to define research at the outset of this book is, we hope you will agree, relatively simple and will help as a reminder of three key elements in undertaking research in educational settings:

Research is systematic enquiry, the outcomes of which are made available to others.

The three elements to this are:

1 Enquiry – this can be taken to mean 'finding out' or 'investigating', trying to develop some new knowledge and understanding.
2 Systematic – for enquiry to be considered to be research, it is necessary that there is some order to the nature of the enquiry, that it has a rationale and an approach which can be explained and defended.
3 Sharing outcomes – the form in which the outcomes are disseminated may vary enormously, but the key point being made here is that, if it is only the researcher her/himself who is aware of the outcomes of the research, then the significance of the activity is very limited and may be better described as a form of reflection or personal enquiry, rather than research.

If one puts this general definition of research into the educational context for practitioners, one can elaborate it slightly by saying:

Practitioner research in education is systematic enquiry in an educational setting carried out by someone working in that setting, the outcomes of which are shared with other practitioners.

The additional elements of this definition are:

1 The qualifier '*practitioner* research'. This is taken to mean that the person or persons undertaking the research are both researching and practising, very often they are 'teacher researchers'. It is usually assumed that the research is being undertaken within the practitioner's own practice, although collaborative practitioner research may suggest a group of teacher researchers working together, investigating practice across a school or college or other educational setting.

2 The phrase 'in educational settings'. As implied above, this is usually taken to be a reference to classrooms, but at this stage it would be desirable to keep a fairly open view about its meaning. It could be interpreted, for example, to include activities in staff rooms, or enquiries with parents or other community members, or indeed to look into the practice of education policy-making, perhaps in local authorities or in government departments.

3 Outcomes to be shared with other practitioners. This relates primarily to the purposes of practitioner research. It is usually, perhaps almost always, the case, that those undertaking practitioner research are seeking to develop and improve their own practice. But this definition reminds us that it should be possible, indeed desirable, for others to benefit from hearing about and responding to the research that has been undertaken.

In this book we explore all of these themes in more detail and look at some of the challenges, opportunities and benefits that may be derived from practitioner research in education.

The term 'evaluation' is often used in educational settings and it is worth considering what the similarities and differences between research and evaluation may be. There is clearly a significant overlap between the terms and indeed many practitioners feel much more comfortable with 'evaluation', which they may see as an integral part of teaching, than they do with 'research', which they may see as an additional activity that somehow goes beyond teaching. Similarly, the term 'reflective teaching' has become very influential in professional discussions over recent years. In some ways this term has been used as a way of promoting an enquiring approach as an integral part of teaching, rather than imposing some sort of additional burden on teachers.

The term 'evaluation' in teaching is commonly used to describe a process through which teachers assess the effectiveness of what they have been doing in the classroom. Following a lesson or series of lessons we might be asking ourselves questions such as:

• What did the pupils/students learn?
• Did the methods that I used for teaching them work well?
• How might I improve my teaching next time?

Such questions can be applied in a simple or in a more complex way. So, 'What did the pupils learn?' may be answered simply by observing pupils' responses during the lesson, or by administering a test or other assessment procedure or by a more detailed investigation. The question about teaching methods implies other questions, such as 'What alternative teaching methods might I have used?' and 'How could I know whether they would be better or not without actually trying them?'

'Reflective teaching' is a term that certainly incorporates an idea of evaluation, but in most definitions is seeking to encourage an even more questioning approach. Typically, it involves teachers asking themselves some deeper questions, involving values. In other words as well as the kinds of questions listed above, we may also be asking ourselves:

- What is it important that these pupils/students should be learning?
- Is the way I am teaching consistent with my beliefs about learning and about the rights of pupils/students?

Such an orientation engages with the purposes of education and with explicit statements of values, as well as questions of effectiveness and efficiency/ efficacy. Reflective teaching is often depicted as a cyclical process, as represented in Figure 1.1.

Among the principles which underlie reflective teaching, according to Pollard and Tann (1993; from whom Figure 1.1 has been adapted) are:

Reflective teaching implies an active concern with aims and consequences as well as means and practical competence.

Reflective teaching requires competence in methods of classroom enquiry, to support the development of teaching competence.

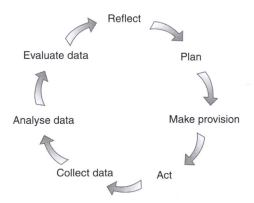

Figure 1.1 The reflective teaching cycle (adapted from Pollard and Tann, 1993)

Reflective teaching has been a very important concept in initial teacher education and evidence of its influence can be seen both in statements of standards for entry into teaching (especially in Wales, Scotland and Northern Ireland), and in the introduction of Master's-level work into teacher education courses. However, it is not only in initial teacher education that a reflective approach has become an important element. Increasingly, the *professional development* of serving teachers and lecturers has also been informed by these ideas. In many countries recent developments in continuing professional development (CPD) have explicitly called for teachers to reflect upon and learn from their practice. A number of research studies have shown how teacher development can be much more powerful when it is based on teachers' own practices (see Day, 1999; Reeves and Fox, 2008). Furthermore, a number of formal CPD schemes have demonstrated the effectiveness of such approaches. Examples in England would include the National Professional Qualification for Headteachers (NPQH), or in Scotland the Chartered Teacher Programme or the Scottish Qualification for Headship (SQH). It may also be that the development of the Master's in Teaching and Learning (MTL) in England will be based on similar approaches.

If we revisit the term 'practitioner research' in the light of these two other concepts, we can certainly say that evaluation and reflective teaching are deeply bound into practitioner research, but we might also suggest that there is more to it than either of those terms implies. The term 'teacher as researcher' emerged very much from the work of Lawrence Stenhouse in the 1960s and 1970s at a time, at least in England, when teachers played a much greater part in curriculum development than they did in the later part of the twentieth century. In his classic text, *An Introduction to Curriculum Research and Development*, published in 1975, Stenhouse sets out in some detail, a model of teacher as researcher. This model is based on a situation in which the teacher her/himself has considerable scope for determining aspects of the curriculum and considerable autonomy in deciding on pedagogical approaches to be deployed. The increasingly prescribed nature of the school curriculum in the UK during the 1980s and 1990s and indeed the control of many aspects of pedagogy led to a model such as this being more or less inoperable. However, recent relaxations in curriculum and pedagogy, such as those encouraged by initiatives relating to creativity in education in England or by curriculum reform in Scotland, create very real opportunities for revisiting and reworking ideas of these sorts.

Indeed, it would be very misleading to suggest that there had been no developments in teacher research during the last part of the twentieth century. Through the persistent and committed efforts of a number of teachers and lecturers the legacy of Stenhouse has given rise to a range of networks of practitioner research in education (some of these are listed at the end of this chapter). In particular the concept of *action research* has been developed to apply within an education setting. Having emerged originally in a community

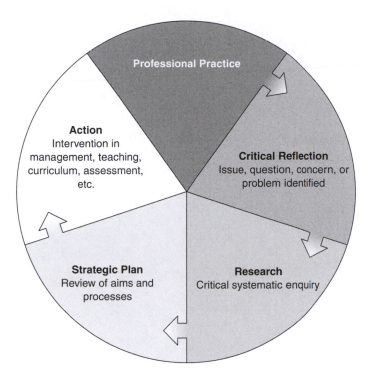

Figure 1.2 A cyclical model of action research

development setting, the notion of carrying out an 'intervention' and assessing its effects in order to refine future action has been very popular in writing about educational change. There are quite intense debates between various schools of thought each claiming the title 'action research', but all of them share a concept again – similar to reflective teaching – of cyclical or spiral development, often going through several iterations (see Figures 1.2 and 1.3).

Figure 1.2 shows the broader conception of action research for practitioners, while Figure 1.3 demonstrates an action research project in progress.

Practitioner research and the teaching profession

In our definition of research at the beginning of this chapter, one of the key elements was the dissemination, or as stated there 'sharing', of findings with others. While this is one of the key distinguishing elements that moves us beyond evaluation or reflective teaching, it is also one of the key elements in reminding us of the social nature of research activity. 'Sharing' is a form of learning for others as well as for the instigator of the research. But it is not necessarily the only social aspect of practitioner research. And the professional development that may be associated with practitioner research

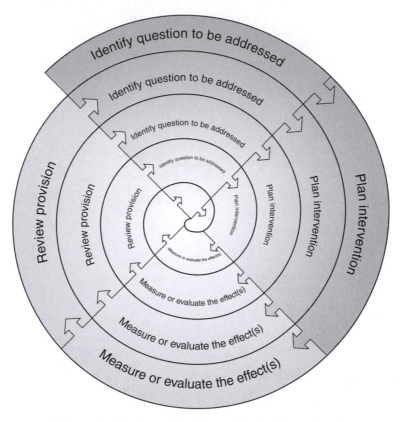

Figure 1.3   A spiral model of action research

may not be for individuals alone, it may well be professional development for a broader grouping of staff, for example, members of a subject department in a secondary school, a team of teachers and assistants in an early years setting, or an inter-institutional network of college lecturers. Furthermore, practitioner research may also be associated with other forms of development such as curriculum development or school/college development. It is to these wider matters of the social nature of practitioner research that we now turn.

   One of the key issues in any form of research is that of 'objectivity'. While we will be addressing this topic in much more detail later in the book (and seeing just how slippery a concept it is), at this point we will limit ourselves to the simple assertion that it is desirable that our research activity is unbiased and dispassionate (that is not to say that our own values are unimportant or that we should not have passion about our research). It is for this reason that many practitioners engaging in research have found enormous benefit in collaborating with others. Specifically, the engagement of a 'critical friend' to work alongside you has proved to be invaluable for many practitioner researchers. Throughout the research process, from initially defining the question you are addressing, through data gathering and analysis, to writing a report on your activity, it is valuable to be able to share your experiences with a colleague, especially one who is both familiar with the setting in which you are working, as well as having some experience themselves in practitioner research. That critical friend can ask questions of you and you can ask questions of her; this may lead to all kinds of insights into your research that might not otherwise arise.

If an individual practitioner researcher can be greatly assisted by the involvement of an individual critical friend, what are the implications of a more collaborative, team approach to research activity? The whole research process may be very different if a team is involved. From the outset, when a group of people are defining what the question to be investigated is, through the design and implementation of the enquiry, through to analysis and writing, discussion, negotiation and collaboration will be necessary. This does not mean that all members of a practitioner research team will be doing exactly the same things in their respective classrooms nor that their roles within the team will be identical. Indeed it may well be that different data collection methods are deployed in different locations and that each member of the team takes a leading role in particular phases of the research. But it does mean that there needs to be some coherence and shared sense of purpose and direction, in order for the research effort to achieve its potential as a collaborative venture.

Here is a description of a collaborative research project taking place in a Scottish secondary school.

The Leadership Group in school C identified four areas they wanted to investigate in a systematic manner. These areas were areas that had provoked some curiosity; they posed 'problems'/questions where there was a need for further information. The Leadership Group were also concerned to encourage the professional development of teachers at a relatively early stage of their teaching career (four to five years' experience). A group of teachers was convened to establish whether there was an interest in forming a research group to investigate the areas prioritised by senior management. A small group of teachers met with a member of the Research Support Team to explore ideas, strategies and methods. Each teacher took responsibility for preparing a draft plan for one line of enquiry. Through an iterative process, with support from the external research mentor, research plans were formulated for each project. The teachers accepted a modest honorarium for the additional work involved in leading these strands of enquiry and agreed a timeline for completion of the work staggered over a year.

The group struggled to find time to meet and share ideas and plans in the early stages. The mentor forwarded relevant research briefings and encouraged

(Continued)

(Continued)

group members to construct a timeline with target dates for the completion of activities mapped against pressure points in the school calendar. The group identified areas where they needed support, for example working with focus groups and constructing interview schedules, and these needs will inform the programme of support for the coming months.

> The biggest thing that we have been finding is that people need to talk to each other and spend time with each other and that is really difficult as a teacher because your job is to teach pupils in a classroom and you are on your own in that. There is very little time to actually speak to other people and spend time with other people sharing ideas and talking. (Classteacher, int.)

The research group plans to hold six-weekly working lunches with the Leadership Group to share work in progress. They are supported by a deputy headteacher who provides coordination and facilitates communication/requests for support/ access to resources.

The headteacher plans to expand the group to include a wider range of staff. It is planned to invite post-probation teachers to participate in the group for specific purposes, for example supporting the lead teacher-researchers where appropriate. It is also planned to recruit more experienced senior colleagues to join the group to encourage cross-departmental and cross-role collaboration. One of the strands of enquiry focuses on primary–secondary transition and this brings a further dimension to the work, strengthening cross-sector links.

One of the common motivations for undertaking a collaborative research project in a school or college is the desire to improve practice. 'School improvement' and 'school development planning' have become key notions in educational management and leadership over the past twenty to thirty years (for example, Harris et al., 2003; Lingard et al., 2003). The process of bringing about positive change in schools and colleges is now recognised as a highly complex task, involving great skill and commitment from the institution's leaders and needing 'buy-in' from the wider school or college community (Fullan, 2001; Hargreaves and Fink, 2005).

Practitioner research is not an essential element of school improvement or development, however it has been demonstrated that it can play a major part in making change more systematic and indeed sustainable. Furthermore it has the additional pay-offs that have been mentioned above, such as contributing to the professional development of the staff involved. We can find numerous examples that have been published – and there are likely to be thousands more that have not been made so readily available – of schools, colleges or departments that have identified areas for significant development and have constructed some kind of action research process to frame the innovation, so that there can be a thorough assessment of the success of the implementation of the change, as well as learning lessons about the viability of future development plans.

For example, in Scotland, the Schools of Ambition scheme was a government-funded initiative to support designated schools in implementing their own 'Transformational Plan'. A university-based research team was commissioned to provide research support for these schools in studying the success of these innovations. This work has been made available in a number of forms (see Learning and Teaching Scotland website: www.ltscotland.org.uk/schoolsofambition/about/schoolsofambitionresearch.asp). It appears that a key element to the effectiveness of the research strand of this work was the way in which the research activity within the school was managed, specifically who was involved in it and whether the senior management members of the school were active in it or not.

Extracts from Annual Report of *Research to Support Schools of Ambition* 2008

There is a need to afford sufficient senior management time to the development and coordination of activities associated with Schools of Ambition. While promoting leadership opportunities across the school community, senior managers lend authority to developments and have a key role to play in synthesising evidence and bringing coherence to the implementation of the transformational plan. (p. 50)

The involvement of a wider constituency of school staff in the planning stages contributes to the sustainability of initiatives throughout the transformation period and enhances the sustainability of changes in the longer-term. Although the original transformational plan may be principally authored by senior management there is considerable scope for devolution of detailed operational planning and the promotion of wider engagement through consultation and action planning. (p. 49)

Evaluation has been enhanced where the School of Ambition plan is aligned with the school development plan. This avoids a perception that there are two different streams of development taking place in school. It also enables the School of Ambition plan to be subject to similar levels of deliberation through established school development planning procedures. (p. 49)

In today's world of high accountability and inspection, it is also worth considering the contribution that institutionally based practitioner research may make to evaluation processes. In England, Scotland and elsewhere, inspection regimes have increasingly used the language of 'self-evaluation', often building on the work of MacBeath and others (MacBeath, 1999). There is now an expectation that schools and other educational institutions carry out regular reviews of their activities, sometimes to the extent of preparing a document that assesses their performance against their own objectives (for example, a 'Self Evaluation Document'). Any institution that has carried out systematic enquiry into its developments and practices will be able to include this work as evidence not only of effectiveness but of a mature self-critical approach.

Practitioner research and education policy

Finally, in this chapter, we wish to discuss the relationship between practitioner research and education policy. So far, in this discussion, the emphasis has been very much about the relationship between research and practice – perhaps not surprisingly, given the focus of this book on practitioner research. One of the criticisms that is sometimes levelled against practitioner research is that its influence is very limited. So, it is suggested that while good quality practitioner or action research may lead to significant improvement in a teacher's classroom practice or even across a department or whole institution, the wider learning and the implications for policy are very limited. Indeed, this argument is sometimes extended to suggest that practitioner research rather than contributing to an extended form of teacher professionalism is actually leading to a more restricted professionalism, where the teacher's contribution is constrained to their own direct field of practice.

Various responses may be made to this criticism. There certainly can be a problem of this nature and indeed it may be that not all practitioners actually wish to influence practice. At the simplest level however, the kinds of ideas about collaborative effort discussed above are likely to lead to wider developments in practice that may indeed amount to a development in institution-level policy.

However, there is a stronger argument about the framing of practitioner or action research that can facilitate a greater engagement with policy processes. If a research study is framed from the outset in relation to wider policy, whether it be policies on the teaching of literacy, policies on bullying and harassment, policies on the management of teachers' time – whatever the area is – then it may well be that the outcomes of the research study will be of much wider interest. Carr and Kemmis (1997) urge that all action research should have a 'critical edge'. Cochran-Smith and Lytle (2009) argue for 'inquiry as stance', that is, that practitioner enquiry should be aiming to bring about desired changes. Indeed, this concept implies a slightly different relationship with policy – almost research as a form of policy implementation.

The point we wish to make here is that practitioner research does not need to be restricted. It can, and we would argue should, play a significant part in bringing about developments in education policy at all levels, from school/college, to the region, indeed to a national and even supra-national level. Sachs (2003) refers to teaching as 'a transformative activity'. Building upon her arguments we would see practitioner research as an essential element of transformative teaching.

In the next chapter we consider some of the purposes of practitioner research in greater detail. We build on the ideas that we have discussed in this opening chapter.

Further reading 📖

Evaluation in education

MacBeath, J. and McGlynn, A. (2002) *Self-evaluation – What's in It for Schools?* London: Routledge.

Reflective teaching

Pollard, A. (2008) *Reflective Teaching – Evidence-informed Professional Practice.* London: Cassell.

Professional development

Campbell, A., McNamara, O. and Gilroy, P. (2006) *Practitioner Research and Professional Development in Education.* London: Sage.

Forde, C., McMahon, M., McPhee, A. and Patrick, F. (2006) *Professional Development, Reflection and Enquiry.* London: Paul Chapman.

Communities of practice, communities of enquiry

Cassidy, C. et al. (2008) Building communities of educational enquiry, *Oxford Review of Education,* 34(2): 217–35.

Wenger, E. (1998) *Communities of Practice: Learning, Meaning and Identity.* Cambridge: Cambridge University Press.

Teacher as researcher

Stenhouse, L. (1975) *Introduction to Curriculum Research and Development.* London: Heinemann.

Action research

Carr, W. and Kemmis, S. (1986) *Becoming Critical.* Lewes: Falmer Press.

McNiff, J. and Whitehead, J. (2005) *All You Need to Know About Action Research.* London: Sage.

Relevant networks

British Educational Research Association (BERA) Practitioner Research Special Interest Group (SIG): www.bera.ac.uk/practitioner.

Collaborative Action Research Network (CARN): www.did.stu.mmu.ac.uk/carnnew.

2

Why do Practitioner Research?

In Chapter 1 we considered the nature of practitioner research and introduced the work of Lawrence Stenhouse. This chapter considers the varied reasons for engaging in practitioner research as a beginning teacher, experienced teacher or school leader. Who engages in research and why?

Research internationally suggests that the quality of teaching is the most significant within-school factor influencing pupil performance (Darling-Hammond et al., 2005; Hattie, 2009; McKinsey & Co., 2007). Research further suggests that engagement in research by teachers has a positive impact on the learning of the pupils in their classrooms (Baumfield and Butterworth, 2005). It is argued that research-engaged teachers have 'a better understanding of their practice and ways to improve it' (McLaughlin et al., 2004: 5). Much recent attention has focused on the need to cultivate a positive disposition to inquiry at an early stage in the professional education of beginning teachers and to promote engagement *in* and *with* research as an integral aspect of professional learning for all teachers across the career span. Professional standards frameworks for teachers cite inquiry as a key professional attribute for all teachers, beginning and accomplished.

> Inquiry stance is perspectival and conceptual – a worldview, a habit of mind, a dynamic and fluid way of knowing and being in the world of educational practice that carries across the course of the professional career – not a teacher training strategy, a sequence of steps for solving classroom or school problems, or a skill to be demonstrated by beginners to show competence. (Cochran-Smith and Lytle, 2009: 113)

It is widely recognised that the needs of today's learners cannot be met through transmission models of teaching and learning. The development of enquiry-based teacher education is consistent with the promotion of enquiry-based learning in the school curriculum. Increasing emphasis is placed on teacher assessment, local curriculum deliberation and enhanced (earned) professional autonomy. Positioning teachers as *learners* and *producers* of knowledge presents a challenge to educational researchers, teacher educators and decision-makers in education. Practitioner research is one way of bringing teachers' voices to policy debates about schooling.

This chapter considers:

- research as part of initial teacher education
- research in pursuit of further qualifications/advanced certification
- research as part of personal or collaborative CPD
- research as a tool for school improvement
- research for policy development.

Key concepts and issues

- Teacher-as-researcher
- 'Enquiry as stance'
- Reflective practice
- Professional development
- School improvement

Some key writers

- Lawrence Stenhouse
- Marilyn Cochran–Smith
- Susan Lytle
- John Mason
- Colleen McLaughlin

Research as part of initial teacher education

The past two decades have seen the progressive introduction of staged career pathways for teachers, based on professional standards. Renewed interest in teacher research and 'teaching as a research and evidence-based profession' (Hargreaves, 1996) has accompanied moves towards integrated professional development frameworks within the UK, across Europe and elsewhere. The introduction of Master's-level credit within postgraduate programmes of initial teacher education (ITE) in the UK has further extended opportunities for research engagement at an early stage in teacher formation. Table 2.1 presents the references to research and enquiry in the professional standards for teachers in England and Scotland.

An enquiry orientation (Table 2.2) in initial teacher education supports the development of reflective practice. Teachers who demonstrate a capacity to reflect *on* and *in* practice may progress to engage in forms of systematic enquiry framed by research questions and conducted over a period of time. In addition to systematic enquiry as a form of professional development undertaken by individuals, some teachers may elect to participate in cyclical enquiry – a series of linked enquiries – undertaken collectively as a form of educational action research.

Table 2.1   Inclusion of research in professional standards frameworks

Scotland	England
Standard for Initial Teacher Education (SITE)	***Standards for Qualified Teacher Status (QTS)***
By the end of the programme of initial teacher education, ***student teachers*** will:	***Beginning teachers***: 'Have a creative and constructively critical approach towards innovation, being prepared to adapt their practice where benefits and improvements are identified' (TDA, 2007: 8).
• know how to access and apply relevant findings from educational research; • know how to engage appropriately in the systematic investigation of practice (GTCS, 2006a: 10); • know how to adopt a questioning approach to their professional practice and engage appropriately in professional enquiry such as action research (GTCS, 2006a:14).	***Core Standards*** ***All teachers*** should: Maintain an up-to-date knowledge and understanding of the professional duties of teachers and the statutory framework within which they work, and contribute to the development, implementation and evaluation of the policies and practice of their workplace (TDA, 2007: 15).
Standard for Full Registration (SFR) ***Registered teachers*** (at the end of induction) have research-based knowledge relating to learning and teaching and a critical appreciation of the contribution of research to education in general.	***Standards for Excellent Teachers*** ***Excellent Teachers*** should: Research and evaluate innovative curricular practices and draw on research outcomes and other sources of external evidence to inform their own practice and that of colleagues (TDA, 2007: 27).
• productively access and relate research knowledge to their teaching circumstances; • discuss critically how systematic investigation of, and reflection on, classroom practice informs and develops teaching and learning (GTCS, 2006b: 9).	
Standard for Chartered Teacher ***Chartered Teachers*** ensure that teaching is informed by reading and research. For example, by	
• engaging in professional enquiry and action research, and applying findings • reflecting critically on research evidence and modifying practice as appropriate.	

Table 2.2   Three forms of professional enquiry

Reflection	Practitioner Enquiry	Action Research
Time limited	Sustained	Series of linked enquiries
Private	Questioning	Cyclical
Inward looking	Outward looking	Collective/collaborative
Not necessarily linked with wider research community	Transactional/dialogue	

Source: adapted from Baumfield, 2009

Research in pursuit of further qualifications/certification

Continued professional growth through a commitment to an 'enquiry stance' is not easy in the face of the day-to-day challenges of classroom life. Concern with teacher quality across the career phases has focused attention internationally on policy levers to incentivise and support the continuing professional development of experienced teachers (Darling-Hammond, 2000; Hinds, 2002; Ingvarson, 2008; Kleinhenz and Ingvarson, 2004). One strategy to enhance teacher quality is the creation of advanced level certification of accomplished teachers. Outside the UK, the USA, Australia, Singapore, Japan and South Korea all offer forms of advanced certification.

Advanced certification in the USA is available through National Board certification. The National Board for Professional Teaching Standards (NBPTS) was established in 1987 in response to the report *A Nation Prepared: Teachers for the 21st Century*. Between 1987 and 1994, the National Board formulated a set of standards for accomplished teaching and a method for identifying teachers who demonstrated these practices. National Board certification is a voluntary two-step process. The first involves completion of six computer-based exercises that measure subject matter knowledge. The second involves preparation of a portfolio that offers an authentic representation of a teacher's skills. The portfolio consists of video records of teaching, written reflections on the learning intentions and outcomes of a selection of lessons, and examples of students' work. Over 74,000 teachers have received National Board certification since 1987. The certification process can take up to three years to complete and carries graduate credit. Many states and local school districts offer some form of financial incentive for those seeking advanced certification. Recertification is required within ten years of the initial award. Enquiring and creative teachers are expected to exemplify the dispositions they seek to cultivate in learners. The core propositions that frame the knowledge, skills, dispositions and beliefs of National Board Certified Teachers (NBCTs) include the following:

- Teachers think systematically about their practice and learn from experience.
- Teachers are members of learning communities.

> As with most professions, teaching requires an open-ended capacity that is not acquired once and for all. Because they work in a field marked by many unsolved puzzles and an expanding research base, teachers have a professional obligation to be lifelong students of their craft, seeking to expand their repertoire, deepen their knowledge and skill, and become wiser in rendering judgments. (NBPTS, 2002: 16)

In the UK, grades and attendant pay scales have been created to recognise and reward accomplished teachers. These vary according to different arrangements for the governance and regulation of teacher education across the UK and include the advanced skills teachers and excellent teacher grades in England (TDA, 2007), the pilot Chartered Teacher programme in Wales (Egan, 2009) and the distinctive Scottish Chartered Teacher Programme.

In England, the Training and Development Agency for School's (TDA) postgraduate professional development programme offers over 35,000 places on subsidised courses leading to postgraduate awards. A school-delivered Master's in Teaching and Learning (MTL) was introduced from September 2010 for newly qualified teachers (NQTs), initially those based in the North West of England or working in National Challenge schools. Developing skills of enquiry and use of evidence are core components of the MTL programme, which will take around three years for candidates to complete.

The Chartered Teacher programme involves of a self-funded Master's degree approved against the Standard for Chartered Teacher (GTCS, 2002), normally completed over a period of between three and six years. The programme is open to all teachers who have reached the top of the main grade teachers' pay scale and who have maintained a CPD portfolio. Chartered teachers receive an enhanced salary without additional management responsibilities. By September 2009, 904 experienced teachers had attained chartered teacher status (from a population of 50,500 school-based teachers). Completion of the Master's component of the Chartered Teacher programme involves undertaking a major work-based project requiring classroom-based research.

> In every sphere of his or her work the Chartered Teacher should be reviewing practice, searching for improvements, turning to reading and research for fresh insights and relating these to the classroom and the school. (General Teaching Council for Scotland, 2002: 3)

In addition to professional qualifications and advanced certification sponsored by government and explicitly linked to professional standards, an extensive range of further qualifications is available to education professionals. These include a wide range of specialist and generic programmes of study leading to university certificates, diplomas and Master's awards (MEd, MA, MSc) as well as expanding provision for Professional Doctorates in Education and doctoral studies for PhD.

Research as part of personal or collaborative CPD

There is widespread recognition that initial 'qualification' (or accreditation) is an insufficient basis for lifelong professional learning. While the UK has not yet instigated the re-licensing of practising teachers that is established practice in the USA and elsewhere, there is an acceptance that qualifying to teach needs to be connected to learning pathways that support continuing professional growth. This position is strengthened by greater access to professions in the related fields of health and social care through the integrated children's service or 'edu-care' agenda. Service integration has been advanced through *Every Child Matters: Change for Children* (DfES, 2004) in England, the development of integrated community schools (ICS) in Scotland and extended school initiatives in Northern Ireland. Many professions in the UK are considering mandatory periodic recertification of practitioners (Department of Health, 2007). Recertification would require practitioners to demonstrate a commitment to professional learning and skills development and to demonstrate that they remain competent to practise post-initial certification. This is both a reflection of demands for public accountability and an awareness of the value of continuing learning for personal satisfaction and effectiveness across the career span.

John Mason (2002) aptly describes practitioner research as 'the discipline of noticing'. For the experienced teacher, regular engagement in practitioner enquiry is a defence against the development of ingrained habits of mind. Mason observes that repeated experience can produce unconscious generalities. Research participation helps the teacher to postpone judgement, uncover assumptions and provides new ways of seeing and articulating practices, values and beliefs. Lee Shulman (2005) has described how difficult it is to learn from teaching experiences because so much of what happens in classrooms instantly 'evaporates'. Practitioner research helps to create a space to stop and look again at existing ways of working.

> Professional practice involves seeing a large number of people (students, clients, colleagues) in similar roles, so it is very tempting to formulate generalisations which seem to help sort out and even predict behaviour … The trouble with 'experience' is that I may be discounting cases that disagree with my generality, and I am at best inferring from a few instances. (Mason, 2002: 219)

A commitment to questioning supports continuing professional development. By formulating research questions, the researching teacher places themselves in the position of *not* knowing. By disrupting the routinisation of teaching, research can help to extend the choices available to practitioners, making them more alert to alternative possibilities.

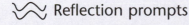 Reflection prompts

1 What generalisations or habits of mind can teachers build up through experience that may become resistant to change?
2 What assumptions do you hold about learners, parents and communities?

Enquiry can also support teachers during periods of external reform that destabilise previous ways of working, contributing to the development of 'adaptive expertise' (see Figure 2.1). Systematic enquiry helps teachers to 'let go', unlearn, innovate and re-skill in cycles of professional learning throughout

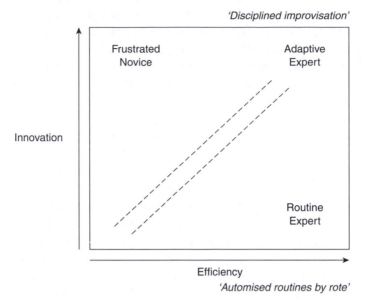

Figure 2.1 Dimensions of adaptive expertise

Source: Darling-Hammond & Bransford, 2005: 49

their careers in response to changing circumstances. In this way, accomplished teachers are able to sustain a commitment to innovation over time.

〰️ Reflection prompts

1 Looking back over the different stages of your teaching career, can you identify scripted, innovative, and adaptive elements of your own practice?
2 How are changes in curriculum and assessment practices introduced?
3 How do changes in pedagogical strategies develop?

So far, we have argued that practitioner research is disruptive because it requires the problematising of day-to-day work. We have also suggested that enquiry helps teachers to formulate considered responses based on principled and structured reflection during periods of change. Engaging in deep forms of enquiry into one's own practice is challenging, especially in institutional contexts that may not support questioning. Despite the considerable challenges and dilemmas of undertaking practitioner research, many teachers note positive outcomes for themselves, their students/pupils and colleagues. Commonly cited benefits of participation include the relevance of teacher-generated enquiries to the local context, the licence research participation gives to reflection in school (space and voice) and the opportunities it presents to work with colleagues to improve experiences and outcomes for pupils.

> The main difference is that you actually have ownership of it. It is my own experiences. It is all very well reading what it says in a book, but will it work under your own scenario? That is the important thing. You can read up on findings but it is the chance to actually test it out. It is the home grown bits that you take notice of. It's your children, your school. (Best Practice Research Scholarship award holder)

> It makes you stop and reflect. When you are teaching day in and day out, you don't have any time to stop and really reflect on what you are doing. Doing this research helps you slow down and think about things much more. (Best Practice Research Scholarship award holder)

For some teachers, enquiry may promote levels of critical reflection that are transformative. Transformative change entails 'teachers making changes in their basic epistemological perspectives, their knowledge of what it means to learn, as well as their conceptions of classroom practice' (Franke et al., 1998: 67). The comments from the teacher below indicate the powerful impact of research engagement for some teachers.

> In terms of what we are doing, we have actually changed. As a result of what we have done, we're not the same people. Our teaching has changed and we can't go back to how we taught before. That's the difference this work has made to us. The research is part of the process of making you think. It's not the only factor but it has helped focus our ideas. We have got an enthusiasm now that hopefully will carry on feeding into our classrooms into the future. A lot more confidence. (Best Practice Research Scholarship award holder)

Research as a tool for school improvement

Schools are increasingly data-driven organisations and teachers are familiar with a range of diagnostic, monitoring and forecasting technologies. Schools' use of data is routinely associated with pupil tracking, target setting, value-added assessments and performance tables. Teachers are expected to use evidence from tracking procedures to regularly adjust their programmes of study, engage pupils in 'learning conversations' and as the basis for planning specific intervention strategies, for example, booster programmes. School professionals are increasingly called upon to develop new skills or commission external consultants to support the baseline measurement and impact assessment of initiatives undertaken, especially where an additional resource has been invested as a catalyst of change. Data use within school self-evaluation attempts to serve the dual purposes of public accountability and school development. A research orientation to self-evaluation helps to extend conventional 'audit' approaches focused on the delivery of *outcomes* to include approaches that also offer rich descriptions of *processes* of change.

> Evaluation should, as it were, lead development and be integrated with it. Then the distinction between development and evaluation is destroyed and the two merge as research. (Stenhouse, 1975: 122)

> It is not the mechanistic completion of progress and success checks that is important, but rather it is the enhancing of the teachers' professional judgement that is the crucial aspect of embedding an ethos of enquiry and reflection within a school. (Hopkins, 2007: 110)

Collaboration between teacher researchers promotes enhanced learning and increases the potential impact on practice. In the extract below a chartered teacher in Scotland describes the benefits of teachers participating in collaborative enquiry.

> It took time to convince the staff that collaborative enquiry meant much more than trying out someone's ideas. We had as a school until recent years 'cooperated' more than 'collaborated' and allowed ourselves to be steered and pushed in the directions demanded of us by policy makers. If a workable strategy was to permeate throughout the school, the teachers and pupils had to have ownership of it. (Chartered teacher, 2008)

There are advantages in convening school enquiry groups to promote and align teacher professional development and whole school development:

- Sharing responsibility – dividing tasks to ensure manageability, range and focus.
- Strengthening relationships – critical friendship, peer support, development of cross-curricular links and relationships across career phases and positions of responsibility.
- Developing capacity – the skill set of individual teacher researchers and building capacity for organisational learning.
- Contributing to sustainability – year-on-year development (staff turnover).
- Eroding teacher privacy and promoting collaboration.
- Enhanced opportunities for teacher leadership.

Opportunities for sponsored teacher research, through the award of research grants, have enabled the participation of teachers at all career stages to embark on small-scale classroom-based enquiries. The evaluation of the Best Practice Research Scholarship programme (2000–04), which awarded grants to support small-scale classroom-based enquires to 4,000 teachers in England and Wales, revealed the involvement of a high number of teachers in non-promoted posts (67 per cent) (Furlong and Salisbury, 2005: 53). The Scottish Schools of Ambition[1] programme (2006–10) also reported enhanced levels of participation from teachers across the career stages and increased levels of peer-led continuing professional development (University of Glasgow, 2009). School enquiry groups can be formed to address specific themes, for example, teaching for understanding, thinking skills, cooperative learning; and allow for participation at different levels, for example, coordinator, core team member, reviewer, analyst. Figure 2.2 below shows the configuration of a school enquiry group within a School of Ambition. The model includes the involvement of the school senior staff/leadership group in the coordinating team with a core team recruiting new members for particular tasks and new ideas.

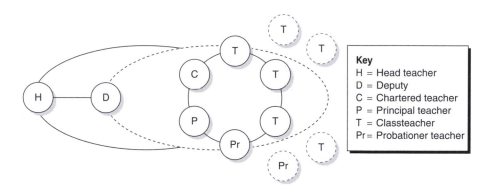

Figure 2.2   Model of a school enquiry group from the Schools of Ambition programme

Collaborative enquiry and school improvement

Examples of UK **school improvement networks** with a research orientation:

School-Based Research Consortia initiative (1998–2001)
Research Engaged Schools Programme (2003–05)
Networked Learning Communities programme (2000–06)
Scottish Schools of Ambition (2006–10)

For accounts from **research engaged schools** see:

GTCE (2006) 'Using research in your school and your teaching. Research engaged professional practice'; online at: http://www.pre-online.co.uk/REpdfs/1_researchinschools.pdf. A booklet produced by NfER and the GTCE that contains examples and introduces some of the challenges and rewards of becoming a research-engaged teacher.

McLaughlin, C., Black-Hawkins, K., Brindley, S., McIntyre, D. and Taber, K.S. (2006) *Researching Schools: Stories from a Schools–University Partnership for Educational Research*. London: Routledge.

(Continued)

(Continued)

For advice on **becoming a research engaged school**:

Leading a Researched Engaged School (2006). A booklet available from the National College for Leadership of Schools and Children's Services. http://www. nationalcollege.org.uk/.

Research for policy development

> It is teachers who, in the end, will change the world of the school by understanding it. (Stenhouse, 1985: vi)

Anderson et al. (1994: 23) have considered the potential of practitioner research to move from an 'academic tradition' to a 'social movement' as teacher researchers find more effective ways of sharing their work. By 'going public' and publishing their research, teachers can contribute to what is known about teaching and learning (Hatch et al., 2005). Teacher research highlights different ways of knowing and invites different forms of representation and dissemination. In the USA, the Carnegie Foundation has undertaken much work to make records of teachers' deliberation on classroom practice more widely available. This includes the development of software tools to help teachers create e-portfolios or multimedia representations of their practice.

Multimedia records of teaching practice

Carnegie Foundation galleries: http://gallery.carnegiefoundation.org/insideteaching/.

For a guide to multimedia representations of teaching see:

Pointer Mace, D. (2009) *Teacher Practice Online*. New York. Teachers College Press.

Dissemination is important in challenging the view that knowledge developed through practitioner research is too context dependent to be important. Cochran-Smith and Lytle (2001) have argued that the generation of local knowledge within communities committed to collaborative enquiry offers the potential to move beyond time-bound models of professional learning based on the novice–expert relation. In place of well-rehearsed divisions between 'knowledge-*for*-practice' (university generated) and 'knowledge-*in*-practice' (apprenticeship models of teacher learning), Cochran-Smith and

Lytle argue for 'knowledge-*of*-practice', that is, both local and public, provocative and cumulative.

> Teacher inquiry is a form of resistance against authoritarian mandates and professional or public apathy. It allows us to rebuild our educational independence in the pursuit of authentic, non-mandated change. (Chiseri-Strater and Sunstein, 2006: xvi)

For some teachers, enquiry is regarded as a professional obligation and reading and research are perceived to enhance the capacity of teachers to lobby for policy change at school, cluster, local authority and national levels.

> It is the role of the Chartered Teacher to ensure that new policies are not simply given to teachers 'ready packaged', in small understandable chunks, requiring no or little interpretation; but instead are read fully and challenged if necessary. Chartered Teachers should be voicing the opinion of the foot soldiers of education, the classteachers, and making it clear how policy can best support good practice in learning and teaching. (Chartered teacher, 2008)

Teacher research and policy

USA   **Teachers Network Policy Institute** (TNPI) aims to 'give teachers an active voice in education policy making so that education mandates are informed by the realities of daily classroom life' (Meyers and Rust, 2003: 157). Fellows of the TNPI conduct action research studies in classrooms and schools.
             National Board Certified Teachers have conducted research reviews of the impact of Board certification on students, practice and the profession (Centre for Teaching Quality, 2008).
England   **National Teacher Research Panel** involves teachers as 'user' reviewers.
Scotland   **Teacher researchers** have participated as members of collaborative research teams examining processes of early professional development and 'accomplished teaching' in funded projects (McNally, 2006; Reeves et al., 2010).

Reflection prompts

1 In your own teaching context, in what ways can teachers influence policy – at school/regional/national levels?
2 On what evidence can teachers draw to make a case for change?
3 What are the main influences on teachers' choice of research 'problems'?
4 What are some of the main inhibitors to change?

Summary

In this chapter, the following key points were made:

- Enquiry-based teacher development is linked with enquiry-based learning.
- Engaging *in* and *with* research can help teachers to become more expert.
- Research encourages informed professional decisions, rather than habitual responses.
- Research requires teachers to re-experience 'not knowing'.
- Research questions posed by practitioners target areas resistant to improvement that warrant systematic enquiry.
- Enquiring teachers, as adaptive professionals, are better able to respond to uncertainty and to become 'agents' rather than recipients of change.

 Questions for further reflection and discussion

- How far can teacher researchers step outside the frameworks that influence their practice?
- How valid is teacher research? Is it research?
- What are the risks of teacher research?
- Under what circumstances can teacher research be empowering?

Further reading

Cochran-Smith, M. and Lytle, S.L. (eds) (2009) *Inquiry as Stance. Practitioner Research for the Next Generation*. New York: Teacher College Press.

Mason, J. (2002) *Researching Your Own Practice. The Discipline of Noticing*. London: Routledge.

Sachs, J. (2003) *The Activist Teaching Profession*. Buckingham: Open University Press.

Useful tools and resources

Rust, F. and Clarke, C. (2009) *How To Do Action Research in Your Classroom*. Teachers Network Leadership Institute. Online at: http://www.teachersnetwork.org/tnli/Action_Research_Booklet.pdf. A useful booklet introducing the key principles and steps involved in designing and conducting classroom action research.

National Foundation for Educational Research (NfER) Practical Research for Education Toolkit series. Online at: http://www.pre-online.co.uk.

The Teachers' Network website contains examples of teacher research and some templates to support planning, analysis and writing inquiry summaries: http://www.teachersnetwork.org/tnli/research/.

Saunders, L. (2007) *Supporting Teachers' Engagement in and with Research*. London: TLRP. Online at: http://www.bera.ac.uk/supporting-teachers-engagement-in-and-with-research/. This concise review contains a useful list of online resources and a bibliography.

Campbell, A. (2007) *Practitioner Research*. London: TLRP. Online at: http://www.bera.ac.uk/practitioner-research/. A two-page 'walkthrough' introducing practitioner research.

Useful websites

The Research Informed Practice Site (TRIPS): http://www.standards.dfes.gov.uk/research/.

Practical Research for Education (NfER): http://www.nfer.ac.uk/publications/topic.cfm.

GTCE Research for Teachers: http://www.gtce.org.uk/teachers/rft/.

GTCNI Access to Research Resources for Teachers Space (ARRTS): http://gtcni.openrepository.com/gtcni/.

Teacher Training Resource Bank (TTRB): http://www.ttrb.ac.uk/.

Centre for the Use of Research and Evidence in Education(CUREE) interactive 'route map': http://www.curee-paccts.com/resources/route-map.

Note

1 For further information on Schools of Ambition see http://wayback.archive-it.org/1961/20100805220151.
http://www.Itscotland.org.uk/schoolsofambition/index.asp.

See also:
Scottish Government (2009) *Schools of Ambition Leading Change*. Available from: http://www.scotland.gov.uk/Publications/2009/04/30095118/0
Scottish Government (2010) *Leading Change Two. Learning from Schools of Ambition*. Available from: http://www.scotland.gov.uk/Resource/Doc/311542/0098307.pdf.

Part 2

What Do We Want to Know?

3

What is a Research Question?

In this chapter we explore the concepts related to research questions: what they are, how they are formulated, how they inform research enquiry, and how you can translate these questions into precise research activities while taking into account a restricted timeline. We show how a slight change in the research focus can significantly alter the design of the study. Throughout the chapter there are guide questions that you can use when reflecting on the feasibility and manageability of the planned research. As a researcher you need to be aware of the issues that might jeopardise your study.

Confucius, a Chinese philosopher, once said that while learning through hearing is soon forgotten, and learning through seeing makes one remember, it is learning by doing that enables a person to gain true understanding. You can apply a similar principle when exploring an educational phenomenon for which first-hand enquiry produces not just knowledge but a genuine appreciation of the matter.

Perhaps this is because systematic enquiry or research goes beyond merely listening and reading – the most basic tasks for knowledge acquisition. Instead, it allows one to be part of a quest that can produce the type of evidence considered well-grounded and trustworthy and which can credibly support or nullify previously held assumptions. Moreover, to be actively involved in the enquiry process is not only a useful way to familiarise yourself with the issues surrounding the area being investigated but it is also an avenue by which legitimate views are established, fresh insights are discovered and further recommendations are subsequently made. Engaging in research is, in fact, a more creative way of learning – through both the research experience and the research findings.

In this section, we will discuss how you can get started in undertaking research by:

- understanding what research questions are
- identifying research questions
- designing research and formulating an outline and a timetable for a research programme.

What is a research question?

> Research questions are the vital first steps in any research. They guide you towards the kinds of information you need and the ways you should collect that information. (Lewis and Munn, 1987: 5)

How do you begin with this process of systematic enquiry called research? You need to have a question or a set of questions to pursue in your enquiry, base the design of the research upon, and address as you analyse the generated data. These questions will guide your study – from beginning to end – acting as an indispensable 'anchor' throughout the research process.

A research enquiry begins with your research questions. They will help you to reflect not only on what counts as evidence but also on the modes or combinations of evidence that could satisfactorily address such questions. These decisions on the evidence required for the study will then critically inform the overall design of your study, specifically the methods and the instruments for gathering data. The suitability of the selected methods and the devised research instruments are to be measured against the question: 'Will they be able to address sufficiently the research questions?' Once the data have been generated, you (as the researcher) will ensure that data is analysed to answer the research questions. Research questions are fundamental in any enquiry; researchers will always consider them in all stages of the research process in order to achieve order and coherence. The importance of the research questions not only as a starting point but also throughout the research is diagrammatically represented in Figure 3.1.

The formulation of research questions, therefore, serves four important purposes:

- to crystallise the focus of the investigation
- to set the parameters of the research
- to inform the design and methods for gathering and analysing evidence
- to steer the whole course of the study.

It is vital that you start your enquiry by having a clear idea what questions you would like to address through your research. Research questions are informed not only by your main interest but also by factors that may impact on the feasibility or manageability of your research.

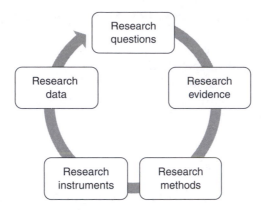

Figure 3.1 Research questions as the starting point and the 'anchor' in the research

Defining your research questions

Exploring possible sources of topics

There are many ways by which research questions are conceived. Let us take a look at some potential sources of initial key ideas based on personal experience that prompted school teachers and college lecturers to undertake their own studies.

> From observation, even the most withdrawn pupils showed some enthusiasm whenever I used the new learning approach when teaching Mathematics. Will this increased enthusiasm impact on their scores? Their attitude to learning? Their overall learning? (A primary teacher)

> After attending a series of seminars on employability, I would like to incorporate some of these ideas in my class, particularly on personal presentation and handling interviews during job application, and find out if my students will find them practically useful as they pursue employment. (A college lecturer)

> Could it be that the extra-curricular activities given to young people after school boost their creativity? (A secondary teacher)

These are in no way unique to these practitioners. Like the primary teacher, your research idea may emanate from a type of *intuitive knowledge* that is acquired through experience and careful observation. This initially involves identification of an existing problem and a viable way or ways of addressing it. Likewise, topics for research often spring from *conference, seminar and/or workshop attendance* since examples of effective practice, innovative concepts and interventions are often shared among the delegates. Such nuggets of wisdom give practitioners ideas and courage to experiment as they attempt to enhance their practice. Equally, practitioners should not underestimate their capacity for gaining strategic knowledge through cognisant *reflection*. For example, reflective teaching, as discussed in Chapter 1, triggers both deep thinking and questioning, which is a fertile source for many potential areas of enquiry.

Lewis and Munn (1987) maintained that *discussions during staff meetings*, for example, can in fact uncover ongoing concerns, which in turn alert teachers to a possible focus for enquiry. *Published reports* or newsletters containing an article on a better approach to classroom management, discipline, or advancement in specific subject areas, among others, may also persuade practitioners to devise and introduce a programme and then monitor and assess its impact through evaluative research. Finally, a focus group discussion (as discussed in Chapter 9) with school staff members and/or pupils may identify issues that are of real concern to the school. This bottom-up approach is considered a 'democratic' way, which is a good rationale for generating a research topic rather than merely being influenced by the school's priorities, the views of the school management team, or the researchers' own views.

As a brief exercise, consider answering the following questions as you seek to identify possible areas of research.

1 Does your position provide you with strategic information that makes you aware of some issues or concerns in your institution?
2 From mere observation, have you noticed associations between theories (proven or otherwise) and practice and started formulating a premise or an assumption?
3 Have you come across new, innovative or exciting ideas in the educational arena recently that perhaps deserve a try?
4 Is there a particular topic that you've been mulling over in the past few months?
5 Have you detected a recurring area of concern from recent staff meetings? In discussion with colleagues in the staff room?
6 Is your school/college taking part in a new initiative that offers a lot of promising benefits?

Consider your answers to these questions and their potential to be developed into a proper research enquiry. You can extend your preliminary thinking by doing any of the following:

- reading further to strengthen your understanding and getting an idea of how studies in the same area were carried out
- discussing a research possibility with colleagues, heads of departments
- reflecting on the personal and/or professional benefits of embarking on a research enquiry.

Reading further
Once you have done the preliminary thinking, it would be useful to check any published material in order to deepen and extend your understanding of the topic. There are various sources to check, for example, local and national newspapers, educational magazines, online educational websites and relevant books. Another source of published material is (either paper-based or electronic) journal articles. These will enable you to appreciate how many studies

have been conducted in your chosen area of interest. These published materials may signal that another study is unnecessary because numerous research studies have already exhausted the topic. In contrast, the conclusions and recommendations of these studies may point to other interesting new areas for enquiry that the practitioner might not otherwise have considered. Reading published reports also shows how an abstract concept is transformed into something specific. You will also gain an appreciation of how research questions are addressed in the research process and of how different research approaches and strategies can be undertaken in the same area.

Discussing with colleagues

Confirming that the topic is of interest to other practitioners, and that it is relevant to the issues faced by the institution, means that it is more likely that you will be able to obtain the support, resources and access you need for your study. From our dealings with teacher researchers, one of the key things that they identified as essential, in school-based research is the unwavering support of the school's senior management team. It appears that research that is valued by the practitioner and at the same time conforms to the school's mission is a very good combination, because it brings benefits to both parties. One secondary teacher shared how a particular research study (undertaken with colleagues) that advocated the notion of 'preparing students for life' also corresponded with the school's objectives.

> these [research] aims are at the fore of everything that we do ... because the pupils are at the heart of what we're all about, so it's to benefit the pupils ... it's not just for pupils while they're at school, it's to allow them to develop skills for life and for work. (Deputy head, Secondary School)

Research enquiry that can satisfy both the interests of the practitioner and of the school can create a real synergy and is thus more likely to be executed successfully.

Reflecting on research benefits

Since research engagement is a serious business, which will inevitably take a lot of precious time and effort, it is worth asking yourself if the topic is sincerely an area of interest to you. A positive answer to the question can help you to stimulate your own thoughts, secure personal and genuine commitment, and keep yourself motivated even when research has become the last item on a long list of day-to-day urgent matters. Blaxter et al. (2001) emphasise the importance of selecting the research topic and they suggest that a potential researcher should also consider how research engagement might lead to enjoying the well-deserved fruits of one's labour, through improving one's curriculum vitae and chances of promotion or even simply contributing to one's personal or professional development. Potential future rewards can also serve as incentives for doing research.

However, it is perhaps the case that some practitioners do not have the luxury of selecting what topic to research but, rather, have been assigned the task of examining a particular phenomenon. However, if the topic is deemed important by other colleagues and/or the school/college management, then such support from colleagues will make the research worth pursuing.

Other crucial factors for consideration

At this stage, your idea, albeit promising, is still a rough research idea. A general idea needs to be suitably narrowed down and translated into a research question or questions. It needs to be refined to generate a focused plan for research that is motivating and relevant, and at the same time realistic and manageable.

Martyn Denscombe (1998: 5) suggests some of the issues to be borne in mind when choosing a research topic include *relevance*, *feasibility*, *coverage*, *accuracy*, *objectivity* and *ethics*. Both the 'addressability' and the achievability of the research questions lie in these decisive attributes. We examine each of these in the following section and then clarify the issues with pertinent examples.

Relevance

The proposed research needs to be seen as a 'well-timed' study given the current issues, policies and general circumstances in education. Whether the research aims to understand or to evaluate, it needs to build upon previous knowledge and use this to establish its significance. The study needs to have a clear and focused purpose that could lead to important research outcomes. In conducting the study, the practitioners may need to be sensitive to the expectations of educational institutions and other stakeholders. There must also be a convincing answer as to why the study needs to take place in a particular place and/or be conducted by you or with other people.

Feasibility

In judging the viability and achievability of the proposed research, the guide questions provided by Lewis and Munn (1987: 17) are very helpful:

- What information do I want? – refers to the nature of the evidence required.
- Why do I want it? – refers to the aptness of the evidence.
- When do I need it? – refers to the timing of research activities and the total timeline for the research.
- How do I collect it? – refers to the approaches, methods and instruments that the research requires.
- Where can I find it? – refers to the sources of evidence (both for primary and secondary information).
- From whom do I get it? – refers to the potential study participants and other gatekeepers of information.

Let us discuss in detail what these questions really mean for you.

1 *What information?* This question clarifies the evidence required to answer the research questions. Your answer to this question will be the basis for gathering either facts or perceptions from primary (for example, survey, interviews) or secondary sources (for example, a literature review) or various combinations of these. When obtaining views, it should be clear if the data gathered were the participants' views (for example, via questionnaires or interviews) or your own views (for example, via observation).

2 *Why this information?* It is possible that a number of research designs could be devised to address the same research question, but weighing up what information could provide the most apt and convincing answer to the question matters. You may need to apply the concept of 'triangulation' or using a combination of data from various sources to increase the credibility or trustworthiness of your study findings.

3 *When do I need it?* You will need to be aware of particular times of the year when you cannot possibly execute certain aspects of the research. In this respect, the school calendar can help decide when best to organise collection of primary and secondary data. Also, it might be necessary for you to incorporate in the design a certain sequence of data collection (for example, a survey with students prior to individual interviews with teachers if the survey is meant to inform the content of the topic guide/interview schedule for teachers). If your study requires the full academic year, you may need to start collecting data just before or shortly after the school starts.

4 *How do I collect it?* Depending on the nature of the evidence that will satisfy the research question, you should employ the most advantageous method of data collection. You will need to prepare a research tool for each method chosen, for example, a questionnaire for surveys or standardised psychometric tests; a schedule for interviews, focus groups or observations; a journal for diary entry. Further, you will need to take into account the criteria for the selected method (for example, the number of respondents and the appropriate sampling technique for a survey; purposive selection of participants when organising focus groups; length of time – both days and hours – for conducting observation).

5 *Where can I find the information?* In research, you will need to be sensitive to what counts as evidence and the best way of obtaining the evidence. Apart from the traditional methods (which are also the most commonly utilised) such sources as school records, essays, official documents, and even your private correspondence between individuals through letters and emails might be accepted as research data. You can also take into account the increasing development of the creative use of images, either as part of the research data themselves or a means of gathering data.

6 *From whom?* Your consideration of what counts as evidence can also be extended to the study participants. In an evaluation of the impact of a new

teaching practice, for example, parents' views may be sought in addition to the pupils' and teachers' perspectives in order to offer a more holistic picture of the phenomenon.

After answering all these questions, the final but nevertheless important question to ask yourself would be the amount of time that you can give to the project while attending to other responsibilities and commitments. Time availability is frequently one of the ultimate deciding factors as to whether or not the research will be accomplished successfully and rigorously.

Coverage

The parameters for the research will be determined by the research questions. Thus, all the instruments should encompass the issues being researched. Research questions will also inform whether your study will be either large scale (findings tend to be generalisable to a wider population) or small scale (insights and understanding may not necessarily be transferable to a different context). Whether a large or a small study, you should aim for a good sample size or an adequate representation of the target respondents to help secure balanced information from a reasonable number of people.

Accuracy

Depending on the sensitivity of the topic, the methods you employ will play a significant role in yielding full, precise and honest responses from the participants. For example, complete anonymity through an online questionnaire may prompt students to express their views more openly than when you and/ or their teacher administer and collect the paper-based questionnaire during classroom hours. The extra care you give to selected questions also assists in encouraging participants to respond to the most vital issues.

Objectivity

Although bias cannot be totally eliminated from research, it is your task as a researcher to be as objective as possible by setting aside your personal assumptions and holding back these assumptions from taking over the research. The key to doing so starts with your awareness and constant reflection on your personal values, beliefs, attitudes and background, which filter the way you perceive things. You should also be prepared to acknowledge the limitations of the study as it might affect the extent of the generalisability of the conclusions and recommendations for the research.

Ethics

Trust and transparency when dealing with the participants need to be established. Additionally, as a researcher, you have the responsibility to protect the identities and interests of the participants by maintaining complete anonymity and an assurance of confidentiality throughout the study. This will not only encourage participants to take part in the study but it will also enable you to discover the views of participants.

There seems to be a lot of consideration required as you clarify what it is you would like to research and what questions you would like to address. Be assured that it is worth the effort. Formulating sound research questions will save you from difficulties and disappointments at a later stage; and going through this process will build your confidence that you are basing your research on a solid foundation. See Figure 3.2 for a summary of the process involved in identifying research questions.

Formulating manageable research questions

So how do you assimilate your preliminary research ideas into these essential considerations and transform them into doable research questions?

Before turning to this, Trochim (2000) suggests three categories of research questions:

- *descriptive questions* – aim to explore or to describe what is currently taking place
- *relational questions* – determine associations between two potentially linked objects, for example, teaching competence and years of service
- *causal questions* – ascertain whether or not one or more variables (regarded as treatment/intervention) lead to the creation of specific outcome(s).

In any investigation, you may use either only one type or a combination of these in formulating your research questions.

Now, here is a scenario: there was an article in a British educational magazine based on a research study undertaken in New Zealand on the learning motivation of very young children. One of the conclusions made in the study was that internal motivation is better than external motivation, although it is the latter that is commonly used in most nurseries and schools through the incentives and rewards system. The article also stressed that internal motivation could be developed from a very young age and have potentially lasting benefits throughout the children's lives.

Let us assume that I were a nursery teacher and I was inspired to undertake a study on the role played by internal motivation on early years learners' performance in school. It is conceivably an interesting and significant study, but first it needs to be narrowed down or reduced to what can feasibly be done within the timescale available, say 12 months. So, how does this work in practice?

Given that I only have a year to conduct this research, the possibility of carrying out a longitudinal study in order to monitor the impact of internal motivation on children as they grow up would be ruled out. Likewise, a comparative study between the role of both external and internal motivation on very

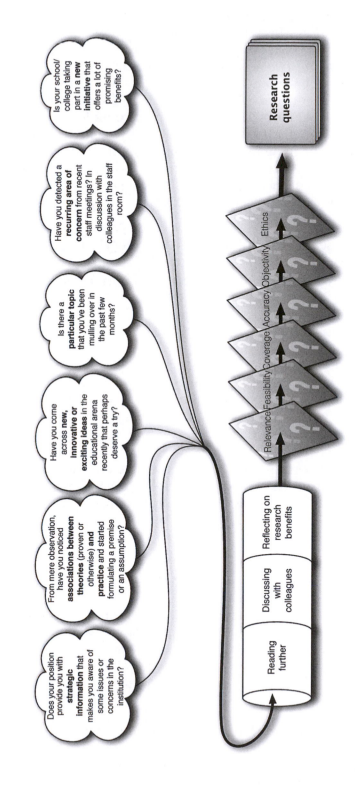

Figure 3.2 A process for identifying your research questions

young children sounds grand and will certainly entail more than the available time, effort and resources. This is too big a study for a full-time nursery teacher so it will need to be narrowed down into a project of a 'workable' size.

Below are examples of two sets of research questions on this subject but with two different foci. If you would like to investigate the different approaches that can effectively enhance early years learners' internal motivation, you might use the questions in example A. This study attempts to understand in general the development of internal motivation among very young children. If, on the other hand, you are more interested in assessing the impact of a certain programme especially designed to instil internal motivation, see the questions in example B. The second study allows me to evaluate the effectiveness of the programme itself against several set criteria.

A: Exploratory research on enhancing early years learners' internal motivation

This type of enquiry is in-depth and exploratory. It aims to discover the ways in which early years learners develop their internal motivation to learn. Data are to be gathered through review of the available literature, observation in class and discussions with parents, teachers and educational psychologists.

1 How is the concept of early years learners' internal motivation generally understood? By teachers? By parents? By educational psychologists?
2 How can the concept of early years learners' internal motivation be developed according to teachers? Parents? Educational psychologists?
3 How is the concept of internal motivation among very young children translated into action?
4 What are the indicators that early years learners are internally motivated to learn according to teachers? Parents? Educational psychologists?
5 How does early years learners' internal motivation influence their learning performance?

B: Evaluative research on the effectiveness of a programme for enhancing early years learners' internal motivation

This study is designed to evaluate an innovative programme intended to instil internal motivation among early years learners. The programme is, therefore, considered an intervention and thus, a pre- and a post-test are to be administered and examined to monitor any changes with the children's level of internal motivation. Similarly, the findings will be compared with the findings taken from a group of early years learners who did not take part in the programme.

1 What does early years learners' internal motivation mean? How can this be assessed?
2 Can the programme raise early years learners' internal motivation? What are the indications that there was an increase?

3 Does the impact of the programme manifest itself immediately? After three months? After six months? After nine months?
4 Can early years learners' internal motivation develop on its own without the programme? Immediately? In three months? In six months? In nine months?
5 How can the programme be enhanced in developing early years learners' internal motivation?

Research questions such as these will inform what other resources are needed for the research or even highlight potential issues. In example B, for example, a lot of organisation may be required for running the programme. Equally, the availability or construction of an appropriate tool for measuring internal motivation is a prime consideration. This type of research is also time consuming for both the researcher and the participants as it requires continual revisits at different stages. The selection of the participants – who will receive or who will not receive the intervention – possibly has ethical implications. It is likely that some of these concerns may pose a problem leading to revision or even reduction of the research questions.

Designing your research

As you can observe, as the intentions of the research are clarified, the research also becomes more focused at the same time. It is important to highlight that the task of defining the research questions, in fact, overlaps with the act of designing the process of the research. Given case examples A and B, the research questions dictate whether a quantitative, a qualitative or a mixed-method approach would be the most rewarding approach. As Cohen et al. (2000) suggest, different research paradigms suit different research objectives and questions. Therefore, 'fitness for purpose' should be your main consideration in making these decisions. This, in turn, informs the selection of the most appropriate methods and research instruments that will enable you to obtain the data that will subsequently be analysed for the purpose of addressing the research questions.

When considering what research design or possible research strategy to employ, Bryman (2004: 56) has provided examples of the most commonly employed research designs, namely 'experimental', 'cross-sectional', 'longitudinal', 'case study' and 'comparative'.

- *Experimental* – This research design is often employed in quantitative enquiries where the impact of an intervention is measured before (pre-test) and after (post-test) by strategically employing two groups of participants, namely the experimental group (those who received/took part in the intervention) and the control group (a group whose members share similar characteristics with the experimental group but did not receive/take part in the intervention). Complementary qualitative data obtained through interviews with both the experimental and control group, before and after the intervention, for example, can substantially augment and explain findings from the quantitative data.

- *Cross-sectional* – Regardless of the research strategy implemented (quantitative or qualitative), researchers need to bear in mind that the data were obtained 'at a single point in time' (Bryman, 2004; Trochim, 2006). This implies that the data collection (for example, questionnaire survey, structured observation, individual interviews, focus groups) within the study is to be administered/conducted with the participants only once. The analogy given is the cross-section of a tree trunk where the data analysis (for example, number of rings, age of the tree) is based solely on a particular section.
- *Longitudinal* – By contrast, longitudinal designs generally involve longer periods for data gathering. Data obtained at different stages are used to monitor emerging patterns or trends. Both quantitative and qualitative data can be obtained through this means depending upon the research tools employed. Longitudinal studies have at least two episodes of measurement (Trochim, 2006) to allow observation of data over time.
- *Case study* – According to Denscombe (1998: 32), 'case studies focus on one instance (or a few instances) of a particular phenomenon with a view to providing an in-depth account of events, relationships, experiences or processes occurring in that particular instance'. Since the investigation is in-depth, this research strategy opts for small numbers and a qualitative type of enquiry through the use of multiple methods.
- *Comparative* – As the name implies, a comparative design considers the characteristics of two or more cases of interest deemed similar or comparable (for example, the educational systems in Scotland and New Zealand – both are small English-speaking countries) by comparing and contrasting acquired data. In making comparisons, both quantitative and qualitative records are used.

Going back to the research questions for the study on early years' internal motivation, the questions require specific research designs. Whereas example A adopted a cross-sectional design, mostly using a qualitative approach, an experimental design with a focus on the quantitative paradigm was employed for example B.

Using example A as a case in point, an outline of a research programme is exemplified in Table 3.1 to illustrate how research ideas can be transformed into actual research activities. We also present the corresponding methods, evidence and research tools adopted for the study to address each of the research questions.

Researchers, either novice or experienced, whether engaged in a small-scale or a large-scale study, will always benefit from conscientious preliminary planning. For educational research to be achievable, it is suggested that planning issues should focus on the practical application (Cohen et al., 2000). This is particularly important for teaching practitioners for whom every hour

Table 3.1 An outline of a research programme

Research questions	Methods	Evidence/data	Tools for data-gathering
How is the concept of early years learners' internal motivation generally understood? By teachers? By parents? By educational psychologists?	Reviewing the literature	Literature data	Books, articles, research studies, educational newspapers and magazines, relevant websites, government publications
	Individual interviews with – teachers – parents – educational psychologists	Qualitative data	Interview schedules
How is internal related to external motivation in terms of very young children's learning development?	Reviewing the literature	Literature data	Books, articles, research studies, educational newspapers and magazines, relevant websites, government publications
	Class observation	Quantitative and qualitative data	Observation schedule
How can the concept of early years learners' internal motivation be developed according to teachers? Parents? Educational psychologists?	Individual interviews with – teachers – parents – educational psychologists	Qualitative data	Interview schedules
How is the concept of internal motivation among very young children translated into action?	Reviewing the literature	Literature data	Books, articles, research studies, educational newspapers and magazines, relevant websites, government publications
	Class observation	Quantitative and qualitative data	Observation schedule
What are the indicators that early years learners are internally motivated to learn according to teachers? Parents? Educational psychologists?	Reviewing the literature	Literature data	Books, articles, research studies, educational newspapers and magazines, relevant websites, government publications

(Continued)

Table 3.1   *(Continued)*

Research questions	Methods	Evidence/Data	Tools for data-gathering
	Individual interviews with – teachers – parents – educational psychologists	Qualitative data	Interview schedules
How does early years learners' internal motivation influence their learning performance?	Reviewing the literature	Literature data	Books, articles, research studies, educational newspapers and magazines, relevant websites, government publications
	Class observation	Quantitative and qualitative data	Observation schedule
	Individual interviews with – teachers – parents – educational psychologists	Qualitative data	Interview schedules

counts. Planning, in fact, helps to save time by managing time-consuming research and dividing the work up into manageable stages. Conversely, embarking on research with no coherent strategy in mind is likely to waste more time in the end.

A research timetable of activities is your blueprint that also serves as a reminder of notional deadlines for each activity for efficient time management. You will need to be mindful of the fact that time for research consists not only of the actual time spent reviewing literature, construction of research instruments, data collection, data analysis or reporting; it also involves planning, obtaining permission, and making arrangements for various aspects of the research. Initial planning is crucial, especially since you are unlikely to have the opportunity to change your methods once you have started with your research, due to time constraints. See the example of a research timetable given in Table 3.2.

Some unforeseen events may occur during the course of the research and this may prompt you to change direction. Required modification may range from changing the mixture of the focus group participants (that is, a minor alteration) to changing the overall design of the research (that is, a major change). For this reason, it would be wise if the timescale is sufficiently flexible to accommodate changes in the research programme should such issues arise.

Table 3.2 A research timetable

Phase	Research activities	Timescale
Phase 1 – *Preparation stage*	Review relevant literature Identify and contact potential participants Get permission from authorities/participants to carry out research Construct research instruments	Summer break
Phase 2 – *Data collection stage*	Classroom observation Individual interviews with teachers Individual interviews/focus group discussions with parents Individual interviews with educational psychologists	Autumn term
Phase 3 – *Data analysis and synthesis stage*	Elementary analysis of numerical data/statistics Thematic analysis of qualitative data (interviews and focus groups) Synthesis of all the findings obtained	Spring term
Phase 4 – *Reporting and dissemination stage*	Write up the research report Present findings to colleagues Present findings at a practitioner research conference	Summer break

Checklist: Readiness to embark on research

As a final check to ascertain your readiness to undertake a piece of research, read the following questions. A positive answer to most of these questions implies a high state of readiness.

Checklist for research readiness	
Does your institution support the conduct of the research?	☐
Does your research comply with the institution's visions, policies or values?	☐
Do you have the support you require from your institution and colleagues to complete the research?	☐
Is the overall research design based on the principle: 'fit for purpose'?	☐
Are you mindful of the parameters and limitations of your chosen design?	☐
Is the research design feasible, realistic and manageable?	☐
Is the timescale adequate for the entire research process to be completed?	☐
Do you have access rights to the potential participants of the study?	☐
Will the research findings offer potential benefits to the parties involved?	☐
Are procedures and practices in place to ensure participants' anonymity and to guarantee the confidentiality of the information they provide?	☐
Are you driven by a strong desire to carry out the research?	☐
Do you have a team of people who can work with you on the research?	☐
Are the resources needed for the research either available or easily accessible?	☐
Are you confident that you have the capacity and the support you require to complete the research?	☐

Further reading

Blaxter, L., Hughes, C. and Tight, M. (2001) *How to Research.* 2nd edn. Buckingham: Open University Press.

Bryman, A. (2004) *Social Research Methods.* 2nd edn. New York: Oxford University Press.

Cohen, L., Manion, L. and Morrison, K. (2000) *Research Methods in Education.* 5th edn. London: RoutledgeFalmer.

Denscombe, M. (1998) *The Good Research Guide for Small-scale Social Research Projects.* Buckingham: Open University Press.

Lewis, I. and Munn, P. (1987) *So You Want to Do Research!* Glenrothes: Barr Printers.

Trochim, M.K. (2006) *Research Methods Knowledge Base.* 3rd edn. http://www.social researchmethods.net/kb/.

Getting it Right! Values and the Ethical Dimensions of Practitioner Research

There has been increased concern about the ethical dimensions of social research in recent years. Two factors which have led to this are, first, the increase in the amount of research activity going on, and second, increased attention to public accountability and individual rights.

Ethics is the branch of philosophy that deals with defining what is good (and what is bad) and with distinguishing the right from the wrong. When we do practitioner research – essentially a very complex and dynamic activity – how can we be sure that we are 'getting it right' – or how can we be sure that we are avoiding 'getting it wrong'? This chapter introduces some of the concepts, principles and practices relevant to taking an ethical approach to practitioner research in education.

> Practitioner research does not begin with the assumption that research purposes are neutral, nor does it assume that the good researcher is studiously agnostic about the questions or outcomes of research. Rather, it is a hallmark of much of practitioner research that the ultimate goal is challenging inequities, raising questions about the status quo, and enhancing the learning and life chances of students. (Cochran-Smith and Lytle, 2009: 102)

At the outset, it is important to remind ourselves that moral questions and questions of values underlie all educational actions. That is, there is always a purpose to education that involves some judgement about bringing about changes in other people. These may be developments in knowledge, understanding, attitudes or indeed values, but it is assumed that these changes are about improvement or betterment. Indeed any education that was leading to damage or harm would not be seen – at least in a liberal democracy – as education. It might rather be seen as indoctrination or brainwashing.

That may sound a simple position to set out, but of course, in reality, there are often enormous controversies about the nature of education, about teaching and learning, about the curriculum and about assessment. Not everyone will agree on what may be judged as improvement or betterment and this reminds us that the values that underlie any educational activity are themselves socially created in particular contexts by particular people, reflecting the values of those people themselves.

Ethics are therefore directly related to values and to defining moral behaviour. The kinds of questions that frequently arise in educational discussion of education and also, as we shall see, in educational research, are whether dubious means may be justified by successful ends. Arguments for corporal punishment, for example, were often of this kind. While physical punishment may cause pain and short-term harm, it was said to be in the long-term interest of the pupil's education.

Growing awareness of human rights is one of the factors that has largely led to a rejection of the means–ends separation, and similarly to a rejection of any element of deception in social interactions, including research interactions. Openness, transparency and trust have become watchwords for ethical behaviour in our society and the rights of children, parents and indeed teachers are frequent topics of discussion.

In this chapter we consider some aspects of ethical dimensions of educational practice before discussing the extent to which they are mirrored, amplified or different when there is a research dimension within such practice. We discuss particular ethical issues that are raised in education research and then in particular within practitioner research. In this section we pay attention to how you may address these issues in your own research. We conclude by suggesting a number of resources that may help you in these matters.

Ethics and educational practice

It is the law that provides the overall formal framework for moral behaviour for all citizens. Laws concerning ownership of property, employment, personal behaviour or violence apply equally to all, including education practitioners. More recent laws in the UK relate directly to relationships between people and to data and information. Each of these may have particular significance in the context of practitioner research (see the appendix to this chapter for more on the significance of three particular pieces of legislation: The Data Protection Act, the Freedom of Information Act and the Race Relations Act). However, one of the distinguishing features of professions in modern societies is that they have a particular code of conduct that applies to them in their occupational contexts. Perhaps the most well known of these is the Hippocratic oath that was traditionally taken by doctors when they entered that profession, but there are similar undertakings expected of lawyers, accountants and, indeed, teachers. Each country within the UK has a formal statement of requirements that must be met and demonstrated by those entering the teaching profession. These cover a whole range of matters such as classroom skills, knowledge and understanding of the curriculum, but they also set out a range of professional issues based, either explicitly or implicitly, on a set of values, including moral values. So, for example, in Scotland the Standard for Initial Teacher Education defines some core professional interests.

Extracts from the Standard for Initial Teacher Education in Scotland

Core professional interests

Programmes of Initial Teacher Education are dynamic, changing and developing. They prepare student teachers to undertake progressively the professional duties required of teachers, and to reflect on the values and principles underpinning the curriculum, on the purposes of education, and on the nature of the education system, not only to respond to changes in the professional context, but also to contribute to that process of change. The range of core professional interests and requirements for the teacher will include:

- taking a professional responsibility for enabling all young people to become confident individuals, responsible citizens, successful learners and effective contributors;
- being accountable for contributing to the education of the whole child or young person, and taking professional responsibility for developing the personality, talents and mental, spiritual and physical attributes of each child or young person;
- engaging with current educational issues and contributing to the processes of curriculum research and development, staff development and school development;
- having confidence in their role in supporting and protecting children, including identifying where children need help and understanding the steps to take in line with child protection procedures;
- understanding the legal and professional aspects of a teacher's position of trust in relation to pupils;
- promoting equality of opportunity among all people in an inclusive society, and actively taking steps to counter discrimination;
- promoting the learning of those pupils who encounter barriers to learning, including those who are in need of additional support in particular areas of the curriculum; and those with emotional and behavioural difficulties. (GTCS, 2006)

In more detail, the value commitments are set out later in the same document:

3.1 Value and demonstrate a commitment to social justice, inclusion and protecting and caring for children.	• Demonstrate that they respect and value children and young people as unique, whole individuals. • Demonstrate respect for the rights of all children and young people without discrimination as defined in the United Nations Convention on the Rights of the Child 1991, the Children (Scotland) Act 1995, the Standards in Scotland's Schools Act etc 2000 and the Additional Support for Learning Act 2005. • Demonstrate commitment to promoting and supporting the Children's Charter and the Framework for Standards for protecting children and young people. • Demonstrate that they value and promote fairness and justice and adopt anti-discriminatory practices in respect of gender, sexual orientation, race, disability, age, religion, culture and socio-economic background. • Demonstrate a willingness to intervene effectively to promote, support, and safeguard the individual development, well-being and social competence of the pupils in their class/register groups, and to raising these pupils' expectations of themselves and others. • Know how to follow local child protection procedures, demonstrate an understanding of their role in keeping children safe and well and of the importance of sharing concerns about the safety or well-being of a child. (GTCS, 2006)

So, the commitment to social justice is very explicit and has ethical implications.

In Northern Ireland the equivalent statement reads thus:

Core Values

The core values of the profession are as follows:

Trust Honesty Commitment Respect Fairness Equality Integrity Tolerance Service

A commitment to serve lies at the heart of professional behaviour. In addition, members of the profession will exemplify the values listed above in their work and in their relationships with others; recognising, in particular, the unique and privileged relationship that exists between teachers and their pupils. In keeping with the spirit of professional service and commitment, teachers will at all times be conscious of their responsibilities to others:

learners, colleagues and indeed the profession itself.

Many of the commitments outlined below are also underpinned by legislation and the profession will always seek, as a minimum, to comply with both the spirit and detail of relevant legislative requirements. (GTCNI, 2007)

However, teachers are not just required to uphold such behaviour and principles on entry into the profession. Such behaviour is required to be maintained throughout teachers' careers. In the UK there is now a General Teaching Council in each jurisdiction (although the English GTC is likely to be abolished), one of whose responsibilities is to devise and uphold a professional code of conduct. These codes of conduct set out the behaviours and dispositions that are expected of teachers in their professional work, covering such matters as relationships with pupils, parents and colleagues, financial integrity and professional honesty.

In England the Code of Conduct which took effect in 2009 sets out eight principles of conduct and practice for teachers:

Registered teachers:

1 Put the wellbeing, development and progress of children and young people first.
2 Take responsibility for maintaining the quality of their teaching practice.
3 Help children and young people to become confident and successful learners.
4 Demonstrate respect for diversity and promote equality.
5 Strive to establish productive partnerships with parents and carers.
6 Work as part of a whole-school team.
7 Co-operate with other professional colleagues.
8 Demonstrate honesty and integrity and uphold public trust and confidence in the teaching profession. (GTCE, 2009)

The particular significance of professional codes of conduct in education is that they recognise the importance of the relationship between the teacher and the taught – analogous in some ways to the relationship between doctor and patient. Teachers are invariably in a position of trust, indeed they were traditionally seen as being entrusted with parental responsibility, *in loco parentis*, as the old saying had it. Even if it is now accepted as being different from a parent–child relationship, there are nevertheless aspects concerning trust and child protection that are very similar. Teachers, however, do additionally hold responsibility for ensuring that their learners are provided with opportunities to learn and they are responsible for assessing that learning. There are elements therefore of power within these relationships which have the potential for exploitation and abuse. There are plenty of examples in English literature that may remind us of these possibilities, whether it be the *Hard Times* of some Dickensian pupils or the dubious influence of Miss Jean Brodie in her prime on the girls who were in her charge.

Occasions where contemporary teachers do breach the professional code of conduct are relatively rare and sometimes attract a considerable amount of publicity. However, that is not to say that it is easy for teachers to behave entirely ethically at all times. Every education practitioner is making hundreds, if not thousands, of decisions throughout their working day. Many of these decisions have an ethical dimension – should I make this provision for child A or for child B, if resources are limited? Should I report my suspicions about bullying to other teachers when I have so little evidence? For readers who have a strong interest in these matters there are sources where the issues are discussed at much greater depth than is possible here (for example, Campbell, 2003; Carr, 1999). The extent to which teachers should be able to articulate ethical matters, that is the extent to which they should be educated in the ethics of education, is a subject that has rarely been discussed (see Mahony, 2009).

Ethics and educational research

So, if teaching is itself governed by codes of conduct which include ethical considerations, what additional issues arise when practitioners embark on research activity?

Most social research involves some form of interaction with people, with 'human subjects'. The most obvious exception would be research that is entirely based on previously published material, such as a literature review (see Chapter 6). But even here there can be ethical matters to be considered, for example, ensuring that full credit is given to the relevant people for previous work and that sources are not presented inappropriately – plagiarism is, after all, in essence a matter of ethics!

There are good pragmatic grounds as well as ethical grounds for ensuring that research designs are carefully thought through. There is no legal obligation on anyone who is approached by a researcher seeking their cooperation – whether it be to fill in a questionnaire, undertake an interview or be subject to observation – to comply with the request. Many of those who are researched will have competing demands on their time or other reasons that may lead them to decline. Being clear, explicit and open with potential respondents is likely to influence people in a positive way towards the research.

One of the reasons that some people may be suspicious is that there have been instances where research has been undertaken covertly. A number of early 'ethnographic' studies involved the researcher entering the research field 'under cover', that is, posing as a normal member of the group concerned, rather than making it clear that s/he was a researcher (for example, Patrick, 1973; Pryce, 1979). Of course, in some settings this may raise not only questions of honesty and deception, but also about personal safety for the researcher. Such an approach after all is not very different from espionage!

There are also tales of researchers who have put research subjects into situations that are deeply questionable morally. The most well-known example of this is the experiments conducted by Stanley Milgram in the USA which put research subjects in the situation of believing they were administering electric shocks to other human beings in the cause of research into pain, when actually the research was concerned with obedience and authority.

As was noted earlier there is much more regulation and guidance now about the conduct of social research. The major UK funding body for social research, the Economic and Social Research Council, recently launched a major initiative that introduced a binding requirement on all applicants for funding to seek ethical approval for their studies through formal procedures within their host institution. It is now the case therefore that every university and other agency that carries out social research has instituted a framework for scrutinising and checking that research designs have been developed in line with good ethical practice.

These frameworks have sometimes been based on existing models applied in medical research, where there has long been concern about use of placebos and about those involved in the trialling of drugs being fully aware of the risks they are taking. Such medical models are not always entirely appropriate in social research, but the same concerns prevail about minimising risk, avoiding harm and maintaining openness and transparency. Within education, and in the light of the earlier discussion about teachers and learners, it must be immediately apparent that the educational well-being of learners must be a very high priority, as well as being concerned about the protection of other human subjects of educational research including parents, teachers and other education workers.

The British Educational Research Association (BERA) and then other similar bodies (such as the Scottish association, SERA) developed ethical guidelines specifically for education researchers. These drew from similar documents developed elsewhere for educational researchers, as well as on guidance developed by similar British societies such as the British Sociological Association and the British Psychological Society.

The ethical principles covered by the SERA (and BERA) guidelines are represented by a commitment to an ethic of respect for:

- the person;
- knowledge;
- democratic values;
- justice and equity;
- the quality of educational research;
- academic freedom.

These guiding principles are applied to four key areas of responsibility on the part of educational researchers, namely:

- responsibilities to participants in research;
- responsibilities to sponsors and other stakeholders in educational research;
- responsibilities to the field of educational research;
- responsibilities to the community of educational researchers. (SERA, 2005)

What we have here is one set of values and one set of responsibilities to various parties. When the two are brought together, what emerges is a series of ethical guidelines that amount to indicating how our actions in relation to the various parties may be shaped by the values. None of the value phrases are simple, they require further definition. If we take 'the quality of educational research' for example, what is meant by this?

In Chapter 1 we suggested that research is systematic enquiry made public. This enquiry must be based on open procedures and that is one of the tests applied through making it public. But does that also mean that the researcher should be neutral and/or objective in their work? Neutrality and objectivity are two concepts that are certainly problematic within social sciences. By contrast, within physical science it is usually assumed that the researcher is a detached observer of physical phenomena, and therefore in a fundamental sense neutral. However, in social research, while the researcher's aims may well include the quest for better knowledge and understanding, there is a usually a social purpose behind the research, whether it be to understand the causes of poverty in order to alleviate them or to understand group interaction better in order to create more harmonious inter-gender relations. Do these social purposes in some way make the researcher something other than neutral, if not in some way biased? Furthermore, when it comes to objectivity, can we expect a social researcher to be entirely detached from the people she or he is investigating? Is there not bound to be some element of empathy, indeed subjectivity, involved in the research interactions? These are challenges to which we shall return in the next section as we look more closely at practitioner research in education.

Ethics in practitioner research

Early examples of practitioner research in education include little or no explicit reference to matters of ethics. For example the classic work by Michael Armstrong, where he was researching and teaching alongside Stephen Rowland in Rowland's primary classroom, makes no mention of such concerns (Armstrong, 1980). Nor, if we look at the range of studies carried out as part of their Master's dissertations by students of Webb (1990), do we see much mention of these issues. Even in a larger-scale study such as Pollard's *Social World of the Primary School*, published in 1984, much of it carried out in classrooms where he was teaching, while considerable attention is paid to theory and methodology, there is little said about any ethical issues that arose during the research.

Somewhat by contrast those researchers who were adopting some form of 'action research' model did tend to concern themselves more explicitly with ethical matters. This is especially notable in the activity that developed on the basis of the seminal work of Lawrence Stenhouse and others at the University of East Anglia. The typical model of research here was not so much teachers undertaking research into their own practice but, rather, university researchers working in classrooms alongside teachers, as 'critical friends' (see Campbell et al., 2004, Chapter 7, for more discussion of this).

The general level of awareness of research ethics over recent years has impacted within practitioner research. Doing research as a practitioner, we cannot ignore our professional codes of conduct, as discussed above. But, because research activity may go beyond what is normally undertaken as a teacher or lecturer (or other professional in an education setting – school counsellor, youth worker, and so on) – there are additional considerations to take into account. These cannot necessarily be separated from the professional considerations but may augment them. Indeed it has been suggested that the dual role of teacher and researcher is itself ethically problematic. As Cochran-Smith and Lytle put it, such critics suggest that: 'When practitioners (especially teachers) are engaged in research, they inevitably face conflicts of interest that jeopardize the best interests of their students' (2009: 47). They argue themselves that actually these 'blended roles' are 'an advantage and a potential window into rich and enhanced insights about practice' (ibid.). This is not to deny that there are some particular ethical challenges in practitioner research – and we shall come to those shortly – but is to suggest that these challenges do not create an insurmountable barrier to successful practitioner research. Rather, if they are addressed they are likely to contribute to the fruitfulness of the outcomes of the research.

However, before turning to the particular issues, there is one more general question to be discussed. Picking up on the earlier point about neutrality and objectivity in social research, we now need to consider whether practitioner research can aim or claim to be either neutral and/or objective. There is a strong body of opinion within the field that suggests actually, the reverse is true. That is, that practitioner research should be very clear that it is concerned to bring about change based on particular value positions.

Some of those who have argued this position call for (practitioner) 'research for social justice'. They argue that it is essential to be explicit about your values, so that no one can say you are concealing your motives. If education itself is about improvement then should not educational research also be about improvement and not simply about 'finding out' or 'improving understanding'? Thus concepts such as 'research for social justice' (Griffiths, 1998; Troyna and Griffiths, 1995) and 'action research for educational change' (Elliot, 1991) have been developed. In such models, not only are values explicitly stated, but the research itself is designed to bring about the promotion or implementation of those values. Such views are also consistent with a view of teaching as a transformative activity (Sachs, 2003).

A more nuanced approach – perhaps some kind of 'halfway house' – may be represented by the view developed by Cochran-Smith and Lytle of 'Inquiry as Stance'. In a fascinating discussion about practitioner research orientations, they argue that practitioner research should indeed have an inherent model of change and development. As they put it, such practitioner researchers:

> have to continuously form and reform the interpretive frameworks that guide their moment to moment actions as well as their deliberate and more considered long-term decisions in the interest of educating for a more just and democratic society. (Cochran-Smith and Lytle, 2009:151)

Ethical issues in practitioner research in education

As Oliver (2008) points out in his overview of ethics in research, ethical issues arise before, during and after the actual research activity within a project. That is, decisions of an ethical nature have to be made as you design your study, as you carry it out and as you report and disseminate it. In the section that follows we identify a number of common matters that may arise within practitioner research projects, when judgements of an ethical nature have to be made.

Access to the research site

Access to the research site is typically seen as an important aspect of any social research. Methods books typically refer to the need to identify and approach appropriate 'gatekeepers', in order to secure permission to carry out the intended work. However, the situation in the context of practitioner research is somewhat unusual. Almost by definition, you as a practitioner researcher are already working within the research site, indeed it is your place of work. Therefore, it might be suggested that access does not have to be negotiated in the usual way. Nevertheless we want to suggest that because of the 'additional' role you are taking on as a researcher, it may well be important that part of securing a strong ethical basis for your research is indeed to go through some procedures that legitimate your research activity and ensure that those around you are aware of this aspect of your activity. Within an early years, school or college setting this will usually entail seeking agreement from your line manager, headteacher head of department, and sometimes your local authority that you may undertake the planned project. It will often be appropriate also to seek agreement from your colleagues, your peers, other teachers, lecturers, ancillary staff, as appropriate. But then the most challenging aspect may be to secure agreement from the learners in your setting, whether they be children or young adults. We deal with approaching individuals for their cooperation in a later sub-section, but here the issue is the gaining of a general agreement that you may undertake the research activity. In all three cases – line manager, colleagues, learners – it is wise to have some form of written statement that you can refer to, either by asking the party concerned to read it or by using it as the basis of an oral explanation. Again, we deal below with the nature of 'Plain language statements' of research activity.

Once the research has started it may be important from time to time to remind those around you of the fact that your research is continuing. In the busy world of education, it is very easy to forget such matters and a fully transparent approach will therefore necessarily involve occasional reminders.

Informed consent and freedom from coercion

If the notion of 'access' to the research site is about securing general agreement for your research to proceed in the chosen location, then there will be further permissions that require to be sought as the research gets underway, depending on the particular methods that you are using. For example if you are planning to undertake interviews then it is good practice to provide a consent form that the interviewee is asked to sign before you start the interview. Figure 4.1 is an example.

The mention of an outline in Item 1 in Figure 4.1 is a reference to a plain language statement which would normally be a statement on less than one side of paper written in easily understandable language, setting out the purposes of your study and the nature of the data gathering that you are undertaking. Either this and/or the consent form should include a commitment from you on the subject of confidentiality and anonymity. Figure 4.2 is an example of a plain language statement used on the same project as the consent form above.

Anonymity and confidentiality

Commitments to anonymity should not be made lightly. Even if you give a commitment not to use the real names of your respondents in the report that you prepare and any publications that may emerge from it, do remember that

University of Glasgow | Faculty of Education

The University of Glasgow, charity number SC004401

Teacher Consent Form

Title of Project: *Glasgow Secondary Schools Partnership Project*

Project Director: Professor Ian Menter

1   I confirm that I have read and understand the outline of the above study and have had the opportunity to ask questions.

2   I understand that my participation is voluntary and that I am free to withdraw at any time, without giving any reason and without consequence.

3   I give my consent for interviews to be audio-recorded and I understand that copies of the interview transcripts will be returned to me for verification on request.

4   I understand that I will not be identified by name in any publications arising from the research, unless I give my express permission.

5   I agree/do not agree (delete as applicable) to take part in the above study.

_____   _____   _____
Name of Participant   Date   Signature

_____   _____   _____
Researcher   Date   Signature

1 for participant; 1 for researcher

Figure 4.1   Example of a teacher consent form

if you are circulating outcomes of your study within your own institution or in the local professional community, it may be very difficult to fully protect the identity of some of the participants. For a start, you yourself as the practitioner researcher at the centre of the study are likely to be named on the front page! if you make reference to the headteacher of the institution, there is only likely to be one of these in your institution.

So our advice is to be realistic about the extent to which you can guarantee anonymity. This makes the matter of trust between you and the people in your research all the more important.

On the question of confidentiality, this too can be challenging in a practitioner research setting. If you carry out an interview with one child in your class who tells you something about another child, for example, how sure

University of Glasgow | Faculty of Education

The University of Glasgow, charity number SC004401

Project Director: Professor Ian Menter
Telephone: 0141 330 3480/ 3450
Email: I.Menter@educ.gla.ac.uk

Title of Project: *Glasgow Secondary Schools Partnership Project*

Information for parents (1)

> *This statement sets out the rationale for this research and indicates what it will involve. Please take time to read the following information carefully. Contact Moira Hulme if there is anything that is not clear or if you would like further information. Thank you for reading this.*

The Scottish Government, in partnership with Glasgow City Council, has commissioned a study of what schools do to improve. The project involves ten secondary schools in Glasgow. The aim of the study is to identify lessons learned that can be shared with other schools in the City and more widely.

Your child attends a school that has recently been involved in making changes. We would like to consult your child about the changes that have taken place.

If you were agreeable, your child would be asked to participate in an audio-recorded small group interview with other pupils of similar age. This informal group interview will last for fifty minutes (maximum) and will be held in school during school hours. A member of the research team will conduct the interview between September and November 2009. You will be asked to sign a consent form agreeing to your child's participation.

Your child does *not* have to take part and can decide to withdraw at any point, without disadvantage.

The findings of the study will be reported to participating schools, Glasgow City Council and the Scottish Government. At no point will your child be identified by name in any publication resulting from this study. If you are interested in any of the presentations or publications, you have a right to see them.

The University of Glasgow Faculty of Education Ethics Committee has reviewed this research.

Thank you for considering your child's participation in this study.

Contact for further information:
Dr Moira Hulme
Faculty of Education
University of Glasgow
St Andrew's Building
11 Eldon Street
Glasgow
G3 6NH
Telephone: 0141 330 3411
Email: m.hulme@educ.gla.ac.uk

If you have concerns about this research contact:
Dr Georgina Wardle
Faculty of Education Ethics Officer
University of Glasgow
St Andrew's Building
11 Eldon Street
Glasgow
G3 6NH
Telephone: 0141 330 3426
E-mail: G.Wardle@educ.gla.ac.uk

Figure 4.2   Example of a plain language statement

can you be that this will not influence the way in which you interview that second child? Worse still, if the second child is aware that you previously interviewed the first child, may they be able to deduce the source of any inferences they detect in the way you ask your questions?

A further complication may arise in respect of issues around disclosure. If during the course of your research activity you become aware of some sensitive information – examples might be accounts of drug misuse by a child's siblings or of domestic violence within a child's household – and you have already given a commitment to confidentiality, then what can be done? It is our view that if your relationship with the respondent concerned is as a teacher as well as as a researcher, then the code of conduct that you would follow in your professional capacity as a teacher has to prevail. It is crucial that any information that you have concerning serious risk to the child or young person concerned, must be shared with the appropriate authority. Therefore it will be important in gaining consent that you do not appear to be relinquishing your existing role and relationship with the learner/child.

Working with children and young people

The meaning of 'informed consent' when working with young people is itself a problematic one. How can a young inexperienced person be deemed to be fully informed about the nature of research and consenting to take part? Well, in reality, this question could be asked about any person being asked to give informed consent. In other words 'informed consent' is not an absolute term. You as a researcher may do your best to inform a possible participant, but you can never be sure either that you have conveyed everything that is relevant, not that they have understood what you have said or its significance. So, from an ethical point of view, what we are saying is that the researcher should be doing her best to inform the participants and should be encouraging them to think seriously about whether or not to give consent. For children this may involve more explanation than for adults and it may also mean careful discussion with parents and/or carers and other adults with responsibility for the children concerned.

Added challenges may arise when children's linguistic development is at an early stage and it may be that reliance entirely on words to negotiate consent is not appropriate. It may be that images of some kind may help the child to understand what is being proposed and asked. Similarly, working with children with learning disabilities can add additional challenges to implementing an ethical approach. How can you as a teacher be confident that a potential respondent has actually understood what you have painstakingly explained to her/him? Is it possible to check their understanding in some way, perhaps through asking some additional questions?

Some studies – and this could include your own practitioner studies – seek not only to invite children to become the subjects of research, but actually to involve them as researchers themselves (see examples of books in the further reading section.) Here, too, a range of ethical considerations must be taken into account. If you want to ask children and young people to gather the views of others, for example, in the playground or the classroom, how can you ensure that the children and young people they are interacting with have been fully informed?

In the end, as we said, it is rarely possible to be 100 per cent confident about the ethical basis of educational research. All that anyone can do is their best to ensure that procedures are understood, that participants are as well informed as they can be, that careful notes are recorded by the researcher on all of these matters and that formal agreements are secured when and where that is possible and appropriate.

(For further insights into challenges of researching with children see Lewis et al., 2004.)

Issues with observation

Observation, whether in classrooms, playgrounds or other settings, is a very common method used in education research. There are all kinds of approaches that are possible (see Chapter 10), but it is worth considering what kinds of ethical issues you may encounter if you choose to use observation as a part of your data gathering.

To start with the obvious, all teachers are continuously observing learners. It is a key element in teaching. Without monitoring and evaluating learners' behaviours and responses it is not possible for a teacher to proceed with her task. So, observation is something teachers take for granted and, to a large extent, it is something that learners implicitly understand is part of their teacher's role. So, what is different when a teacher is observing for the purposes of research? Well, not necessarily a great deal. But the significance of that question really depends on what the focus of the research is – what the questions are that the teacher is investigating. It may well be that if the research question is very much within the 'conventional' domains of pedagogy and curriculum, very few, if any, additional questions arise. However, if the teacher is researching something which is not part of the normally taken for granted business of the classroom, then it may be that s/he should make it very clear to learners that part of what is being observed goes beyond the normal expectation.

A teacher who is seeking through her research to assess differences in boys' and girls' responses to a particular element of the curriculum may well wish to explain to the learners that this is one reason for her carrying out observations. As a 'rule of thumb', as with so much that we have said in this chapter, it is almost always best to be open with the learners and to explain the nature of your interests as you pursue the research, whether it be through observation or through other techniques.

Publication and authorship

Ethical issues may also arise at the end of a research study, at the time when you are writing up and disseminating, and perhaps publishing, the outcomes of your work. Clearly, all that we have said before about anonymity and confidentiality becomes very important again at this point as you ensure that you hold to the undertakings you have made to the participants in your research. But the original work that you have undertaken is now your own intellectual property and you have rights over it as well as responsibilities. You will wish to ensure that your own name and position are accurately reported in any papers or articles or reports on your work that emerge. However you will also need to ensure that any work by others that you have referred to is also properly attributed to them. This is likely to be especially pertinent in the context of any literature review that you write. There are many conventions for the formal recording of references – most education research uses a version of the Harvard system. But it really is most important that you mark any direct quotations you use from other people's work, for example, by the use of quotation marks and/or through indenting quoted sections, as well as by giving an easily traceable reference, including the page number for the extract you have used and an accurate citation of electronic sources.

Ownership of intellectual property is not always a straightforward matter. You may have collaborated in some way with others while carrying out your research. It is desirable that any issues around joint ownership of research material and eventually of joint authorship, are discussed at the outset. It can be quite difficult to raise these matters only at the end of a process. If you are working in a team that wishes to share ownership equally, that may still create problems. The order of the listing of authors of a report or an article may not seem significant, but in some circles it certainly is. Very often it is the first named author who is assumed to be the lead author with major responsibility for a piece. You may wish to have an agreement in your team to take it in turns to be listed first, or you may decide to reject such conventions and always go for an alphabetical listing.

Researcher bias

It is assumed that researchers seek to avoid bias in their enquiries. In the context of research, bias may be taken to mean undue influence of the researcher's own predispositions or prejudices on some aspect of the procedures that are being carried out. This could occur at any point in the research process from the very identification of the research question, through the research design, to the drawing up of research instruments, to the writing up and dissemination of the work. Bias is to be avoided because it reflects covert distortion of the 'reality' that the research is seeking to analyse. Very often when unbiased research gets into the hands of the press or politicians it may be that the interpretation of the research is subject to bias (this is picked up in Chapter 14). But for our purposes here we seek to help you to avoid accusations of bias in your work as a teacher researcher.

Throughout this chapter we have sought to promote the view that research cannot in some way be 'value-free'. All aspects of the research process are based on judgements made by the researcher that will reflect his or her own values. But what we are saying is important is that each researcher endeavours to bring those guiding values to the surface, to make them explicit so that the participants and eventually the reader can be clear 'where you are coming from' and can then make their own judgements about the value of your research and its 'authenticity'.

Feminist and anti-racist perspectives

Anti-sexism and anti-racism are but two examples of 'value positions' that may influence a research study. They are both concerned with social justice and may be treated either as 'givens' or as 'purposes' of research.

If they are treated as givens then that would suggest a shared assumption that we will be endeavouring to ensure that all aspects of the research we are undertaking will be based on a commitment to gender and 'race' equality. So, while that is a reasonable expectation of all research within a democracy, it is nevertheless a reminder that we should be seeking to avoid unconscious bias or discrimination. Does the language of a questionnaire implicitly favour girls over boys or does our focus group technique allow white students more verbal 'space' than students from black and minority ethnic (BME) groups? In a sense these are not specifically research issues – they are issues that all teachers should be aware of.

On the other hand we may wish to undertake research that is actually designed to address issues of sex and/or racial discrimination, in which case we treat these as values behind the purpose of the research. So you may wish to explore the effects of different gender groupings on pupils' learning in technology lessons, having noted that girls appear to be doing less well, compared with their achievement in other subjects. Or you may have read some of the research that indicates that many (white) teachers interact differently with pupils from BME backgrounds (Gillborn, 1995) and wish to assess your own interactions in relation to ethnicity. In either of these cases you will be designing a study that is intended to lead to greater social justice within your classroom.

Conclusion

There is no doubt that matters of ethics and values in educational research are complex. For a practitioner researcher there is the additional complexity of being both practitioner and researcher. The overarching principle set out in this chapter has been to call for as much transparency, clarity and explicitness as is possible. You can never be certain of getting everything right, but if you do your best to work through the ethical challenges and to tease out questions of values, it is very unlikely that you will not get the support of those around you. The general guidelines drawn up by Hopkins in the 1980s should still prove helpful:

An ethics checklist for education practitioner research

1 Observe protocols.
2 Involve participants.
3 Negotiate with those affected.
4 Report progress.
5 Obtain explicit authorization before you observe.
6 Obtain explicit authorization before you examine files, correspondence or other documentation.
7 Negotiate descriptions of people's work.
8 Negotiate accounts of others' points of view.
9 Obtain explicit authorization before using quotations.
10 Negotiate reports for various levels of release.
11 Accept responsibility for maintaining confidentiality.
12 Retain the right to retain your work.
13 Make your principles of procedure binding and known. (Based on Hopkins, 1985)

For a more detailed checklist, that reflects some of the recent developments of thinking about practitioner research, here is one adapted from Zeni et al. (2001: 155–65):

• What professional problem does your research address? How was this determined? Who owns the problem? Is it a problem in your own practice, suggested by the School Improvement Plan, school inspection report and/or national policy priorities?
• What is your role in the setting where the research will take place? What do you bring to the research – personally, culturally and professionally? What is your position in relation to dimensions of cultures such as gender, ethnicity, age, community, social class, and family?
• How does your research differ from the ways in which you would normally document your practice? (Bounds of 'accepted practice'.)
• Which participants at your school or college have read your proposal? Which ones have been informed of the research orally in some detail? Which ones know little or nothing about your project? Reflect on the decisions behind your choices.
• Does your study evaluate your own effectiveness or a method to which you are committed? How will you handle the temptation to see what you expect

to see? How will you obtain other perspectives from people who do not share your assumptions?

- Who will be touched by your research? What are their roles? Which people do you have power over? Which people have power over you? What shared understanding do you have with these people? Do you have personal bonds, professional commitments? Will this research strengthen this trust or possibly abuse it?
- What are the possible benefits of your research for participants and the wider school or college community?
- How will you protect the people from whom you collect data? What are the limits to anonymity? Does anonymity conflict with intellectual property rights (the right to be acknowledged)? Will you use composite portraits, pseudonyms, interchange gender, and so on?
- Have you considered different kinds of consent, for example, the consent to participation and consent to publish specific material from specific people? How *informed* is informed consent?
- Does your local authority/district/trust have a formal review procedure? If you are conducting research as part of an award bearing course, are you familiar with the ethical approval application process?
- Will stakeholders view a draft of your report? Will this improve accuracy or compromise candour?
- Consider why you chose some data to report to the wider community and why some is left in your files. Consider the politics of the way in which you focus your story.
- How do your line managers/senior management team view your work? Are colleagues supportive or suspicious? Is your work part of organisational quality control? How safe do you feel in the institutional setting pursuing this research? Will you be free to report your findings to a wider audience?
- Is the research sponsored through a small grant from an external funding body, an honorarium from your employer or release time? What are the supporter's expectations? Consider possible implications of sponsorship.

If you are undertaking your research as part of a university based award-bearing programme, then in addition to satisfying yourself that you are following ethical procedures you are likely to be required to demonstrate this formally to the university, through the submission of an ethical approval form. Each university has its own particular procedure for this, but it is likely to involve the completion of a form to be submitted to a university or faculty committee. You may also be expected to supply copies of your plain language statements, consent forms and perhaps examples of questionnaires, interview schedules or other research instruments. While this can sometimes feel like a burdensome bureaucratic exercise, it does have the advantage – once your research has been approved – of legitimising your activity. Any significant changes you make to the research design will also require returning to the committee for additional approval.

Further reading 📖

Campbell, A. and Groundwater-Smith, D. (eds) (2007) *An Ethical Approach to Practitioner Research.* London: Routledge. This is a very valuable collection that picks up many of the issues in this chapter and discusses them in more detail. Many of the contributors are leading practitioner research scholars.

If you wish to consider the question of ethics and teaching (that is, the professional dimensions) more fully then both of the following are very worthwhile:

Campbell, E. (2003) *The Ethical Teacher.* Buckingham: Open University Press.

Carr, D. (1999) *Professionalism and Ethics in Teaching.* London: Routledge.

Finally, a book which addresses questions around social justice and educational research is:

Griffiths, M. (1998) *Educational Research for Social Justice.* London: Open University.

Other useful sources include:

Farrell, A. (ed.) (2005) *Ethical Research with Children.* Maidenhead: Open University Press.

Haynes, F. (1998) *The Ethical School.* London: Routledge.

Israel, S.E. and Lassonde, C.A. (eds) (2007) *The Ethical Educator.* New York: Peter Lang.

Zeni, J. (ed.) (2001) *Ethical Issues in Practitioner Research.* New York: Teachers College Press.

Further reading on *children and young people as researchers*:

Kellet, M. (2005) *How to Develop Children as Researchers.* London: Paul Chapman.

Thomson, P. (ed.) (2008) *Doing Visual Research with Children and Young People.* London: Routledge.

Save the Children/Joseph Rowntree Foundation (2000) *Young People as Researchers: A Learning Resource Pack.* London: Save the Children.

Resources

BERA Guidelines: http://www.bera.ac.uk/files/guidelines/ethica1.pdf.

SERA Guidelines: http://www.sera.ac.uk/docs/Publications/SERA%20Ethical%20GuidelinesWeb. PDF.

Appendix

Data Protection Act 1998

As a researcher you may well be gathering personal information about particular people. The Data Protection law seeks to ensure that you do not misuse such data.

The basics

The Data Protection Act requires anyone who handles personal information to comply with a number of important principles. It also gives individuals rights over their personal information.

Your rights

Individuals have a wide range of rights under the Data Protection Act, including access, compensation and the prevention of processing.

Your legal obligations

If you handle personal information, you have a number of important legal obligations. All the details are here.

Guidance

The ICO produces detailed guidance which provides organisations and individuals with all the information they need to know about the Data Protection Act.

Enforcement

The ICO has legal powers to ensure that organisations comply with the requirements of the Data Protection Act.

For more information see the government website: http://www.ico.gov.uk/what_we_cover/data_protection.aspx.

Freedom of Information Act 2000

Any records or data concerning individuals may be required to be released to the individuals concerned. However, this also gives you rights as a researcher to ask for information from public bodies, which may be very helpful to your research activity. Some extracts from the government website follow (http://www.ico.gov.uk/what_we_cover/freedom_of_information.aspx).

The basics

The Freedom of Information Act deals with access to official information and gives individuals or organisations the right to request information from any public authority.

Your right to know

The Freedom of Information Act gives you the right to request information held by public authorities, companies wholly owned by public authorities in England, Wales and Northern Ireland and non-devolved public bodies in Scotland.

Your legal obligations

All public authorities and companies wholly owned by public authorities have obligations under the Freedom of Information Act.

Race Relations Amendment Act 2000

This is just one example of equalities legislation that could have a bearing on research practice. Similar legislation exists in relation to disability, gender and sexuality. As you can see from the information below, provided by the Department for Children, Schools and Families, research could be a very helpful activity in ensuring a school or college's compliance with the race relations legislation. On the other hand, any research that – albeit inadvertently – promoted *in*equality of opportunity could be subject to litigation.

The Race Relations Act 1976 as amended by the *Race Relations (Amendment) Act 2000* gives public authorities a statutory general duty to promote race equality. The aim of the general duty is to make promoting race equality central to the way public authorities work; and this includes schools. The general duty says that the body must have 'due regard' to the need to:

- eliminate unlawful racial discrimination; and
- promote equality of opportunity and good relations between people of different racial groups.

In addition the Act places specific duties on schools to help them meet the general duty. They are a means to an end; that is, they should result in and improve the educational experience for all children, in particular those belonging to minority ethnic groups. It should not become a bureaucratic exercise. These specific duties are:

- to prepare a written statement of the school's policy for promoting race equality, and to act upon it;
- to assess the impact of school policies on pupils, staff and parents of different racial groups, including, in particular, the impact of attainment levels of these pupils;
- to monitor the operation of all the school's policies, including, in particular, their impact on the attainment levels of pupils from different racial groups; and
- to take reasonable steps to make available the results of its monitoring.

For more information see: http://www.education.gov.uk/schools/pupilsupport/inclusionandlearnersupport/a0012538/race-relations-amendment-act-2000.

Part 3

What Do We Know Already and Where Do We Find It?

5

What Do We Know Already?

As you conduct your research, there are probably other 'untapped' sources of information around you which can enrich your research in various ways. You need to take these resources into account before obtaining further data. In this chapter we look at information available to you through your formal and informal experience, as well as existing data which can be credited as *secondary data*. This can be an effective way to build on what is already known, while capitalising on information that you have the right of access to, and the right to use.

As you reflect on the readily available information that you could use in conducting your research and addressing your research questions, it is worth asking the following questions:

- Taking cognisance of my role in the school, do I know of any information that might contribute to addressing my research questions?
- Is this information available from my own class/school records? My class? My school? Other schools? The education authority overseeing our school? Other government agencies? Or any other sources?
- Is the information in the public domain or is access restricted to a few individuals only? If so, will I need to negotiate with the gatekeepers of the information?
- Does the information contain raw data and require further analysis or does it exist in organised tables and diagrams that can easily be utilised for my research?

In whatever forms these data exist, they can potentially be used as secondary data for a research study and can offer substantial information to complement your primary data. In fact, the use of existing data is regarded as one of the methods of data collection.

As previously discussed, research involves reflection. Such reflection can help you to make important decisions as to whether previous knowledge and understanding could help inform a study. A careful appraisal of what might count as evidence can help you in answering the research questions. Different ways of first-hand data gathering – also referred to as the *primary data* – are explored in Chapters 7 to 11 but you should neither ignore readily available information (counts as secondary data) nor underestimate its usefulness. Such information often complements and validates the findings of the main study and thus contributes considerably to the credibility of the findings. There are also occasions when these data sufficiently address the research questions and become the basis for the study itself.

What are secondary data?

We know that a large amount of data is collected on a regular basis, 'as part of routine data management and administration activities' (Smith, 2008: 8), individually or collectively, in order to serve personal or wider ends. Depending on the nature of the data, they can either be publicly available through paper-based resources (for example, published documents) and/or electronically accessible (for example, website resources), or could exist but not be publicly accessible.

All educational institutions keep a variety of records in relation to their pupils. Likewise, colleges have their management information systems. Education authorities, government agencies and organisations also create distinct databases that contain very rich information. Academic groups and research bodies, on the other hand, often hold archives of research data based on previously conducted studies. Unsurprisingly, these datasets serve different purposes and may be used:

- to become aware of the profile of the student body
- to observe a changing trend from one year to another (achievement and attainment, attendance, detention and exclusion, retention and withdrawal)
- to monitor supply and demand concerning course provision
- to ascertain growth or improvement in specific areas (for example, intake to courses)
- to prepare educational reports, evaluations, and assessments
- to advance research in specific fields.

Each of these types of data can potentially be employed in research as secondary data. In general, the term *secondary data* refers to the information that has already been collected, but for a different purpose. This principle concurs with what Glaser and Hewson, cited in Smith (2008), say about the usage of secondary data in research:

the study of specific problems through analysis of existing data which were originally collected for another purpose. (Glaser, 1963: 11)

the further analysis of an existing dataset with the aim of addressing a research question distinct from that for which the dataset was originally collected and generating novel interpretations and conclusions. (Hewson, 2006: 274)

Although it may appear that secondary data are merely extracted from old data to serve a new purpose, perhaps applied to new settings or further analysis for a completely different study, secondary data are nevertheless considered legitimate data for research (Blaxter et al., 2001). Analysis, albeit secondary, requires the same rigour as the analysis of primary data, whether the original researcher or a practitioner such as you undertakes it. It is, therefore, unsurprising that secondary analysis has gained 'a central role in contemporary social research' (Kiecolt and Nathan, 1986: 9). It is also worth mentioning that with secondary data, you may need to be a bit more creative with your analysis, taking into account that the data were originally collected and utilised for a different reason, which may bear no relationship to the research that you are about to undertake. Nevertheless, these secondary data when appropriately used could enhance your study.

Secondary data can be treated as evidence and incorporated as part of the research. Information may be either quantitative (numerical) or qualitative (textual) or a combination of the two. They consist either of raw data or are in ready-to-use tables and diagrams that can easily be adapted for the study. The decision as to what is acceptable as secondary data will depend entirely on the objectives of the research.

It is always worth considering the incorporation of secondary data into your research, as they are likely to satisfy one or more of the following conditions:

- They can effectively set the context for the study. Such data can contribute to making a strong case as to why further exploration in this area is imperative.
- They are a very good supplement to your primary data making the study richer, more focused, and coherent. Combined use of primary and secondary data may offer triangulated, balanced and credible research findings.
- In exceptional cases, they can be a good alternative if collecting primary data proves extremely difficult, costly or time-consuming. When timescale and research resources are very limited, carefully selected secondary data may be used to address the objectives of the research.

Kiecolt and Nathan explicitly elucidated the last point in terms of secondary survey analysis.

The primary advantage of secondary survey analysis is its potential for resource savings. Secondary research requires less money, less time, and fewer personnel and is therefore attractive in time of economic fluctuations, when the funds available for research are limited or uncertain. (1986: 11)

At the same time, the use of secondary data may have restrictions or limitations that you will need to acknowledge in your report. It is equally possible that there are risks that may potentially jeopardise the research. For example, you should be cautious in using secondary data under the following circumstances:

- The data came from untrustworthy sources. Factually incorrect evidence may implicate or raise serious questions about the validity of the research findings.
- The data are too old (and are no longer applicable to the context of the study). Such data may therefore lead to misleading conclusions and/or recommendations.
- The data are not comparable with the current study (if your aim is a direct comparison of the data). Again, the additional information merely raises questions on the credibility of the information provided and of the overall research.
- The data are not suitable for public dissemination and disclosure of the information requires the consent of the relevant individuals. The data may contain sensitive and/or personal information, which may infringe participants' privacy and thus contravene the Data Protection Act 1998.

In the next section, we explore the extensive types and examples of what can be categorised as secondary data. We also present and discuss real scenarios where secondary information is employed in research.

Types and examples of secondary data

Generally, secondary data are divided into two categories: (1) quantitative data and (2) qualitative data. Whereas *quantitative secondary data* include existing data in numerical or statistical forms and are often contained in databases, tables or diagrams, *qualitative secondary data* are information in textual form that can be found in a wide range of documents including personal letters, emails, biographies, diaries and minutes from meetings. Smith (2008: 5) also suggests that '[n]on-numeric or qualitative secondary data, can include data retrieved second hand from interviews, ethnographic accounts, documents, photographs or conversations'. Needless to say, there seems to be an endless list of potential secondary data depending on the research questions posed. Once you have identified the appropriate type of secondary data needed for your research, the next task will be locating the source and ascertaining the availability of the data.

If you work in a school, think of all the information that is collected, gathered and recorded on a year-on-year basis or for a specific purpose. Such information is probably provided by the pupils themselves, obtained from pupils' official records, from pupils' school activities, from their parents/carers or from their teachers. They may exist in hard copy or electronically (on CDs and DVDs, school computers) and kept in official reports or databases. It is likely that this information has already been used for a different purpose

Figure 5.1   General statistical data

and perhaps it has already contributed to key decisions made by senior members of staff. In spite of how the information was used previously, if the information is 'fit for purpose', it can still serve as a key element in your research.

It is also possible that this information is located in separate databases and therefore, merging of datasets would be a prerequisite to analysis. Alternatively, the data may come in aggregate form and thus selection or even separation of the data variables will first be required. Consideration of what information is needed should always be informed by the focus and objectives of the research.

Below are examples of quantitative secondary data.

General statistical data

Statistics (for example, census and survey data) are regarded as official data that are available at a local, regional and national level (Figure 5.1). This information is routinely published by governments at regular intervals and is likely to be in the public domain. Increasingly, this statistical information is becoming more accessible via the Internet in the form either of tables or charts (as part of research/policy reports or databases). These data facilitate both simple monitoring of emerging patterns and trends and/or comparisons of more complex information for longitudinal studies. If data can be extracted from databases, then they have the additional advantage of being able to be processed as statistical data since databases offer more flexibility than already made-up tables and diagrams. Data from databases can also be sorted according to region or other demographic variables.

In this regard, such websites as the Office for National Statistics are a valuable source of information (www.statistics.gov.uk).

Specific statistical information

Official published documents from various educational agencies and organisations often contain specific numbers and figures suitable for certain studies (Figure 5.2).

Figure 5.2 Specific statistical information

Assessment reports for schools and colleges published by Her Majesty's Inspectorate (HMIe) or the Office for Standards in Education (OFSTED) as well as various reports published by the government, Learning and Teaching Scotland, and the Department for Education, among others, fall under this category.

Additionally, important statistical information on Scottish higher education institutions and colleges can be found in designated databases (Infact, FES online, EMA online, FEGIS) located on www.sfc.ac.uk. The Scottish Qualification Authority's (SQA's) Business Intelligence Services (BIS) database (www.sqa.org.uk/sqa/3773.html) is also a very good resource for the entire portfolio of qualifications available since 1986. Alternatively, summarised statistical data are available through the SQA's BIS Research.

Demographic information from institutions

In schools, general information relating to pupils and staff members is all recorded (and safeguarded) and can offer valuable information to support the research. This information may include gender, age, year level, postcode, family background, employment experience, receipt of learning support, and so on, all of which may be variables potentially relevant to the research (Figure 5.3).

Information of this type can be useful as a point of comparison or in assessing the representativeness of the sample, if the study involves a survey, for example.

Specific information from institutions

Apart from the general information, schools and colleges also produce (and publish) specific information (Figure 5.4) – some of which relates to assessment/examination results, attendance, withdrawal, exclusions, discipline/referrals, number of students who have learning difficulties, number of students taking a vocational course, number of teachers participating in a school event. Even minutes from meetings (with other staff members, the senior management team, and educational authority staff members), planning documents (for example, position and briefing papers) are potentially useful.

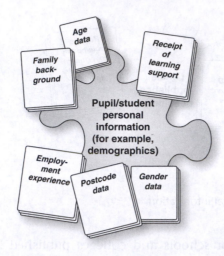

Figure 5.3   Demographic information from institutions

Figure 5.4   Specific information from institutions

Other information from school/college websites and other publications

School websites (Figure 5.5) should not be underestimated as they can provide both contextual information (useful when setting the background for the study) and probable secondary data (in support of the findings from the primary data and/or in explaining the research findings).

Figure 5.5   Information from the school/college website

Websites also often contain past and current school/college initiatives that can be linked to the research being undertaken. In ascertaining the importance or impact of the study, explanations can be enriched by specific information that can only be found on an institution's website (for example, school activities and programmes), its links and related publications.

Other information from government White Papers and legislative documents

This type of secondary information can be equally beneficial in presenting the policy context of the research and how the findings of the study relate to current practices and educational legislation (Figure 5.6).

For example, after the recent overhaul of the school curriculum in Scotland, documents relating to the Curriculum for Excellence are potentially useful resources for research studies undertaken by school practitioners, especially if the study explores an innovative approach to teaching.

Figure 5.6   Information from government White Papers and legislative documents

Figure 5.7   Archived data from academic sources

Archived data from academic sources

Secondary information is also widely available through conventional resources such as books, peer-reviewed articles, published research reports, and educational magazines and newspapers (Figure 5.7). In addition, government-sponsored national studies are good examples of secondary data of this type. Due to the rigour and national representation employed with some large-scale surveys, for example, in the Programme for International Student Assessment (PISA), such data can be regarded as official data. Data generated for each country are therefore ideally placed for creating the context in a smaller relevant study within the same country or even in validating its findings, whenever appropriate.

These academic resources are increasingly becoming available online, making access a lot easier for busy teaching practitioners. One advantage of using them is that the information provided is often linked to another related study, a similar case or even a contrasting point of view – all of which can enhance the interpretation of the research findings.

Since the quantitative approach in research has a much longer tradition in the social sciences (Kiecolt and Nathan, 1984), it is not a surprise that '[s]econdary analysis is best known as a methodology for doing research using pre-existing statistical data' (Heaton, 2004). Yet, in qualitative terms, previously collected data can also be re-analysed for a new study. Table 5.1 is a list of probable sources of secondary data according to Heaton (2004).

As you can see, sources of secondary research data are almost endless. The rule of thumb, however, is that when considering such data, you should always reflect on the focus and objectives of your research. As a practitioner researcher, it is more likely that your use of secondary data will be informed not by a favoured research approach (that is, quantitative, qualitative or mixed), but by what will contribute to addressing your research questions as

Table 5.1 Examples of pre-existing qualitative data used in social research

Type	Sources of secondary data
Non-naturalistic or artefactual data (solicited for research studies)	Field notes
	Observational records
	Interviews
	Focus groups
	Questionnaires (responses to open-ended questions)
	Diaries (solicited)
	Life stories
Naturalistic data (found or collected with minimal interference by researchers)	Life stories
	Autobiographies
	Diaries (found)
	Letters
	Official documents
	Photographs
	Film
	Social interaction

Source: adapted from Heaton (2004: 5)

well as what secondary data are available and accessible to you. As a practical example, if you are proposing to undertake a small-scale research project on your school's attempt to improve attendance, then the school's attendance records will help considerably not only in setting the context of the study, but also in substantiating any changes that take place as a result of the intervention employed.

How do we use secondary data?

There are two common ways of using secondary data:

Presenting original data – tabular, numerical or textual information are presented in their original format. The source of the data will need to be acknowledged.

Re-analysing existing data – school databases and textual information (even those previously analysed for a different purpose) can be re-analysed on their own or in conjunction with data generated from the current study.

Whether data are presented in their original form or re-analysed further, they can be utilised:

- as part of the literature or policy review when presenting the context of the research
- as a means for justifying the method and techniques (for example, primary research) employed
- along with the primary data as evidence to support the argument within the research
- as an alternative for primary data.

In whatever form secondary data are utilised, you, as a researcher, need to treat secondary data carefully to ensure that the information is not taken out of context when supporting a different argument to what it was used for before. You will need to be ready to defend and explain why you have decided to integrate these secondary data into your research. Decontextualisation of supporting evidence invites open criticism. More crucially, doing so compromises the validity and reliability of your study and thus undermines the whole of the research.

Here are two real scenarios (drawn from the Schools of Ambition project) where school practitioners made use of some existing data in their research.

 Case A

As part of their research, this comprehensive secondary school evaluated the effectiveness of the vocational education offered. In addition to questionnaires and focus groups with pupils, teacher researchers also analysed the data contained in the school records, which yielded the following useful information:

- the number of pupils who registered for a vocational course for four consecutive years
- the number of vocational courses offered for every year concerned
- the number of pupils who registered for each vocational course
- the number of pupils in S3 and S4 who studied a vocational course.

The findings from both the questionnaire and focus groups (primary data for this study) revealed a general enthusiasm from the pupil cohort to be part of a vocational programme in their secondary school. Additionally, there were some supportive secondary data that pupils were satisfied with the quality and usefulness of the vocational programmes offered.

The acquisition of these additional data from the school records validated such claims. The information gathered was analysed and subsequently illustrated in bar graphs. The increasing demand by pupils registering for vocational courses strongly concurred with the claims made based on the primary data. This is a good example of how both primary and secondary data can complement each other very well, and thus strengthen the research findings.

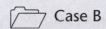 **Case B**

Three neighbouring secondary schools in the same educational authority centred their research on assessing the effectiveness of 'restorative practice techniques' that they promoted and widely employed throughout the school. They wanted to see if there would be an observable reduction in the number of incidents relating to school discipline. They therefore collected and analysed the following data obtained from the school records for four consecutive years:

- number of punishment exercises/disciplinary referrals
- number of detentions
- number of exclusions
- number of violent incidents
- number of racist incidents
- number of sectarian incidents.

Based on the available information, the three schools created a sophisticated database for recording the data on a monthly basis. For example, the database was designed to give a breakdown of data according to gender, year level, and other relevant variables.

In this research, the analysis of secondary data was seen as critical for establishing any trends such as when incidents were most or least likely to occur (that is, time of the year; first few years/middle years/last few years) as they could have been affected by when restorative practice techniques were implemented. Schools also aimed to explore, through the database, whether or not the trends achieved from each school could be associated with the model of restorative practice training received by the staff members in each school.

These quantitative secondary data can be compared among the three schools as they endeavour to learn from the similarities and differences in the findings. Alternatively, the data from all participating schools can be aggregated to afford a bigger picture of the issues facing the schools and the overall impact of the administered intervention in that particular local educational authority.

Other considerations for using secondary data

A decision as to whether or not to incorporate secondary data in the research is worth discussing with your research partner or with the research team. This is because the use of secondary data could become a key component of the study. It may require independent investigation, analysis, synthesis and writing up. It may, therefore, have implications on the team's capacities and resources, as well as the ethics and timescale for the research.

Resources

Secondary data (if obtained as raw data) are useful but will require rigorous analysis in the same way as primary data. It is worth checking if the team has the capacity to tackle this additional task as part of the research. If the analysis requires more in-depth statistical analysis, for example, it is worth ascertaining if this will pose a potential problem for the team. Perhaps support is in place for this particular need and therefore no difficulty is anticipated.

Ethics

In using secondary data, it is advisable that you ensure that you have the right to access the information by checking if you need to seek permission from the participants prior to using the data. If you were given access to the raw data, which may include participants' personal details, you should observe anonymity and confidentiality in compliance with the Data Protection Act 1998. As far as ethical considerations are concerned, secondary data will need to be handled in the same way that primary data are handled. (Please refer to Chapter 4's ethics section for a more in-depth discussion of the topic.)

Timescale

Incorporating secondary data into the research could easily alter notional deadlines for completing each aspect of the study and eventually affect the timescale of the whole research study. Most research studies are guided by the timescale and deadlines set by those who have instigated or commissioned the research. Therefore, you should carefully consider, preferably with the other members of the team, if inclusion of secondary data in your research will be worthwhile. These considerations are a reminder to all researchers that there is always a balance to be struck when contemplating whether or not it is worth including secondary data.

In the event that the practitioner research studies are independently funded by the schools themselves, the timescale issue may become a minor one. Judging the potential contribution of the secondary data to the overall research may convince everyone that an extension of a few months is worth the effort.

Checklist: Examples of secondary data

Here are some questions to reflect on as you consider assimilating secondary data into your research. A positive answer to most of these questions will not only give you confidence about whether or not it is appropriate, but also guide you in how you can use them more effectively in your research.

Checklist for considering examples of secondary data	
Using your 'insider knowledge', is there any readily available data that are both appropriate and useful in the context of your research?	☐
Can secondary data help you in setting the context of your research?	☐
Can secondary data complement the primary data as you answer your research questions?	☐
Do you recognise the limitations of secondary data in your research?	☐
Are you able to obtain the secondary data that you require? If so, do you have the right to access this information?	☐
Will you get support in the analysis and interpretation of the secondary data?	☐
Will the timescale allow you to incorporate the collection, analysis and writing up of the secondary data into your study?	☐
Are there any issues about the anonymity and confidentiality of the information provided by the participants that you will need to address prior to using secondary data?	☐

Further reading

Blaxter, L., Hughes, C. and Tight, M. (2001) *How to Research*. 2nd edn. Buckingham: Open University Press.

Heaton, J. (2004) *Reworking Qualitative Data*. London: Sage.

Kiecolt, K.J. and Nathan, L.E. (1986) *Secondary Analysis of Survey Data*. Thousand Oaks, CA: Sage.

Smith, E. (2008) *Using Secondary Data in Educational and Social Research*. Maidenhead: Open University Press.

6

How Do I Do a Literature Review?

Whatever you intend to research, someone will probably have been there before you. You need to know what they have already found and published. This chapter introduces some of the processes involved in reviewing existing literature. It briefly describes ways in which you can search for and describe what others have written on your chosen subject.

Key terms and concepts

Annotated bibliography

Narrative review

Systematic review

Reference management

Key word strategy

Inclusion/exclusion criteria

Literature search log

Synthesising results

Purposes of the literature review

There are a number of reasons for undertaking a literature review. It can be an end in itself but, for the purposes of this chapter, we will assume that you intend it to be the starting point for your own research. First, you need to summarise the state of existing knowledge, and identify any gaps in that knowledge so that you can justify and explain what it is that you are planning to do. What you're trying to do with your literature review is to say, 'This is what we know, so far, and this is what I'm trying to find out. This is how it has been done before and this is how I am planning to do it'.

It may be that you only have a very general idea of the topic that you wish to explore. In this case, examining the existing literature will help you to refine your ideas about that topic and hone in on the specific aspects of it that you wish to research in more detail. It is also very likely that by examining the work of those who have gone before you will gain ideas about the theories they have used and the ways they have gone about gathering data and analysing the data they have gathered. You may wish to use these and adapt them for your own use, or you may react against them and decide that there is some other way you wish to undertake your research. Whatever you decide, it is a good idea to relate what you do back to the previous research you have read. By doing so you will refine your research questions and be clear about what it is that you are trying to do.

In summary, a good literature review should help you to:

- summarise the current state of knowledge
- identify gaps in the knowledge
- find ideas for the topic of your research
- find ideas for the theoretical or analytical frameworks which you will use
- find ideas for the methods you will use
- formulate your research questions.

See Figure 6.1 for a visual representation of this.

Types of literature review

There are several types of literature review which you can produce. The simplest of these is an *annotated bibliography* which consists of a list of publications together with your notes on their significance. Annotated bibliographies provide a useful reference source but do little to synthesise what you have read.

Annotated bibliographies

Changing Teacher Roles, Identities and Professionalism: http://www.kcl.ac.uk/content/1/c6/01/41/56/bibliography.pdf.

The Teacher Education bibliography: http://www.tlrp.org/capacity/rm/wt/teg/.

At the very least you should be trying to produce the story of what is already known, how significant it is, what is yet to be discovered, and why it is important to discover this. This is the basic background to your research. This second type of literature review tells the story so far: it is commonly called the *narrative review*.

You will also come across other types of literature review such as the *systematic review*, *meta-analysis* and *best evidence synthesis* (Table 6.1). Each of

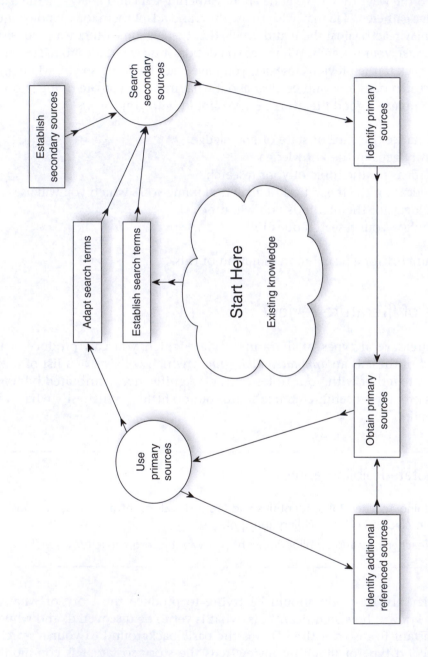

Figure 6.1 Literature review process

Table 6.1 Examples of literature review reports

Systematic review

Totterdell, M., Woodroffe, L., Bubb, S. and Hanrahan, K. (2004) 'The impact of Newly Qualified Teacher induction programmes on the enhancement of teacher expertise, professional development, job satisfaction or retention rates: a systematic review of research on induction', in *Research Evidence in Education Library*. London: EPPI-Centre, Social Science Research Unit, Institute of Education.

Best evidence synthesis

Robinson, V., Hohepa, M. and Lloyd, C. (2009) *School Leadership and Student Outcomes: Identifying What Works and Why Best Evidence Synthesis*. Auckland: Iterative Best Evidence Synthesis Programme, New Zealand government. Available from: http://www. educationcounts.govt.nz/_data/assets/pdf_file/0015/60180/BES-Leadership-Web.pdf.

Meta-analysis

Guskey, T.R. and Kwang Suk, Y. (2009) 'What works in professional development?' *Phi Delta Kappan,* 90(7): 495–500.

Hattie, J. (2009). *Visible Learning. A Synthesis of over 80 Meta-Analyses Relating to Achievement*. London: Routledge.

these is highly technical and is not the sort of thing to be attempted by a lone researcher. They are all attempts to produce completely objective summaries of existing knowledge free from all possible sources of bias, but none of them are completely uncontested, and they are not foolproof. Systematic reviews require a team of researchers, complex protocols and a great deal of time if they are to be undertaken properly. Meta-analyses use complicated statistical techniques to combine the results from a number of quantitative studies in an attempt to extend the generalisability of the individual results. Best evidence synthesis uses concepts from the legal world and the theory of legal evidence in order to decide the weight which should be given to individual results when they are combined, but it depends upon sophisticated judgements about the quality of those results, and it is not yet a widely accepted method.

Focus and scope

As with almost all aspects of doing research, it is important that you define the focus and scope of your area of interest before you begin. This, of course, is a counsel of perfection, but you should at least try to be as clear as possible.

- What exactly is the issue you're trying to investigate?
- In what context?
- How have others defined it?

As you read through the literature, you will probably find that some of these things are not as clear as you first thought, so you will have to refine your ideas. For example, in a review of the literature on student dropout, it soon became clear that student dropout could be defined in many different ways. A student could simply leave the course and discontinue their education, but what about the case of a student who changed courses midway? Should this be counted as a dropout from the first course? Or what about the student whose studies were interrupted? These issues of definition had to be addressed and explained. Also, what type of students were we talking about? The different contexts of part-time further education, vocational education, and higher education, both full-time and part-time, were all relevant but had different implications for what we meant by dropout. There was also the problem of the terminology used: as well as 'dropout' the literature could refer to 'student retention' or 'student wastage', each of which had its own slightly different definitions. In fact, the terms of retention and wastage were used in the final review in preference to dropout. We have more to say about selecting the terms used when searching literature later in this section.

You also have to think about the scope of the literature you will search (Table 6.2). Are you only interested in literature which refers directly to your own educational system (for example, Scotland), or do you want to extend your search to other related systems (such as England and Wales), or even further afield (such as Europe, the USA or anywhere in the world)? Are you only interested in research written in English, or can you include other languages? How far back in time do you want to extend your research? Are you only interested in recent research? If so, how recent? As a rule of thumb you may decide that you wish to include literature from the last 10 to 15 years in your search. Whatever temporal scope you fix upon, you may nevertheless find that there are some older classics that you also want to include. Take care that you do not end up trying to include everything that has ever been written about your topic.

Identifying and obtaining appropriate literature

The dawn of the digital age has seen remarkable changes in the accessibility of (and proliferation of) all kinds of information, including the publication of educational research. It has consequently become both easier *and* harder to find relevant literature as part of your evidence-based practice: easier in the sense that with so much educational research available electronically via the Internet, there will be published information somewhere which is relevant to even the narrowest of niche investigations; harder, in that it can often seem that the quantities of information are simply overwhelming, and that one 'cannot see the wood for the trees'.

Table 6.2 Parameters of a search on 'accomplished teaching'

Date limitations	2003–09
Geographical limitations	International literature, UK and beyond
Sector/pupil age range	Early years First school Primary/Elementary Middle school Secondary/High school
Language	English language publications
Key words	Effective (teach$) Expert Accomplished Advanced Exemplary Excellent Chartered Teacher leaders National Board
Excluded	Policy documents (professional standards review and accreditation) Book reviews Studies with a pre-service focus Studies with a PCE (post compulsory education) focus Studies with a narrow curricular/school 'subject' focus

A number of strategies can help, however:

- Do not be distracted: keep in mind all the time what it is you are investigating and stay tightly focused on that.
- Just as in the physical world, librarians and other information professionals can be your guides through the information jungle: for best results, search a limited 'subset' of the whole Internet, as offered by various intermediary websites.
- Keep in mind the distinction between looking for information *about* available research findings (through secondary sources), and the findings themselves (primary sources), even though both may be available through the medium of the Internet.
- Think carefully about the search terms you use, and adapt them as necessary as your searching progresses.
- Assess the quality of the information you retrieve: quality may far outweigh quantity in terms of the usefulness of the review.
- Think of the process as a cyclical one, rather than one in which a determinate set of key words leads directly to an ordered and self-contained set of key literature.

A wide range of secondary sources of information is available to search electronically on the Internet (some for free, others not), and in order to conduct an efficient and effective literature search it is worthwhile familiarising yourself with a number of these (try to avoid relying entirely on one such source, as this may introduce unnecessary bias into your findings), and searching a number of overlapping sources allows one to 'triangulate', to confirm the veracity of your search results.

Bibliographic information is, essentially, information about primary sources of information (the books, articles, reports, and so on themselves), and is the stock-in-trade of secondary information sources. Basic bibliographic information (often augmented by such things as keywords and abstracts) would include titles, authors, enclosing volumes, publication dates and publishers – the information contained in a standard reference of the type found at the back of most scholarly reports and articles.

Before looking at a few of the secondary sources available in more detail, we need to consider a still broader type of resource which may be useful not so much in conducting your research strategy as in the initial *design* of it. These 'tertiary' resources, for want of a better name, would include websites or pages (often referred to as 'portals' or 'gateways') which point the user to the subject-specific secondary sources in a particular field of knowledge, or act as 'broker' by searching them simultaneously. For UK education, the main ones at the time of writing are the Intute Education Gateway and the Educational Evidence Portal. However, the Internet is a rapidly changing environment, and resources of all kinds come and go, are 'reinvented' and merge with other resources, so, as the saying goes: 'your mileage may vary'. The main point to take away is that such 'tertiary' resources exist, and may play a useful role, particularly in the initial stages of your investigation.

Abstracts are short précis of scholarly journal articles which commonly appear at the start of the article, but will often be made more widely available to help potential readers to ascertain whether a particular article will be relevant to them or not, before going to the trouble (and expense) of obtaining a copy. Generally (though not always) abstracts are written by the author(s) of the article, and thus one might expect them to be a useful and accurate summary of what follows; alas, this is not always the case, but where it *is*, the abstract may be sufficient to garner all the necessary facts about a particular bit of research, in order to cite it in one's own work. A well-written abstract will contain all the relevant key words and concepts, as well as salient details about the methods and approaches employed for the authors to arrive at their (stated) conclusions (Figure 6.2).

Abstracts, along with titles, will thus often provide a 'way in' to key literature, and publishers of scholarly journals will usually make the abstracts to their journal articles available to as wide an audience as possible (as part of their business model), both via their own websites and via online

Furlong, John and Salisbury, Jane (2005) 'Best practice research scholarships: an evaluation', *Research Papers in Education*, 20(1), 45–83.

The Best Practice Research Scholarship programme (BPRS) was one of a series of initiatives designed by the English Department for Educational Studies (DfES) between 2000 and 2003, to support teachers' continuing professional development. Each year, around 1,000 Scholarships of up to £3,000 each, were awarded to serving classroom teachers to engage in supported, school-focused research. This paper reports an evaluation of the national scheme during its last year. Documentation from a stratified random sample of 100 proposals and reports were examined and case studies undertaken in a sub-sample of 20 schools. The paper describes the major features of the scheme including topics studied, research methods employed, and the occupational position of teachers involved. In order to establish a basis for an evaluation of the scheme, the paper explores the nature of the projects and the extent to which they could be characterised as research. It is argued that for most teachers, the primary purpose of the projects was not to contribute to the public stock of knowledge but to improve practice within their own schools. The criteria for evaluating projects, it is argued, should therefore include their impact on teachers' own professional development, on their teaching practice, on pupils, on parents, and on their colleagues. Evidence is presented to suggest that projects did indeed appear to have considerable impact on all of these factors though only in a minority of cases was the evidence considered to be robust. The paper goes on to raise questions about the problematic nature of quality in teachers' research and the associated difficulties with 'dissemination'. The paper concludes by exploring the different factors that might affect the success of teachers' research including mentoring, finance and their occupational position within their school.

Key words: Action research; Evaluation of; Impact of; Teacher research

Figure 6.2 Example of an abstract

databases. Again, the distinction needs to be made clear between journal publishers' websites and general/commercial online databases; the former can provide useful information in the form of abstracts, but are in no way representative of the sum of all knowledge in a particular field since they reflect the contents of a subset of the relevant journals which happen to be produced by that particular publisher. It is seldom, if ever, the case that a single scholarly journal is the only place where journals in a particular field of knowledge might be published.

The *Intute Education Gateway* (http://www.intute.ac.uk/education/) provides details and links to high-quality Internet resources within the field of educational studies which are judged to be useful by UK-based subject specialists. Because this is the Internet, the 'list' of resources is being constantly monitored and updated. The target audience (that is, those for whom the service is funded) are 'students, staff and researchers in higher and further education [in the UK]', but this is a free service and is available to anyone with access to the Internet. Included resources are evaluated and categorised, to ensure quality and ease of identification. Intute also provide tutorial content, to help the beginner find their way around the subject, and improve their Internet skills in relation to it. (One important aspect covered, for the beginner, concerns the importance of, and techniques in, judging the relative quality of different sources of information available on the Internet.)

The UK *Educational Evidence Portal* (EEP) (http://www.eep.ac.uk/) was established by a consortium of education bodies to help education practitioners (principally), and other professionals and lay people, 'to find educational evidence from a range of reputable UK sources', but without the need to search each of those sources separately. Instead, the site allows you to do a 'meta'-search of all the sources at once (or any combination of them, if you so choose). The sources include various bibliographic and other databases, as well as the publications sections of a number of key organisations' and agencies' websites, and represent a broad cross-section of published output which is felt to be of sufficient quality and relevance to support those engaged in evidence-informed practice in education.

To make the process of conducting a literature search easier, one feature of the EEP is that it uses standardised key terms from the *British Education Thesaurus*. For the purposes of information retrieval, a thesaurus can be thought of as an arrangement of keywords, such that the relationships can be seen between them: broader terms, narrower terms and synonymous terms (with 'preferred' and 'non-preferred' equivalents indicated). The EEP shows those terms which relate to items in its own bibliographic database (which can be searched alongside the 'meta'-search outlined above), but the full British Education Thesaurus can be accessed online, via the website of the British Education Index, its authors. The British Education Thesaurus provides valuable help in formulating your search terms, by helping you to adjust the level of specificity to increase or decrease the number of 'hits', and by indicating other similar key terms which you might not have considered using.

The *British Education Index* (BEI) itself is a subscription-only bibliographic database covering all aspects and levels of education, with an emphasis on British and other European, English-language publications. Many libraries have such a subscription, so you may already have entitlement to access it, particularly if you have borrowing rights at a higher or further education library. Also on the website, and free for all to access, however, is a suite of other resources, including the British Education Thesaurus, outlined above, along with a suite of databases which can be searched simultaneously (or separately) via a 'meta'-search like that of the EEP. (Confusingly, the EEP 'meta'-search includes these BEI resources, so perhaps *it* should be called a 'meta-meta'-search.) The BEI resources available in this way include a database of documents in the field of education which are available on the Internet, and 'Education-Line', a database of (quality-assured) 'grey' literature, such as conference papers, discussion papers and other unpublished or non-commercially published corporate-type documents. Depending on the nature of your enquiry, these kinds of documents can be a rich source of evidence.

The free online services from BEI also include a search of very recently added entries to the main commercial database, prior to their publication in the next iteration of BEI.

The *Education Resources Information Center* (ERIC), is described as the 'world's largest digital library of education literature', including journal articles, reports, books, policy papers and other materials. It contains well over a million records in its database of materials relevant to the full range of education professionals, not just academics. Where available, links to the full text of the resources described are given. And best of all, it is completely free to use for anyone with Internet access. The catch? Well, it is more something to be aware of: this database is produced in the USA and funded by their government, so its primary audience is a North American one, which means that the inclusion of bibliographic references in its collection is strongly biased towards the needs of that audience. In addition, keywords, for example, will generally reflect the concepts and terminologies familiar to a US audience (and that includes things as simple as differences in spelling). That said, there is no reason not to be able to find useful material for a literature review just because one is not a US citizen: it is just that caution needs to be used in selecting keywords and search terms, and an awareness of the inherent bias towards particular materials should be counterbalanced by the use of other databases in addition to ERIC. Like the British Education Index, ERIC also has an online thesaurus as part of the website, and this should probably be consulted when selecting keywords and thinking about search terms.

Some academic and research journals are published independently, for example by a learned society, but the costs of doing so mean that by far the majority of journals are published by one of a small handful of publishing companies (often on behalf of learned societies). This serves to make the journals much more widely accessible than they might otherwise be, but clearly comes at a financial cost, which is generally (though not always – more on free access journals later) passed on to the consumer (in this case, the individual conducting a literature search). Individual journal articles and volumes they are contained in, are often prohibitively expensive for the lone researcher/ literature reviewer on a budget, but as has been said already, in many cases you may not need the whole article to glean sufficient information to conduct your review, and in other cases you can use information initially gleaned for free, to home in on a more narrowly focused set of key papers which you can then obtain.

Companies which publish a wide range of journals will usually have a database on their website to allow you to look for relevant articles by searching in titles, abstracts, and lists of selected keywords (sometimes called 'descriptors') relevant to the individual articles. In this way, you can read the abstracts of potentially relevant materials and narrow your search down to just those you think will be most directly relevant. (You need to remember when doing this, however, that you are not searching across all journal articles in a particular subject field, but only those articles in the field *which happen to be published by that one company*.)

Tip   If you are generally interested in research in a particular field, you can very often sign up to a free service offered by the publishers to be notified of relevant articles in that field newly published by them.

Particularly if you like a bit of detective work, you may be able to use the names of authors (and their academic institutions) from bibliographic database search results, to find further information from other free sources, before deciding on the 'must read' articles, central to your investigation. Such sources might include conference papers from around the same period (which may well overlap substantially in their content), and which might be available from the BEI website, as described above, or from the institutional online repositories of academic authors' home institutions (many universities now have such a resource available via their websites). These latter may even contain exact reproductions of published journal articles, for which permission to reproduce has been sought from the journal publisher. Institutional repositories may also contain conference papers, research reports (published and unpublished), and other working papers and discussion papers.

Of course, if you are studying at an institution which has granted you student access rights to their own library resources, the above 'work-arounds' may well be unnecessary, as the library may have a subscription to the journals in question. You would certainly be wise to check whether such access is available, remembering that a library may have access to only a finite period of back issues, rather than from issue 1 of volume 1 right through to the present.

Reading and recording the literature

As you read through the literature it is very important that you keep a careful record of what you have read (Figure 6.3). Do not think you can rely on your memory. Even if something has impressed you deeply it is very easy to forget exactly where you have read it; so write it down! Make sure you keep a careful note of where it can be found, and use a consistent referencing system so that you, and others, can find it again. You will need to record such things as the writer's name, the title of the article or book, the name of the journal in which

Reference: (full citation)	Day, C., and Gu, Q. (2007) 'Variations in the conditions for teachers' professional learning and development: sustaining commitment and effectiveness over a career', *Oxford Review of Education, 33*(4), 423–43.
About the study	
Purpose What are the main aims?	Research focus: Identification of factors contributing to variations in teachers' effectiveness in different phases of their professional lives working in a range of schools in different contexts (VITAE).
Participants Chartered/main scale/AST etc.	300 elementary and secondary school teachers in 100 schools.
Pupil year group/curriculum area	Mixed, elementary and secondary school.
Location where the study was undertaken	Seven regions of England, UK.
Duration of project Timescale, ongoing	Four-year project.
Research design, method(s) Data sources, data collection methods, sample size, response rates	Longitudinal, multisite, mixed method study funded by the DfES. Method included twice yearly, face-to-face semi structured interviews; document analysis and interviews with school leaders and groups of pupils. Measures of effectiveness included: progress an attainment through baseline test results national curriculum test results at the end of the year. Detailed holistic profiles of teachers' lives and work, drawing on quantitative and qualitative data, were constructed over time.
Key findings *Impacts* for participants, learners, organisations, etc. Key challenges and *implications*	Teachers' capacity to sustain commitment is influenced by professional life phase and identities that are mediated by work and life context, specifically fluctuating *personal, situated and professional* dimensions. Performativity agendas and efficiency concerns challenge existing notions of professionalism. VITAE research findings challenge the *linear* conception of the relationship between experience and proficiency and expertise; and break the 'unhelpful connection' between career stage and professional development stage. Recommends the provision of '*responsive and differentiated support to meet teachers' professional and personal learning needs at different times in their work and lives*' (p. 439). '*The success of professional development (planned interventions in teachers' learning lives) is dependent on the opportunities for professional learning (unplanned, unrewarded and often implicit) which occur in their everyday context*' (p. 430).
Researcher comments Strengths, issues affecting interpretation of the findings, limitations	Mixed method, large-scale longitudinal research design.

Figure 6.3 Annotated record of a retrieved study

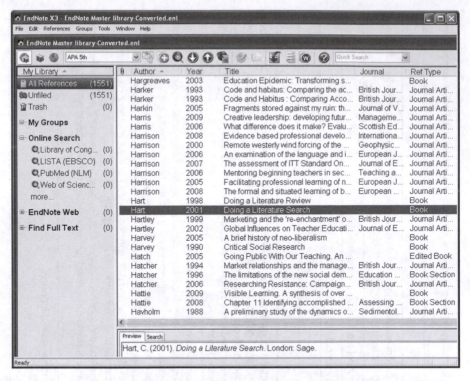

Figure 6.4 Managing records using an EndNote library

Source: EndNote ® © 2010, Thomson Reuters

you found an article, chapter or page numbers, and the date of publication. You will also want to make notes on why a particular article or book is important to you. What does it say? You can make your own notes and summaries, and you can copy out quotations, but make sure you clearly distinguish between your own words and those of the author. The traditional way of doing this was to write all this information down on index cards. Nowadays there are computer database programs to help you keep records of the literature you have searched. You can adapt a general database program for your own needs, but there are also specialist bibliographic databases available. Have a look at software for reference management, for example, EndNote (http://www.end-note.com/) (see Figure 6.4) or Reference Manager (http://www.refman.com/).

Judging the quality of the literature

In screening the records retrieved by your search, you will need to make judgements about quality. In your review, you will screen out studies that do not meet the quality criteria you set. There is no universal agreement on quality standards in educational research. Educational research is a broad church encompassing basic (conventional university-based) academic research, applied and practice-based research and evaluation (policy) research. The American Educational Research Association (AERA) defines 'scientifically based research' as research that uses 'rigorous, systematic, and objective methodologies to obtain reliable and valid knowledge'. Specifically, such research requires:

(A) development of a logical, evidence-based chain of reasoning;

(B) methods appropriate to the questions posed;

(C) observational or experimental designs and instruments that provide reliable and generalisable findings;

(D) data and analysis adequate to support findings;

(E) explication of procedures and results clearly and in detail, including specification of the population to which the findings can be generalised;

(F) adherence to professional norms of peer review;

(G) dissemination of findings to contribute to scientific knowledge;

(H) access to data for re-analysis, replication, and the opportunity to build on findings. (http://www.aera.net/uploadedFiles/Opportunities/Definition ofScientificallyBasedResearch.pdf)

These criteria are not the only criteria used to judge the quality of educational research, much of which is not based on experimental designs. Furlong and Oancea (2006) offer the following dimensions for consideration in assessing the quality of applied and practice-based research:

- trustworthiness
- contribution to knowledge
- explicitness in designing and reporting
- propriety – adherence to ethical codes of practice
- salience/timeliness
- purposivity – fitness for purpose
- specificity and accessibility
- concern for enabling impact
- flexibility and operationalisability.

In assessing the methodological quality of retrieved records, you may find the general questions posed by Fink (2010: 63) useful. Make a note of any particular strengths or limitations of the methodological approach of each study in your annotated records.

- Is the study's *research design* internally and externally valid?
- Are the *data sources* used in the study reliable and valid?

- Are the *analytic methods* appropriate given the characteristics and quality of the study's data?
- Are the *results* meaningful in practical and statistical terms? (Fink, 2010: 63)

Synthesising the findings and producing the report

When you have (1) conducted a systematic search for relevant literature that meets the criteria of the review; (2) collated a set of annotated records for each study retrieved; and (3) your search reaches saturation point and you are not retrieving any new material or insights, you are now in a position to review the corpus of material and complete the construction of your argument. You will by now appreciate that this is not a neat linear process, but a process of iterative review. The literature will be revisited as you progress through your study and gain further insights.

In constructing your report you will need to consider:

- The aims and purpose of the review – the parameters and rationale.
- A summary of existing work on the topic – methodologies used and arguments made. Identification of main 'landmark' studies (and gaps in existing knowledge).
- *Critical* evaluation of previous work on the topic (not just a descriptive account *of* research and policy literature but demonstration of critical engagement *with* research). The warrant and evidential basis of claims made.
- General and specific conclusions about the work done to date on the topic (adapted from Hart, 1998: 172–207).

In writing your report, you will want to show that you have taken a systematic approach. In the example below a student teacher, Louise Jamieson, provides an account of the search method she used when completing her undergraduate dissertation on factors influencing attainment in Scottish primary schools.

Example: Review Method

When researching the available literature on socio-economic status and educational attainment in the Scottish primary school, the following methods were employed for the review.

- Research evidence was obtained by keyword searching of various databases and the internet for relevant journal articles (see table 1 for keyword searching).
- Data was organised using an electronic research diary to support the management of the literature references.

- Data was screened for inclusion/exclusion through the aid of abstracts and research titles. Hart (1998) suggests that using the abstracts of articles provides the reader with a short summary of the main ideas and findings included within the full article, permitting the reader to decide if it is worth reading in full. This was very beneficial when screening the available literature.
- The dates of the articles were also used as a screening technique. The criteria for inclusion/exclusion outlines that literature written within the last ten years would be used to address the research questions, while research before 2000 would be carefully considered to gain the most relevant information for the literature review.
- Many of the other journal articles cited in the literature review have been obtained from internet searches, educational and research websites and are listed in the references section.
- Key policy documents have also been included from the Scottish Government website, Learning and Teaching Scotland, the Scottish Executive Education Department, Department for Children, Schools and Families and the Centre for Educational Sociology (CES).
- Books used for the dissertation are also included in the reference section.

Louise Jamieson, *Equal Educational Opportunities for all? A Study of Socio-economic Status and Inequalities in Attainment in the Scottish Primary School*. BEd (Hons) Dissertation (2010), University of Glasgow.

EXAMPLE: REVIEW RECORDS

Source/ Database	Date	Keywords	No. of Hits	No. Included in Review
Informaworld Swetswise	10.09.09	Socio-economic status AND inequalities in attainment AND Scottish primary school	58	2
ERIC	10.09.09		446	5
British Education Index	15.10.09	Socio-economic status AND inequalities in attainment AND Primary school	7	0
ESRC Data Archive	15.10.09	5–14 National Testing system AND measuring attainment	124	3
	03.02.10	Assessment is for Learning AND measuring attainment	24	1

(Continued)

(Continued)

Source/ Database	Date	Keywords	No. of Hits	No. Included in Review
		Inter-agency working AND social justice AND Scottish primary schools		
Scottish Government Website	10.09.09	Socio-economic status and inequalities in attainment	206	3
	05.02.10	Additional support for learning in Scottish Primary schools	6593	2
	10.02.10	Educational interventions tackling attainment inequalities	527	8
	10.02.10	North Lanarkshire Council tackling inequalities in attainment	10	2
Learning and Teaching Scotland Website	08.02.10	Curriculum for Excellence assessment	8134	3
	16.09.09	Socio-economic status and inequalities in attainment	4	2

Louise Jamieson, *Equal Educational Opportunities for All? A Study of Socio-economic Status and Inequalities in Attainment in the Scottish Primary School.* BEd (Hons) Dissertation (2010), University of Glasgow.

Summary ☐

In this chapter the following key points were raised:

- The purpose of a literature review is to establish what is known, the current state of knowledge about a topic.
- The literature review can be seen as an inquiry method in its own right.
- There are different types of review: annotated bibliographies, narrative reviews and systematic reviews.
- A good review involves critical evaluation or argumentation. It is not just a descriptive account of previous studies on the topic.

- Reviews should involve evaluation of the methods and findings of previous work – are they trustworthy and plausible?
- It is important to state clearly the focus and scope of the review. This delimits the enquiry and makes it manageable. Set clear inclusion and exclusion criteria and pilot these to refine your search.
- Decide on the quality criteria to be applied in your study and justify these.
- Keep a careful record of all items retrieved through key word database searches. Organise records to construct your argument around key themes and issues in the literature.
- Construct the final report to show that you have conducted a systematic and comprehensive search that has identified the main positions, key arguments and significant gaps in current knowledge on the topic. Show that you are a knowledgeable and credible contributor to your field of enquiry.

Further reading

Fink, A. (2009) *Conducting Research Literature Reviews: From the Internet to Paper*. 3rd edn. Thousand Oaks, CA: Sage.

Hart, C. (1998) *Doing a Literature Review: Releasing the Social Science Research Imagination*. London: Sage.

Hart, C, (2001) *Doing a Literature Search: A Comprehensive Guide for the Social Sciences*. London: Sage.

Pears, R. and Shields, G. (2008) *Cite Them Right: The Essential Referencing Guide*. Durham: Pear Tree Books.

Ridley, D. (2008) *The Literature Review: A Step-by-step Guide for Students*. London: Sage.

Useful websites

INTUTE Education and research methods: http://www.intute.ac.uk/education/.

Educational Evidence Portal: http://www.eep.ac.uk/.

Internet for Education online tutorial: http://www.vts.intute.ac.uk/tutorial/education.

British Education Index (BEI): http://www.leeds.ac.uk/bei/index.html.

Centre for the Use of Research and Evidence in Education (CUREE) Interactive 'route map' to research resources: http://www.curee-paccts.com/resources/route-map.

General Teaching Council for England Research for Teachers: http://www.gtce.org.uk/teachers/rft/.

Teacher Training Resource Bank: http://www.ttrb.ac.uk/.

Evidence for Policy and Practice Information and Co-ordinating Centre (EPPI-Centre): http://eppi.ioe.ac.uk/.

Part 4

How Will We Find Out?

7

Questionnaires and Questionnaire Design

Questionnaires are one of the most frequently used methods in educational research, and are often used as part of a survey. They form an important part of practitioner enquiries. They have strengths and weaknesses, advantages and disadvantages and we explore these in this chapter. We include an account by a secondary school teacher, Jane Carson, of her use of a questionnaire with her colleagues.

Surveys are most commonly used to collect quantitative information about people in a population. Surveys of human populations and institutions are common in political polling, health, social science and marketing research. A survey may focus on opinions or factual information depending on its purpose, and many surveys involve administering questions to individuals.

When the questions are administered by a researcher, the survey is called a *structured interview* (see Chapter 8) or a *researcher-administered survey*. When the questions are completed by the respondent, the survey is referred to as a *questionnaire* or a *self-administered survey*.

No doubt you will have had many experiences of filling in a questionnaire yourself, whether it be as part of your work as a teacher or as a consumer. As you read over this chapter thinking about questionnaire design, do reflect on these experiences. Did you find the questionnaires easy to fill in? Were there questions that you did not really understand? Did you mind giving up the time to respond?

Advantages and disadvantages of a questionnaire survey

In this section, we consider the advantages and disadvantages of questionnaires, in practitioner research, by comparison with other research methods.

First, we list what are commonly seen as some of the benefits and advantages that may derive from the use of questionnaires:

- Survey questionnaires are flexible in the sense that a wide range of information can be collected. They can be used to study attitudes, values, beliefs, and past behaviours.
- They are relatively easy to administer – though not necessarily easy to design.
- They can be used to collect large amounts of data in a relatively short period of time.
- Although much practitioner research is relatively small-scale, surveys do make larger samples possible. Statistical techniques can be used to determine validity, reliability and statistical significance.
- 'Closed' questions make for rapid data analysis – but it is also possible to include 'open' questions that are more complex to analyse.
- There is an economy in data collection due to the focus provided by standardised questions. Only questions of interest to the researcher are asked, recorded, codified and analysed. Time is not spent on 'tangential' questions.

On the other hand, here are some of the disadvantages of questionnaires:

- They depend on the subjects' motivation, honesty, memory, and ability to respond. These subjects – your respondents – may not be aware of their reasons for any given action. They may have forgotten their reasons. They may not be motivated to give accurate answers, in fact, they may be motivated to give answers that present themselves in a favourable light.
- Questionnaires – especially self-administered ones – rely on the respondent being able to read and understand the questions. It may be quite challenging, for example, to design effective questionnaires for younger children or for students with learning disabilities.
- Although the individuals identified for a survey are often a random sample, errors due to non-response may exist. That is, people who choose to respond on the survey may be different from those who do not respond, thus biasing or skewing the findings.
- You cannot spontaneously follow up answers within a questionnaire (as you may in an interview) and so the responses you get are constrained by the decisions you have made about the design of the questionnaire.
- You cannot get a sense of how wholeheartedly or confidently the respondent is providing their answers. It is a relatively 'mechanistic' form of data gathering.

Some of these difficulties or disadvantages may be at least partly overcome if the researcher is administering the questionnaire face to face rather than leaving the respondent to self-complete. A researcher-administered questionnaire may thus lead to:

- fewer misunderstood questions and inappropriate responses
- fewer incomplete responses
- generally higher response rates and better information on non-response
- greater control over the environment that the survey is administered in
- additional information being collected from respondent.

But also may lead to:

- respondents being unwilling to discuss sensitive topics with a stranger (or with a teacher!)
- interviewer bias (for example, answers influenced by a desire to impress the interviewer)
- generally being much more time-consuming to run.

In much practitioner research, if you do decide to use a questionnaire then it may be that you wish to administer it to a relatively small number of pupils/students, say, or colleagues in your school or college. If that is the case then it may well be possible for you to administer it face to face and thereby it becomes a more flexible and adaptable tool than the self-administered questionnaire.

As a practitioner researcher what are the reasons that you might wish to use a questionnaire as part of your study? Well, they can be a relatively straight-forward way to do some background enquiry to ascertain whether the problem you think you have identified for your research is actually a real one. So, you might put out a questionnaire to all pupils in your school, say about pupil participation in school activities, when your main project is actually to be an in-depth study of your own class. You would then use the results of the wider survey to help you refine the subsequent research activity with your own class. Alternatively, you might choose to use a questionnaire after you have completed some in-depth work with a smaller sample, because you want to find out whether what you have come up with in your small-scale study may be of relevance to other teachers and in other settings.

Or, within the confines of your own small-scale study it may simply be that the most straightforward way of gathering some of the data is through admin-istering a questionnaire. If you want to know what your students think about the series of lessons you have just taught, it may actually be easier for them to give honest answers through an anonymous questionnaire rather than through a class discussion or focus group where they have to look you in the eye!

However, if you do have good reason to administer a questionnaire, whether to a large or a small sample, these are some of the features to consider (some of them are quite offputting):

- Respondents are more likely to stop participating midway through the survey (drop-offs).
- Respondents cannot ask for clarification.

- Possible low response rate.
- Often, respondents who choose to return a survey questionnaire can represent extremes of the population – skewed responses (often associated with low response rates).
- Allows shy respondents to answer sensitive questions in private.
- No interviewer intervention available for probing or explanation.
- Respondents can read the whole questionnaire before answering any questions.
- Free of interviewer bias (but not free of questionnaire designer bias).

Ways of collecting survey/questionnaire data

There are several ways of administering a survey/questionnaire. You can use questionnaires over the telephone, by post, by electronic means, by handing them out or indeed, as we have said, they can be administered face to face, in the form of a structured interview. We consider each of these in turn.

Telephone

- Encourages sample persons to respond, leading to higher response rates.
- Interviewers can increase comprehension of questions by answering respondents' questions.
- Fairly cost efficient, depending on local call charge structure.
- Good for large national (or international) samples.
- Some potential for interviewer bias (for example, some people may be more willing to discuss a sensitive issue with a female interviewer than with a male one).
- Cannot be used for non-audio information (graphics, demonstrations, body language).

In practitioner research you would of course only be likely to use telephone as the medium if you were carrying out a survey beyond the walls of your own institution, and this is also true of the use of postal surveys.

Postal

- The questionnaire may be handed to the respondents or mailed to them, but in all cases they are returned to the researcher via mail.
- Cost may be reasonably low, if you can make use of bulk postage rates.
- Long time delays, often several months, before the surveys are returned and statistical analysis can begin.
- Not suitable for issues that may require clarification.

- Respondents can answer at their own convenience (allowing them to break up long surveys; also useful if they need to check records to answer a question).
- No interviewer bias introduced.
- Large amount of information can be obtained: some mail surveys are tens of pages long.

If your survey is within your own school or college then you might well use the internal mail or at least 'pigeon-hole' system to collect questionnaires.

Online/Internet surveys

You can send a questionnaire as an attachment to an email. The respondent can then complete it and return it to you electronically or, if they prefer, they can print it out, complete it by hand and then post it back to you. However there are also ways of administering questionnaires on a website. You make the URL available to the respondent who can then log in and complete the questionnaire from their own computer. This may be preferable to the email option because interactive HTML forms can be used. It is usually relatively inexpensive to administer and can produce very fast results. If you are piloting the questionnaire with a small sample first then it is very easy to modify it before distributing it to the full sample.

Managing, analysing and reporting the data can be automated and/or easily exported into a format which can be read by statistical analysis software, if you are using it (see below). It has been suggested that using e-based questionnaires may skew responses towards a younger demographic profile – but, if you are surveying young people (for example, students), this may be a very real advantage.

There are software packages available that provide a basic questionnaire framework that can be tailored to your needs. These include Zoomerang and Survey Monkey.[1]

Personal on-site survey

In this approach, respondents are interviewed in a person, in a setting which is familiar to them (for example, in school or perhaps parents may be interviewed in their own home). Some factors to consider include:

- Very time-consuming.
- Suitable when graphic representations or demonstrations are involved and the researcher may be able to note body language.
- Often suitable for long surveys (but some respondents object to allowing researchers into their home for extended periods).
- Skilled interviewers can persuade respondents to cooperate, improving response rates.
- Potential for interviewer bias.

Methods used to increase response rates

As mentioned earlier, response rates are an important consideration and different approaches tend to lead to different levels of response. The lower the response rate of course, the less confident one can be about the results that emerge. So what steps can you take to encourage the highest possible response rates? Some of the techniques that have been found to be helpful in some contexts include:

- Brevity – if it is possible to limit it to a single page, do so.
- Setting a suitable deadline for the questionnaire to be returned – this will depend a lot on who your sample are and what the context of your study is, as well as how long it is likely to take to complete the questionnaire.
- Incentives – in practitioner research it is unlikely to be appropriate to offer financial reward but you could consider non-monetary incentives such as commodity giveaways (pens, notepads) or entering respondents into a lottery, draw or contest – but there will be ethical dimensions to consider here (see Chapter 4).
- Preliminary notification – clear advance warning to the planned respondents and good organisation can make a considerable difference – people will be better disposed to cooperating if they have confidence in you.
- Personalisation of the request – address specific individuals.
- Follow-up requests – if you have a way of checking who has and has not responded in a survey then you can send out reminders, which often do jog people's memories.
- Affiliation with universities, research institutions, local authority or charities – if your research has the support of one such body it may be helpful to mention this when you are approaching potential respondents – it may add to the perceived status of your work.
- Emotional appeals – while we know how incredibly busy some of our respondents may be, it is possible to start bringing an emotional dimension into the request. This is best avoided of course, but everyone – researcher and researched – is human, and sometimes it seems almost unavoidable. But do consider the ethical dimensions again.
- Convincing the respondent that their response could help to 'make a difference' – that the research is important and aims to lead to educational improvement.
- Guarantee anonymity to respondents – (we can see from Jane Carson's account below that she was quite surprised that this was a concern in her school).

Effective questionnaire design

Good *questionnaire construction* is critical to the success of a survey. Inappropriate questions, confusing ordering of questions, incorrect scaling or bad questionnaire format and presentation can make the survey valueless. A useful method for checking a questionnaire and making sure it is accurately capturing the intended information is to pre-test or pilot it among a smaller subset of target respondents, under conditions as similar as possible to those that will prevail for the main survey.

The research objectives and frame of reference should be defined beforehand, including the questionnaire's context of time, budget, intrusion and privacy. Do think carefully about the issues.

Specific points

- Unneeded questions are a waste of time to the researcher and an unwelcome imposition on the respondents. All questions should contribute to the objective(s) of the research.
- Respondents should have enough information or expertise to answer the questions truthfully. The topics should fit the respondents' frame of reference. Their background may affect their interpretation of the questions.
- Questions and prepared responses to choose from should be neutral as to intended outcome. A biased or leading question or questionnaire encourages respondents to answer one way rather than another. Even questions without obvious bias may leave respondents with expectations.
- The order or 'natural' grouping of questions is often relevant. Prior questions may bias later questions.
- The wording should be kept simple: do not (normally) use technical or specialised words.
- The meaning should be clear. Ambiguous words, equivocal sentence structures and negatives may cause misunderstanding, possibly invalidating questionnaire results. Double negatives should be reworded as positives.
- If you are asking respondents to use numbers, for example in ranking items from most to least important, say on a scale from 1 to 5, be clear whether it is 1 or 5 that represents 'most important'.
- Care should be taken to ask one question at a time. If a survey question actually contains more than one issue, the researcher will not know which one the respondent is answering.
- The list of possible responses should be inclusive. Respondents should not find themselves with no category that fits their situation. One solution is to use a final category for 'other'.
- The possible responses should be mutually exclusive. Categories should not overlap. Respondents should not find themselves in more than one category, for example in both the 'married' category and the 'single' category – there may need to be a 'not living with spouse' category.
- Writing style should be conversational, yet concise and accurate and appropriate to the target audience.
- Most people will not answer personal or intimate questions.

As with interviewing, questions that you ask may be open or closed, the former inviting the respondent to use their own words, the latter asking them to respond more simply. It is possible to have a question that combines closed and open approaches, for example:

Which of the following best describes your views on the television viewing of the children in your class (please tick one):

☐ Most children watch more than two hours of television at home after school each day.
☐ Most children watch between one and two hours of television after school each day.
☐ Most children watch less than one hour of television at home after school each day.

What are your opinions about the television viewing habits of the children in your class?

In Table 7.1 we demonstrate that there are several different types of structured questions that can be included in a questionnaire. We suggest here four different types – all are in some sense 'closed' – and provide some examples of each type. The design principles we have discussed above, for example about the need for clarity and for avoidance of ambiguity, apply to all of them, but the way in which the data are coded and analysed will differ (see Chapter 12). When you are designing a questionnaire do think about what type of question is best for the particular issue you are focusing on and think through how you will analyse the responses.

Table 7.1   Designing Your Questionnaire

Structured questions	
Types of questions	Format
1 Dichotomous questions	Please enter your gender:
	☐ 1 Male ☐ 2 Female
	Do you find learning support materials at your college adequate?
	☐ 1 Yes
	☐ 2 No
2 List or multiple choice	What made you want to take the course? *Please tick all that apply*

(Continued)

Table 7.1   (Continued)

Structured questions	
Types of questions	Format
	☐ 1 To learn new skills and knowledge
	☐ 2 Personal interest
	☐ 3 I liked the subject
	☐ 4 To gain a qualification
	☐ 5 To increase my job prospects
	☐ 6 Something else, please specify
	Which of the following additional support materials was the most helpful in preparing for the exam? *Please tick only one box*
	☐ 1 Paper-based resource materials
	☐ 2 Electronic materials
	☐ 3 Old exam papers
	☐ 4 Examples of exam questions
	☐ 5 A guideline in answering exam instructions
	In what category does your job belong?
	☐ 1 Management, professional & administrative support
	☐ 2 Research and teaching
	☐ 3 Honorary, visiting and associate
	☐ 4 Security and janitorial
3 Questions based on level of measurement	From the following list of factors, choose the THREE which you feel have the strongest impact on student retention: *1 = strongest, 2 = second strongest, 3 = third strongest*
	☐ 1 Student attitude
	☐ 2 Quality of the learning process
	☐ 3 Good relationship between lecturers and students
	☐ 4 Additional learning support
	☐ 5 Financial assistance
	Please tick one of the given options where *1= Strongly Disagree, 2 = Disagree, 3 = Neutral, 4 = Agree, 5 = Strongly Agree*
	Work apprenticeship …
	1 enables me to combine theory and practical application
	☐ 1 ☐ 2 ☐ 3 ☐ 4 ☐ 5
	2 means an unnecessary effort on the part of the learners
	☐ 1 ☐ 2 ☐ 3 ☐ 4 ☐ 5
	3 helps me to meet people with the same vocational interest
	☐ 1 ☐ 2 ☐ 3 ☐ 4 ☐ 5
	4 widens my understanding of the practical application of the job
	☐ 1 ☐ 2 ☐ 3 ☐ 4 ☐ 5

Table 7.1   (Continued)

Structured questions

Types of questions	Format
	Please state your opinions on the learning support provided by the college. Please tick each statement that you agree with: ☐ 1 The problem of adult literacy is a serious concern in Scotland. ☐ 2 The adult literacy problem is a by-product of a defective educational system. ☐ 3 The adult literacy problem requires a whole-nation approach. ☐ 4 Most learners who lack literacy skills suffer from dyslexia. ☐ 5 The adult literacy problem is a characteristic of educational deterioration. ☐ 6 The adult literacy problem is difficult to deal with because of the stigma attached to it.
4 Filter or contingency questions	Have you participated in a staff development course in the last six months? ☐ 1 Yes (If yes, please go to Question 6) ☐ 2 No

When you have achieved your basic questionnaire design and have decided on the essence of the questions you want to ask, think carefully about your respondent group and how the questionnaire will appear to them. This is partly about layout and presentation, but it is also very much about the actual words you used.

- Are you using language appropriate for the particular group of people?
- Are you demonstrating sufficient respect for them and their (hoped for!) cooperation with you by completing the questionnaire?
- Does your questionnaire set out what it is you are asking them to do and why you are doing the study?
- Would it be a good idea to have a covering letter that is separate from the questionnaire, with some explanation of these matters and perhaps indicating how much time you think it will take them to complete?

Sampling

As Cohen et al. (2007: 100) put it: 'The quality of a piece of research stands or falls not only by the appropriateness of methodology and instrumentation but also by the suitability of the sampling strategy that has been adopted.' This is just as true of small-scale practitioner research as it is of large-scale studies.

When you administer a survey using a questionnaire, one of the most important questions you have to decide on is *who* you will administer it to. Part of the answer to this will be a decision also on *how many* to administer. The answer to that may depend on the rate of response that you predict. If you are keen to get 50 returns, how many will you have to send out? And, of course, the response rate will relate closely to the mode of distribution/administration of the questionnaire, as we discussed above.

Sometimes the answers to all of these questions will be very obvious. For example, if you wish to use a questionnaire to evaluate a course that you have taught you will probably want to ask all of the students who have followed the course to complete it. When you send a questionnaire to the full population, that is called a census. But if you are wanting to gather the views of parents of young children about the teaching of literacy skills, do you distribute it to all of the parents in your school or just to those of children in your own class? Or do you also want to ascertain the views of parents at other schools, perhaps for comparative purposes? And do you want the views of fathers and mothers/female and male carers? There are many decisions to be made. But there are some principles (Table 7.2) that can be applied in order to help you decide.

Table 7.2 Sampling techniques

1 **A simple random sample**. Each unit in the population has an equal chance of being selected. First, you have to create a list of all the members of the population (for example, all the students in the college). Then you prepare a set of random numbers corresponding to the size of the population that you have. (It is better to create the list using Excel, you can then generate random numbers in the next column quite easily.) The participants will then be selected based on the number allocated to them.

2 **A systematic random sample**. If you want a sample of 20 from an alphabetical list of 100 people, dividing 100 by 20 equals 5, that is you need to select a fifth of the full population. Then select any number between 1 and 5. Suppose you pick 4, that will then be the starting number on your list. Then you will select every fifth name – number 9, 14, 19, 24 and so on, until you reach the last one, number 99.

3 **A stratified sample**. Groups or strata (for example, each dominant programme group) will be your starting point. If group A has 300, group B has 200, group C has 100, you may decide to take 10 per cent from each, so you end up taking 30 from group A, 20 from group B and 10 from group C – again randomly, but ensuring that your sample has the same proportion from each group, giving you a sample that is representative of the full population.

4 **A cluster sample**. Used where there are 'natural' groupings that are evident in a statistical population. Using this, you can consider counting the number of classes for the whole college, selecting the classes randomly (taking into account your sample size) and administering the questionnaire to all of the class members of the classes selected.

Table 7.2   (Continued)

5   **Census**. If budget, time and resources permit, it would be good to conduct a census. This is particularly appropriate if you are administering the questionnaire online since including everybody and analysing the data will not normally incur more time, money or effort. This also means that you do not need to worry about sample size and sample representativeness since you are including all the students in your school.

6   **Purposive sample**. A sample in which respondents are selected by some purposive method. For example, 50 engineering students who are a mixture of male and female students, younger (less than 30 years old) and older (30 and more) who continued and discontinued their studies after meeting the qualifying date.

Case study of the use of a questionnaire

Having now set out a whole range of principles and guidance on questionnaires and questionnaire construction let us now read an account from a teacher of her use of a questionnaire with staff within her own school.

 Jane Carson, Wallace Hall Academy,[2] Dumfries and Galloway

This questionnaire was distributed to all 51 FTE teachers at Wallace Hall Academy in September 2009. I had hoped to ascertain teachers' current values and practices regarding a number of issues surrounding the Teaching for Understanding (TfU) project at the school. I wanted particularly to find out about current practice with regard to assessment, planning curricular units, collaborative practice within the school, whether teachers saw themselves as learners and what they thought about the learning culture in the school. I also wanted to know what teachers knew about the TfU framework at the beginning of the project. I also needed to find out some biographical information regarding teachers' professional role, the nature of their current post and their years of service within the profession. 34 questionnaires were returned.

How Do Teachers Learn to Teach for Understanding?
A collaborative teacher research project at Wallace Hall Academy

Please complete and return by Friday 9th October

> **Please read the following statements and tick the appropriate box to indicate your level of agreement.**

(Continued)

(Continued)

SECTION A: TEACHERS' BELIEFS AND PRACTICES REGARDING

Assessment	Strongly Agree	Agree	Unsure	Disagree	Strongly Disagree
1 I consider the most worthwhile assessment to be assessment undertaken by me	☐	☐	☐	☐	☐
2 My assessment practices help pupils to learn independently	☐	☐	☐	☐	☐
3 My pupils are encouraged to view mistakes as valuable learning opportunities	☐	☐	☐	☐	☐
4 Pupils are helped to understand the learning purposes of each lesson or unit	☐	☐	☐	☐	☐
5 My pupils' learning objectives are determined mainly by the prescribed curriculum	☐	☐	☐	☐	☐
6 Assessment provides me with useful evidence of my pupils' understandings which I use to plan subsequent lessons	☐	☐	☐	☐	☐

Additional comments:

Planning

I regularly plan lessons/units of work in the following ways:	Strongly Agree	Agree	Unsure	Disagree	Strongly Disagree
1 Making a unit booklet					
2 Using grid plans					

I regularly plan lessons/units of work in the following ways:	Strongly Agree	Agree	Unsure	Disagree	Strongly Disagree
3 Through discussion with colleagues					
4 Thinking about a topic by myself					
5 With pupils					
6 Trial and error					
7 Other, please specify					

	Strongly Agree	Agree	Unsure	Disagree	Strongly Disagree
1 Making a unit booklet					
2 Using grid plans					
3 Through discussion with colleagues					
4 Thinking about a topic by myself					
5 With pupils					
6 Trial and error					
7 Other, please specify					

Additional comment or description of how you currently plan lessons/units of work:

Working collaboratively with colleagues

I regularly work collaboratively with colleagues in the following ways:	Strongly Agree	Agree	Unsure	Disagree	Strongly Disagree
1 Planning lessons/units of work together	☐	☐	☐	☐	☐
2 Observing each other teach	☐	☐	☐	☐	☐
3 Discussing pupil behaviour	☐	☐	☐	☐	☐

(Continued)

(Continued)

	Strongly Agree	Agree	Unsure	Disagree	Strongly Disagree
4 Discussing pupil learning	☐	☐	☐	☐	☐
5 Discussing professional learning	☐	☐	☐	☐	☐
6 Reflecting on practice together	☐	☐	☐	☐	☐
7 Cross-curricular planning/teaching	☐	☐	☐	☐	☐
8 Other, please specify	☐	☐	☐	☐	☐

Additional comments:

Professional learning	Strongly Agree	Agree	Unsure	Disagree	Strongly Disagree
1 I regularly think about my own learning as a means of improving how I teach.	☐	☐	☐	☐	☐
2 I am still a student of my own subject.	☐	☐	☐	☐	☐
3 I regularly generate new lesson materials and teaching approaches.	☐	☐	☐	☐	☐

Additional comments:

The learning culture in the school	Strongly Agree	Agree	Unsure	Disagree	Strongly Disagree
1 Pupils are clear about the purposes of what they are learning.	☐	☐	☐	☐	☐

The learning culture in the school	Strongly Agree	Agree	Unsure	Disagree	Strongly Disagree
2 Pupils are helped to become independent learners.	☐	☐	☐	☐	☐
3 Throughout the school, people research, inquire and reflect critically on practice.	☐	☐	☐	☐	☐
4 Teachers are open to change, but critical as to what is most important in terms of learning.	☐	☐	☐	☐	☐
5 Teachers in school learn together, exchanging ideas and practice.	☐	☐	☐	☐	☐
6 There is a strong ethos of mutual support among staff.	☐	☐	☐	☐	☐
7 People talk about and value learning, not just grades, marks and test scores.	☐	☐	☐	☐	☐
8 This school is characterised by people deciding and acting together.	☐	☐	☐	☐	☐
9 There is a strong shared sense of where we are going as a school.	☐	☐	☐	☐	☐
10 All staff have opportunities for continuing professional development.	☐	☐	☐	☐	☐

Any additional comments:

(Continued)

(Continued)

SECTION B: TEACHING FOR UNDERSTANDING

> In 2–3 sentences please state your responses to the following questions.

1 What do you understand the Teaching for Understanding Framework to be?

2 What do you see as the potential benefits to yourself as a teacher through the adoption of the framework?

3 What do you see as the potential benefits to learners through your adoption of the framework?

4 What do you see as the potential inhibitors to teachers' adoption of this approach?

SECTION C: ABOUT YOU

> Please circle the most appropriate description(s) in response to each of the next three questions.

1 Which of the following best describes your current professional role?

- Probationer
- Class or subject teacher

- Class teacher with special curricular or non-curricular responsibilities
- Cross-school responsibilities with a reduced class teaching role
- Learning Leader/Faculty Head/Principal Teacher
- Deputy
- Headteacher

2 What is the nature of your current post?

- Full-time permanent
- Part-time permanent
- Full-time temporary
- Part-time temporary
- Supply
- Other, please specify _____

3 How long have you been working as a teacher?

- 0 to 2 years
- 3 to 5 years
- 6 to 10 years
- 11 to 15 years
- 16 to 23 years
- 24 to 30 years
- 31 plus years

Would you be willing to participate in a group or individual interview of 20–30 minutes duration (max)? Please tick either or both boxes. Cover may be available for this.

Group interview   **Individual Interview**

THANK YOU VERY MUCH FOR TAKING THE TIME TO COMPLETE THIS QUESTIONNAIRE.

With hindsight I wonder if I was trying to find out too much in one fell swoop, but I really felt that I needed to try to establish some sort of baseline or picture of practice as it stood before the TfU framework was adopted by staff in their planning and teaching of units of study. Without this I wouldn't be able to measure or see any changes that had occurred because of the Teaching for Understanding project.

Why I chose to use a questionnaire

Advantages: able to get views of lots of people and anonymity.

I wanted to gather information (views and opinions) from quite a large number of people – all of the teaching staff in the school. Using a questionnaire was the obvious choice to try to find out what a large

(Continued)

(Continued)

number of people thought about a particular topic. It also provided anonymity for the teachers who were being surveyed. This was quite an important consideration for me as I wanted to find out what people really thought about Teaching for Understanding and what they valued in their everyday practice. Looking at the responses to the open questions I feel that people were quite honest and open. I think teachers often feel worried about expressing a negative opinion regarding their own work, but the whole point of the project was to look openly at our practice and share our ideas and evaluate what was working or not working. The anonymity of the questionnaire gave staff a way to express their honest thoughts and opinions without having to worry about being 'negative' I suppose.

With regard to the collaborative practice part of the questionnaire, I found it really useful to speak to colleagues and check that I hadn't missed any types of collaborative work that went on. The dialogue with colleagues about what I should put in prompted lots of interesting discussion and that in itself was useful in helping me to sharpen ideas and get a picture of what was going on in the school in different subject areas. It was also helpful with regard to getting the wording of questions right. Because I had discussed wording with colleagues I felt that the questionnaire would be much easier for other folk to understand. Sometimes if you're working just by yourself you end up becoming quite obscure. You sort of know what you want people to say/you know what you're getting at but it's not always that clear for somebody else. Spending a bit of time looking at wording with other people definitely helped me and helped others understand what I was doing.

I included a section on the learning culture within the school. I found it in 'Learning How to Learn; Tools for Schools' by Mary James et al. I hadn't planned on finding out about this but while I was researching questionnaires, I came across this little section and I thought that it might be really useful. I wondered if the learning culture in the school will have changed as a result of the Teaching for Understanding project? On the down side it made the questionnaire quite long but I thought people were only ticking boxes here so it would be worth the time if the information proved interesting in the end.

Limitations: it took a lot of thought/time to prepare and analyse, answers were quite superficial and often the responses created more questions that needed answers.

I found it really difficult to put the questionnaire together even though I had quite a good idea of what I wanted to find out (I emailed my university 'mentor'). I looked carefully at other 'professional' research studies that were in some way similar to what I was trying to do on a small scale and tried to use the language and format they had used. I also discussed and checked ideas with colleagues to make sure that I hadn't missed anything. Looking at the 'Assessment' section of the questionnaire now, I see that I have just really asked a random set of questions about assessment that don't give a picture of current practice. It does provide some interesting information though. However, if I ask the same questions again after teachers have used the TfU framework, the responses might be different, so there's always hope!

What was really interesting was the reaction I got from some staff about numbering the questionnaires. People were worried about anonymity. Although I had put a letter in the envelopes with each questionnaire explaining what the questionnaire was for, how it would be used and reassuring staff about anonymity, some were still worried about protecting their 'privacy'. I sent an email to all staff with assurances that information would be completely confidential and that numbers were just used to identify different pieces of information. Once the questionnaire was completed I shared the results via GLOW[3] on our school page and I think staff were reassured that no one individual was identified as having said this or that. I don't think it will be so much of an issue with the next questionnaire. I think the process itself has gone some way in helping staff be a bit more open with each other about what they are doing in the classroom and how they operate within the school. Also, I found that the questionnaire prompted quite a bit of discussion between different groups of staff across different subject areas. I don't think it was always positive, but that didn't matter. Lots of staff were talking about their work in a way that maybe they hadn't done before. I was heartened by the number of people who agreed to take part in interviews and express their opinions/thoughts/ideas openly.

I also did a sort of mini pilot which was great. There were a couple of spelling mistakes that I hadn't spotted. Also, and I really learnt from this, one of my colleagues said that the response options given at the top for each question (Agree, Not Sure, Disagree etc) didn't quite work for one set of questions. At the time I thought they were fine and had spent so much time on the questionnaire that I was desperate to get it out there. In the end I regretted not changing the options to more suitable responses. It may have made a difference to the responses that staff gave. It's definitely worthwhile spending lots of time getting the questions just right. I think it makes a big difference to the quality of information that you get back.

Administering the questionnaire

Timing was an issue. I thought quite carefully about exactly when I would actually give out the to try to maximise response rate. We were preparing for the move to the new school, thinking about planning for Curriculum for Excellence and had all the pressures of everyday life in a school. I spoke to colleagues about when they thought it would be best to give

(Continued)

(Continued)

out the questionnaires and also asked people personally at a staff meeting just to be polite!

Analysing the results

Once I had the returned questionnaires it was quite daunting considering the amount of information I had got back. I followed the advice given in *Using Questionnaires in Small Scale Research* (Munn and Drever, 2004) and made big grids on squared paper. I colour coded responses in certain categories so that it was easy to see how many people had said what. I showed the grids to the Action Research group and that was great too, because they saw patterns that I hadn't noticed. I actually really enjoyed putting all the responses together and seeing what was going on in the school.

So, you can see from Jane's account, how many of the issues discussed above were very real for her. This was a successful survey overall and helped enormously in achieving the objectives of Jane's study. As you will have gathered it was not the only thing she did and there was follow-up with the generation of more qualitative data through the use of interviews and focus groups. Here are some questions that will help you reflect on Jane's experiences.

1 What kinds of questions did Jane use? (see Table 7.1 above)
2 What was the balance of open and closed questions?
3 What was her sampling approach? (see Table 7.2 above)
4 How do you think she analysed the returns?
5 How did the questionnaire and the data derived from it, relate to the rest of Jane's study?

She mentioned something about how she organised and analysed the questionnaire data and this is something we return to in Chapter 12.

Conclusion

As we have noted, questionnaires are a very common feature of much research. Indeed to the lay person, questionnaires very much represent social research. There are many other methods that social researchers – including practitioner researchers – can use. This chapter has shown that there are many possible pitfalls in using questionnaires – they are more difficult to use than is sometimes recognised. But if they are appropriate as part of your study and if you take appropriate care and consideration in preparing them, then you can certainly gain insights and benefits from their use, as Jane Carson demonstrated in her case study.

Further Reading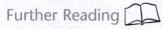

Gillham, B. (2008) *Developing a Questionnaire.* 2nd edn. London: Continuum.

Munn, P. and Drever, E. (2004) *Using Questionnaires in Small-Scale Research.* Glasgow: SCRE Centre, University of Glasgow.

Notes

1 See surveymonkey.com and zoomerang.com; there are also some websites that compare these two packages that may help you decide which one to use.
2 Wallace Hall was one of the 'Schools of Ambition' designated by the Scottish government that received support for implementing a transformational plan and was supported in researching the implementation of that plan.
3 GLOW is the Scottish schools' digital network.

8

Interviewing

This chapter is a guide to interviews in practitioner research. It gives an understanding of when it is appropriate to use interviews to gather information, what types of interviews can be used, their various advantages and disadvantages, how to design interviews and what can influence the effectiveness of those interviews. We draw on our research experience for examples and insights on using interviews in real educational settings.

You will benefit from consulting Chapter 9 on focus groups, for issues also pertinent to interviewing, particularly selecting informants and interpersonal dynamics, and the section on qualitative analysis, in Chapter 13, on how to deal with the information gathered from interviews.

Why use interviews?

A research interview is a dialogue aimed at eliciting information on a certain topic or topics of interest to a research enquiry. Arksey and Knight, in their very accessible book on interviewing written with small-scale research in mind, state that interviewing, rather than a single method, is a family of research practices which have one thing in common, namely a discussion between people with one being the researcher; the person conducting a 'systematic enquiry' (Arksey and Knight, 1999: 2).

One reason for the popularity of interviews as a research method is their flexibility. As with all qualitative approaches, interviews are one of a range of methods intended to gather information that is illuminative and goes beyond the descriptive in order to help us understand why people think or act in certain ways or to help explain why something has or has not worked.

Interviews are best used when the research questions require you to elicit information on people's perceptions, attitudes and meanings. The information, gathered using interviews, therefore, is not meant to provide generalisable findings but rather to enhance understanding of social actions and processes.

The explanatory power of interviewing means that it can complement quantitative methods such as surveys by helping to clarify research issues, informants' views and their frames of reference so that appropriate and meaningful survey questions can be designed. Interviews can also be used following surveys to help interpret and understand some of the more ambiguous findings that arise from quantitative analysis. Informants' accounts can be compared and contrasted and triangulated with other evidence gathered from surveys, observations and documentary sources. This process helps promote the robustness of the research findings.

The interviews may also prove relevant and provide useful information where interviewees lack the ability or motivation for completing questionnaires, for example, those with limited literacy skills, or those with special education needs.

Some examples of when interviews might be appropriate to use include:

- to help inform the types of survey question wording and terminology that are appropriate to use with particular groups
- to explore the results of a survey in order to understand the reasons for people's responses
- to promote understanding of young people's perceptions and rationale for their behaviours in certain settings
- to help understand why respondents pursue particular objectives or undertake particular actions
- to help understand events following an observation
- to explore in detail how and why educational programmes have made a difference to the lives of stakeholders.

Advantages of interviewing and issues for consideration

Many of the advantages of interviewing concern the flexible nature of the method and the limitations can often be addressed with careful planning or offset by complementing the approach with other methods.

Advantages of interviewing

- Interviews allow people to provide their views in their own terminology. This allows us to understand better the meanings underpinning people's actions and illuminates their attitudes, motivation and rationale.
- The interactive nature of the interview allows the researcher to adapt the questions to suit responses and so elicit relevant information and gain greater insights.

- Interviewees through actively discussing the research topics can shape the research and highlight unforeseen, yet relevant issues.
- Interviewees can provide detailed answers which are embedded in contextual information, again helping us to understand more about the factors and processes that influence actions and attitudes.
- Unlike self-completion questionnaires, interviewees can ask for clarification which helps you gather more accurate information or helps you to realise the questions need refining.

Issues for consideration

- The time taken to conduct interviews and analyse the information can make the method time-consuming and expensive.
- The interview is a social interaction which can both enhance but also hamper the gathering of information. For example, interviews can be vulnerable to personality differences, power dynamics, gender and generational differences, and so on. The skills and experience of the interviewer, however, can offset these factors.
- The socially interactive nature of the interview also means that certain topics that are sensitive can be difficult to discuss face to face. Again, the skills and experience of the interviewer can help overcome some of these issues. Careful planning should mean that potential sensitivities can be anticipated and variations to the method (for example, use of more anonymous qualitative methods such as telephone interviewing) can be used to reduce anxieties of informants. If time permits, the researchers can build rapport and trust with the informant and thus encourage frankness.
- If the interviews are conducted by more than one interviewer, there is a possibility that each will ask questions differently or not probe sufficiently, resulting in variations in the level of detail across the interviews and the interpretation of questions by the informants.
- Like focus groups, interviewing requires skill and awareness on behalf of the interviewer to avoid influencing the interviewee. For example, an interviewer might indicate his or her own views on what is being said through non-verbal expression or tone of voice and this might then influence the interviewee's responses.
- Interviews are good at telling us about people's reasons, interpretations and attitudes. If you are interested in a more complete understanding what has happened in a particular setting, such as in an evaluation of a school-based initiative, you will have to compare a range of interviewees' accounts and also triangulate with other methods such as observation and documentary analysis.

Different types of interviews

There are various types of interviews that differ mainly in terms of their structure. The structure and design of the interview, as with all research instruments, largely reflects the nature of the research questions/theoretical framework. The extent to which something is already known about the research topics and, therefore, the level of information required. Interviews can range from very structured (for example, verbal questionnaires) to almost conversational approaches. Most often researchers will adopt a balance between these two; the semi structured approach. Here we focus mainly on this versatile approach but we also outline structured and unstructured interview formats.

The structured interview

This is often referred to as an 'oral questionnaire'. This type of interviewing is most commonly used in market research and political opinion polls. Sometimes this approach might be used when the interviewee is not sufficiently literate or able to complete a written questionnaire. The interviewer will not deviate from the wording of the questions and closely follows strict protocols concerning question routing depending on the responses given. These interviews usually require responses to predefined categories and produce largely quantitative data.

The ethnographic or unstructured interview

When relatively little is known about the research topics then unstructured interviews are appropriate. Here the interviewer has no predetermined script and no agenda other than to understand the views of the interviewee. This is most commonly used when very little is known about the research area and an exploratory approach is needed to map out how those in a research setting perceive their world. The interview will often be informal and appear conversational. Such interviews typically produce a significant volume of rich qualitative information which the researcher hopes will result in 'illumination'.

In the unstructured interview, the researcher wants the interviewee to talk around some broad areas of interest to the research to allow the research approaches and understanding to be refined. Ethnographic interviews were pioneered in the early 1960s by qualitative researchers, particularly Aaron Cicourel (1964). The questions are not predefined and can be spontaneously generated from the interaction between the interviewer and interviewee (Patton, 1990).

This method is useful in exploring complex behaviours and perceptions while minimising any a priori categorisation which might limit the field of inquiry (Punch, 1998). In such exploratory research, the interviewer may use only a limited number of questions or topic areas. For example, during the initial stages of a research study or evaluation on how the curriculum is being reflected in schools' planning and classrooms, researchers might want to explore with local policy-makers and school staff what they see as curriculum priorities and the approaches used in schools to reflect these. Life history research will also typically use this type of interview.

Ethnographic interviews are useful when the researcher can stay in or revisit the research setting over a period of time and speak to the interviewees to refine the question wording and build rapport. This process can also be informed by observation of the research setting during this time. While the researcher can use the freedom of this method to explore the issues salient to the interviewee, this process can take time and generate a great deal of information.

While this method is called unstructured interviewing, the researcher will usually begin with some main questions or topics to begin the discussion and key issues he or she wants to explore if the interviewee does not naturally cover these. Depending on how the discussion proceeds the interviewer will intervene with other questions to probe further.

The less structured an interview is, the more skill the interviewer requires to recognise when to probe for more information and to manage the interaction to ensure the interviewee is productive but is not intrusive. Where more than one interviewer is involved in gathering information then careful planning and liaison are required to ensure interviewers have a shared understanding of the general areas of information to be collected from interviewees.

In an unstructured interview the topic guide can vary greatly. In some cases it may look similar to a semi-structured interview with discrete topics the researcher wants to cover. However, where the researcher has very little idea of the key issues, processes and perceptions of those in the research setting then the interview might be based on a conversation guided by the researcher using a vague set of ideas on which to begin the discussion. The subsequent questions will emerge from the interaction and themes that arise. When conducting unstructured interviews it can be distracting to take notes, therefore, you will require a reliable, and preferably digital, recorder. If this is impractical, you will need to develop ways to remember key points and write these up as soon as possible following the interview.

One example of an unstructured interview guide used during the initial stages of a study to explore young people's views on what they saw as key life skills is provided in Figure 8.1. Some points for consideration are provided as annotation.

> **Topic Guide**
>
> Q. Our research project is looking at the skills young people use in their everyday life. This can cover a wide range of situations but perhaps I can start by asking you to describe typical day for you?

Depending on what activities are highlighted by the interviewee, the questioning would elicit whether the interviewee thought they drew on any particular skills and knowledge the interviewee draws on to accomplish the various activities and tasks in his or her everyday life. An example of a subsequent question is:

> Q. Do you think there are any particular skills you use when you are doing that kind of activity?

For each skill highlighted by the interviewee the interviewer might probe how these have been acquired. For example:

> Q How do you think you've developed this skill?

The interviewer would be interested in exploring whether there was any formal or informal influences in the development of the highlighted skills.

Depending on the aims of the research the interviewer might also want to explore whether the interviewee feels he or she needs other skills to negotiate everyday life and address their aspirations. For example

> Q. We've been talking about skills people use in everyday life, in different circumstances and settings. Do you think there are any skills you feel you need but that you don't yet have?

The interview would usually conclude by thanking the interviewee for their time and reminding him or her how they can find out more about the research should they wish.

Figure 8.1   Example of unstructured topic guide

The semi-structured interview

For this type of interview, the researcher has a sketch map of the territory to be explored, but the freedom to explore it as he or she will. The map or agenda is shaped by the research objectives but it is open to negotiation with the interviewee. The semi-structured interview aims to explicate the interviewee's understanding of the research topics, and therefore produces qualitative information. (See also Drever, 2003: 13–15.)

Different modes of interviews

In addition to the different types of interview, there are various ways interviews can be conducted such as face to face, telephone and video. These are sometimes called 'modes' of interviewing. Other than face-to-face interviewing, telephone interviewing is perhaps the most common mode. Structured and semi-structured interview approaches can be successfully conducted over the telephone and this mode has the particular advantage of reaching geographically diverse interviewees without incurring the costs and time involved to travel. An example of when telephone interviewing would be used in practitioner research would be a study that required gathering qualitative information from a range of teachers; headteachers or educational policy personnel in one's own local authority or even across local authorities.

The preparation and design of telephone interviews requires the same considerations as face-to-face interviews addressed elsewhere in this chapter. The conduct and interaction over the telephone, however, creates certain advantages and challenges. For example, interviews over the telephone can avoid the influence of many potentially distracting or biasing visual and non verbal factors such as appearance and involuntary responses to what someone is saying. Power differences can also be offset to some degree. On the other hand, when conducting telephone interviews the interviewee and interviewer cannot see each other and this can sometimes hinder the smooth flow of the discussion as pauses and silences are less easy to interpret, ie is the silence due to someone thinking over a question or is he or she waiting for the next question. Similarly if the interviewer is silent while note taking, the interviewee might be confused. This can usually be addressed by telling the interviewee that there might be short silences during the interview because of your note taking.

Cheap yet effective devices that attach to telephones and digital and tape recorders are available in major electronic retailers and allow the recording of telephone interviewing. This can reduce your reliance on detailed note taking during the discussion and so promote listening and more natural communication. However, the use of such recording devices which are not visible to the telephone interviewee highlights the need for explicit ethical protocols to ensure the interviewee is aware of your recording and has given his or her formal consent to be recorded.

Interviewing using a video link has become far more accessible to researchers as video communication software such as Skype has become available along with most desktop and laptop computers now having video cameras included or easily attached. Essentially, as long as the video link is robust and there is little or no time lag or dropout, interviews conducted using video link are almost the same as a face-to-face interview with all of the associated advantages and limitations.

Carrying out a semi-structured interview

When people think of an interview they perhaps first think of the one-to-one, face-to-face discussion where the interviewer uses a list of flexible questions to gather information from a person (the informant) who can provide responses using his or her own words and as much detail as they feel necessary. This is the semi-structured interview and it is arguably the most common form of interviewing in social and education research.

The semi-structured interview is used when the researcher already has some thoughts on what the main research topics that will address the research questions and objectives of his or her study. This type of interview uses a list of questions to promote some level of standardisation between the interviewees and to help remind interviewers to cover the key topics. Each question in this type of interview will often use sub-questions or probes to help further explore particularly relevant comments made by informants or to stimulate discussion if the informant requires more clarification.

Usually, semi-structured interviews will have a limited number of topic areas with corresponding questions and related probes. The questions used in a semi-structured interview are not a script but rather a set of reminders on the key topics the researcher wants to cover. The interviewer has flexibility in the way in which the questions are asked and in what order they are covered and will adapt to suit what the interviewee is saying. The interviewer can also introduce additional topics as necessary. These might be closely related to the original interview topics but can also include new topics when the interview highlights unforeseen yet relevant issues and information. The interview questions are also sufficiently broad and flexible to allow the interviewee to introduce information and comments they see as relevant.

Designing a semi-structured interview

Once the decision has been made that semi-structured interviewing is an appropriate method to help address your research objectives and questions, there are a series of steps to address to design your topic guide and plan the interview. These steps are illustrated here using an actual interview guide as an example.

1 First you will need to think about an appropriate preamble that will inform the interviewee:

- about the focus of the research, why it is being conducted, why they have been approached for interview and what will happen to the findings
- that their participation is completely voluntary and they can choose to stop the interview at any time
- that any information gathered from the interview will be treated in confidence and all findings produced will be anonymous. If for any reason this is not possible, then this could be made clear to the interviewee.

Preamble

As the Schools of Ambition programme (SoA) is coming to an end we are working on the final report. Recent discussions with the Scottish Government have highlighted the value of conducting reflective interviews with key staff in a limited number of Tranche 1 and Tranche 2 schools. The aim of these interviews is to gather insights from Headteachers and other relevant staff/partners on the impact of the Schools of Ambition programme on the more quantitative measures such as positive destinations, attainment and school roll. This information will supplement the wide range of other data and evidence on the impact of the programme.

We have selected a small number of schools to reflect the range of geographic and demographic contexts.

All reporting of the findings from this strand of the research will not name any individual or school.

Figure 8.2   Preamble for a semi-structured interview

This information should also be provided in a brief, clear language leaflet that outlines the research aims, approaches and who they can contact if they have any queries or concerns about the research.

Figure 8.2 is an example of a preamble from a semi-structured question guide used to gather information from headteachers as part of a major education initiative.

2   The next stage is to create a series of interview questions that will elicit useful information from interviewees relating to the main research objectives; in effect mapping the actual questions to be used in the interview on to the main research objectives.

Below are the main research objectives for the previous example, and presented in the next section are the actual interview questions used to gather information to address the objectives.

Research objectives example:

- To gather insights from school leaders on the impact of a national education initiative (in this case the Scottish Schools of Ambition – SoA – programme) designed to facilitate whole school change and transformation against each school's agreed targets and aims.
- To explore in more detail school leaders' views on the initiative's impact on quantitative measures such as positive destinations, pupil attainment and school roll. This information will supplement the wide range of other data and evidence available on the impact of the SoA programme.
- To gather final reflections from school leaders on the wider impact of the SoA programme including for pupils, staff and the wider community.
- To identify key factors that have influenced the impact of the programme and its sustainability.

The interview questions and probes

The above research objectives are reasonably explicit and can be used to frame the interview questions. However, for each question it is likely that you will want one or more sub-questions or probes to remind you to delve further on related aspects of the main questions that might be pertinent to your research. Often more than one interview question and associated probes might be needed to fully address a research question.

Wording and language level

Whether you require semi-structured or loosely structured interviewing the question guide is essentially a checklist to ensure the necessary questions are covered. However, as you design the questions you will need to consider what knowledge and awareness the interviewee is likely to have concerning the question topics. For example, are you talking to him or her about something he or she is likely to have detailed knowledge or actual experience of, or are the topics something he or she has not experienced but has particular beliefs on? The greater level of knowledge and experience the interviewee has then the more likely you can probe for further details.

Ideally, you might consult those who are being researched to help design the interview questions and research instruments. This will not only promote their engagement but also make the questions more relevant to the target informants and reflect their frames of reference and terminology. In qualitative research it is common for the first exploratory interviews to help inform refinements and additions for the later interviews. This allows hitherto unforeseen yet salient topics to be included or alterations to questions that people find difficult to understand.

Clearly, because the interview is semi-structured and flexible, there can be variation in the order in which questions are covered in order to follow the flow of the interviewee's discussion. During an interview, people might jump to related topics and issues they feel are natural and, while relevant, this might not always follow the order on the topic guide. This is natural but this process needs to be managed, by listening to what is being said, addressing questions out of sequence on the guide and noting which questions still need to be covered.

Figure 8.3 is an example of a semi-structured interview guide used in the research project given as an example previously in this chapter.

Selecting interviewees

Interviewing is usually conducted as part of a qualitative research approach, therefore you are not selecting a sample from which you can generalise and produce findings that have statistical significance. Rather, the selection of informants aims to reflect the characteristics of the range of the group being studied but also include those people who are likely to provide the necessary range-relevant illuminative insights on the focus of the research and research

1. Identify key informants' positions and role played in the SoA. Were they involved in SoA evaluation activities?

2. Looking at the printout showing data for your school, what effect do you think the SoA project has had on:

- Positive destinations of pupils

  Probe: – whether SoA focus in school focussed on this

  – other factors that might have influenced this dimension

  – if appropriate, why quantitative measures might not tell the full story concerning impact here.

- Pupils' attainment

  Probe: – whether SoA focus in school focussed on this

  – other factors that might have influenced this dimension

  – if appropriate, why quantitative measures might not tell the full story concerning impact here.

- School roll

  Probe: – whether SoA focus in school focussed on this

  – other factors that might have influenced this dimension

  – if appropriate, why quantitative measures might not tell the full story concerning impact here.

3. Overall, how would you summarise the difference the Schools of Ambition programme has made to the:

- the pupils and staff within the school?

- the wider community (including parents, primary schools, partner organisations, colleges and employers etc)?

- the culture of the school.

4. Do you feel the changes are sustainable?

  Probe: – if yes, what factors are contributing to supporting sustainability?

  – if no, what would be helpful (assuming it's not just money) or needs to be in place to ensure sustainability?

5. Are there any particular factors that have helped or hindered the effectiveness of:

- Transformational Plan activities

- Evaluation activities.

6. Finally are there any other comments you would like to add?

Thank you very much for your cooperation.

Figure 8.3 Semi-structured interview guide

objectives. For example, if you were interested in understanding key stakeholders' views on what difference a whole school leadership programme had made in a school, you would seek to include representatives from:

- the young people who had participated in the course with representation relevant ages, gender and ability
- the parents of pupils involved in the course

- Senior Management Team and staff who were involved in the planning and teaching of the course
- staff who teach those involved in the programme
- depending on the course objectives, ie promoting wider pupil confidence, aspirations and contributing to school ethos, then you would seek to interview other staff such as classroom assistants, janitorial, administration and support staff.

The number of interviewees required, depends on the focus of your research and how many people you need in order to reflect the range of relevant stakeholders' who can provide information on the focus of the research. For example, pupils, staff, parents and, if necessary, taking into account gender, age and status, and so on. However, more often than not, the practical concerns of time, funds and resources will also limit the number of people you can interview. The final selection, however, will have to be justifiable and any limitations for what can be claimed from the findings made explicit. You might also wish to look at Chapter 9 on focus groups where the issue of sampling in qualitative research is also covered.

Planning and arranging the interviews

Usually it is helpful to send interviewees a list of the main questions prior to the interview along with a brief outline of the research. This will give people time to think about the topics and, if necessary, gather any useful information they wish to draw on during the interview. The information about the research provided in plain language should duplicate the information provided in the interview preamble and inform interviewees about the purpose of the research, what will happen with the findings, how long the interview is likely to last and details on confidentiality. It is helpful to gather basic biographical information from interviewees in advance to save time during the interview itself. Before the interview takes place you have to ensure that the interviewee understands the information you have provided about the study and has given his or her consent to your use of the information provided. Therefore, a formal consent form for the interviewee to sign should also be prepared.

Preparing for the interview

When used appropriately, interviewing can be a particularly powerful and flexible research method. However, even when you are confident that this method is appropriate to gather the information you want, there are other considerations to take into account before you interview people. Interviews are essentially an interpersonal interaction and dialogue, and are influenced by a range of factors, some of which can be more or less anticipated and addressed in the design of the interview. As humans and social 'actors' we engage in discussion and dialogue with a range of people every day, so does this mean everyone is able to conduct social research interviews? The research interview, while similar to everyday discussions you might have with others, is different in that you are seeking to systematically elicit information from a range of people on particular topics that can be analysed with the findings that hold up to the scrutiny of others.

Interviewers should have skills in communicating, listening and taking notes. When conducting loosely structured interviews, these skills are particularly important. It is also helpful if the interviewer has a good knowledge of the topics being covered as this will help him or her know when to probe further when salient issues emerge during the discussion. Kvale's (1996) excellent guide to interviewing has provided a list of ten criteria that make for an effective interviewer:

- Knowledgeable: is thoroughly familiar with the focus of the interview; pilot interviews of the kind used in survey interviewing can be useful here.
- Structuring: gives purpose for interview; rounds it off; asks whether interviewee has questions.
- Clear: asks simple, easy, short questions; no jargon.
- Gentle: lets people finish; gives them time to think; tolerates pauses.
- Sensitive: listens attentively to what is said and how it is said; is empathetic in dealing with the interviewee.
- Open: responds to what is important to interviewee and is flexible.
- Steering: knows what he/she wants to find out.
- Critical: is prepared to challenge what is said, for example, dealing with inconsistencies in interviewees' replies.
- Remembering: relates what is said to what has previously been said.
- Interpreting: clarifies and extends meanings of interviewees' statements, but without imposing meaning on them. (Kvale 1996: 148)

The interview interaction and therefore, the amount and quality of information gathered, can also be enhanced when there is a rapport or affinity between interviewer and interviewee. The extent to which the latter can be engineered varies and it is arguable that, rather than trying to manufacture rapport, you should be aware of the interpersonal variables that might affect the interview dynamic. These variables might include: real and perceived power, status, ethnicity, gender, age and personality. Any reflections and observations you might have on the interviews can be noted in a research diary and these insights will be useful during the analysis of the interviews.

The potential range of informants (such as young people, professional peers, parents, organisational representatives) and the diverse topics addressed mean that interviewer skills and experience are at least as important as the design of the questions used. Therefore, as with focus group methods, you have to ensure that you, or those conducting interviews on your behalf, have at least a basic skills set and relevant sensitivities concerning conducting research interviews. An awareness of protocols to adopt if certain contingencies emerge because of disclosed information is also important. For example if information gathered highlights a child protection issue does the interviewer know what procedures to follow?

It is also important that if there are a number of interviewers conducting the interviews then you have to ensure that there is a level of consistency in the way the questions are asked. Otherwise, asking a question using different words or emphasis might mean interviewees have a different understanding of what you want to know. Approaches to address this involve training sessions in which the interview is rehearsed and providing interviewers with guidance on how to phrase questions and deal with follow-up probes. In addition, the interviewers can meet to ensure they have shared understanding of what each interview question means and what it is attempting to elicit. Having a shared understanding across interviewers on the questions is especially important when using a loosely structured interview where the interviewer is using a list of key topics rather than specifically worded questions. Using such topics allows the interviewer to frame the question using terms and language they feel suits the interviewer and the emerging findings but needs particular skills to probe and follow developing themes of interest to the research.

Interviews conducted as part of practitioner research in schools and the workplace can face particular challenges because the information gathering involves peers gathering information from one another. Such research, particularly that which is evaluative in nature, can mean that certain ethical and sensitive issues have to be taken into account in addition to the usual methodological considerations.

Professionals interviewing their peers

When teachers want to gather information from their peers as part of their research for whatever reason, the planning and conduct of the research will have to take into account potential tensions that might arise because of individuals' status, concerns about anonymity and what will happen to the information they provide. These anxieties can be exacerbated when interviewing colleagues face to face.

Context is also important. For example, if the focus of the research is likely to highlight issues concerning school or course management or the efficiency of teaching then those individuals involved in these activities might well be anxious about how the findings will affect their reputation. However, in schools and establishments where the ethos promotes reflection and collegiality then peers at various professional levels will be more likely to welcome interviews, observation and other research that focuses on their practice. However, if such an ethos is absent there is little the interviewer can do to engineer it.

While some of these variables can be difficult or impossible to remove completely, their impact can be reduced. For example, anxieties about the research findings affecting professional standing can be addressed to some extent by clarifying and emphasising the ethical safeguards in place that will ensure the interviewees' rights and promote confidentiality.

The power dynamic that can emerge when there is variance between the interviewee and interviewer's professional status is perhaps more difficult to address in interviews, especially when the interviewee and interviewer are in a professional relationship. Here, the interview protocols, consent form and preamble are important in establishing that the research is not about the two people engaged in the interaction but is using the process to gather insights on the research topics. If you allow the interviewees to read and review the interviewer's notes or transcript, then this can also help to balance the power relationship.

Pupils interviewing their peers

In some practitioner enquiry and research there can be benefits to involving young people as interviewers when the aim is to gather information from pupils. In some cases, pupils might be more willing to provide information on their views and experiences to peers they trust rather than to adults because of established rapport and shared experiences. However, should the support of pupils to interview their peers be sought then you would have to be aware of some of the potential issues that can arise. First, you would have to ensure that you helped develop their interviewing skills and awareness of the dos and don'ts of interviewing and provide some role play of examples. The age and maturity of the young people will influence the extent to which they can be expected to conduct less structured interviews and use probing. However, just as important is establishing young people's appreciation for the ethical guidelines to be adopted. In particular, the selection and training of young people to be interviewers has to take into account the individual's reliability in terms of adhering to guidelines on confidentiality and respecting the rights of others to express certain views. Certainly, you would have to take particular care before asking younger pupils to interview their peers on more sensitive topics. It is interesting to note that where schools and the curriculum focus on promoting leadership and broad 'citizenship' life skills, it is more likely that pupils will acquire the abilities and dispositions that enable them to play a more active role in the design and conduct of research and enquiry in their schools.

Conducting the interview

At the beginning of the interview it is usually necessary to gather descriptive information on the interviewee such as their position and relevant characteristics so that you have a record for your analysis. You might want to consider gathering basic descriptive information on the interviewee in advance of the interview to save time during the interview but also to help with your selection process and planning on how to conduct the interview. Protocols to ensure anonymity and confidentiality should be stressed, this is essential especially if you need to collect actual names and personal details. If you do not already know the interviewee then initial impressions are important in establishing rapport and respect.

Guidelines for successful interviews

The effectiveness of using interviews to gather information can be influenced by a range of factors that cover the characteristics and attributes of the individuals concerned, from the skill of the interviewer through to practical concerns such as the time and location of the interview. Drawing on the author's experience of interviewing and relevant literature, the following lists of considerations have been developed as a guide to conducting effective interviews.

Recording the interview

- Ensure that the interviewee's formal and written permission to record their comments has been obtained and that he or she is aware of the research aims and what will happen to the information provided.
- Check all recording equipment in advance. Ideally use a digital recorder, because these devices can record in high quality and recordings do not suffer from the hiss and distortion found on tapes. The digital files are easily transferred to computer to assist transcription and analysis. These recorders are also usually small and therefore unobtrusive but offer many hours of recording, and battery life is considerable. Before the interview, check whether the batteries have sufficient charge and that there is sufficient memory space. Also check other settings where necessary such as microphone sensitivity.
- In addition to recording the interview electronically, take concise notes. This helps keep check of responses and sometimes record your reflections during the interview but it is also a crucial back up record should the recorder fail. Most interviewers have stories of conducting all necessary pre-checks of their recording equipment, yet it still failed and without taking notes they would have lost fascinating information.
- Sometimes interviewees may feel reticent, for whatever reason, about being recorded and unable to give full and frank responses. In such cases, detailed note taking is all the more essential.
- Decide in advance of the interviewing whether the research objectives require that the interview recordings will be fully transcribed and reflect this in the research costs and timetable.

Interview question guide

- An interview guide with a limited list of topics with key questions and their associated sub-questions and probes is important as a reminder to follow up important issues. While this guide is flexible to allow following up relevant information, you will also have to strike a balance and ensure that you do not lose track of the key research aims and so collect irrelevant or unnecessary information.

- The questions should be relevant to the interviewee to keep him or her engaged.

Introductions and establishing rapport

- Use introductions and conversation to help relax the interviewee. Keep the interview friendly but not too informal.
- The interviewer's dress and appearance should be appropriate to the context.
- If possible, conduct the interview at a time and location that are chosen by the interviewee. This will help place him or her at their ease.
- Begin with checking that the interviewee knows the purpose of the research and has seen the research plain language information sheet or leaflet.
- Check that the interviewee has given formal permission to take part and have their comments recorded using notes and/or electronically.

Conducting the interview

- Encourage the interviewee to draw on their experiences and ask for specific examples. This helps avoid vague responses and promotes greater illuminative insights.
- Listen carefully to what the interviewee is saying and indicate that you are paying attention.
- Probe for specific answers and examples, especially when the responses are vague or too general.
- Periodically check the interpretation of what is being said. For example, 'Can I just check that what you are saying is …'.
- Avoid questions that the interviewer is likely to find sensitive or, if such questions are necessary, ensure that the interviewee is aware that these questions are to going to be covered. Also, introduce sensitive and more complex questions later in the interview when the interviewee is more at ease. Depending on the nature of a 'sensitive topic', it can be helpful to phrase such questions so that they avoid the interviewee discussing his or her own behaviour but cover the topic using hypothetical examples.
- While interpersonal interaction can never be totally controlled, you can reduce some factors that will exacerbate interviewer influence. When topics are controversial you should avoid, as far as possible, making verbal value judgements or verbal and non-verbal signs that indicate that the interviewer is approving or disapproving of the interviewee's answers.
- Where interviewees struggle to provide a response, try re-phrasing the question without altering its meaning.
- Do not help interviewees to provide an answer, including finishing his or her sentences.

- Avoid asking ambiguous questions.
- Be aware of your preconceptions and whether these are influencing how you ask questions or your decision to pursue certain responses and topics.
- Do not ask leading questions, for example, 'What's problematic about the current curriculum?' rather than a less leading 'Does the current curriculum present any challenges?'
- Do not extend the interview beyond the agreed time limit unless the interviewee makes it clear that they are happy to do so.
- The duration of interviews will often be around one hour but this can be extended if the interviewees feel strongly about, or are particularly interested in, the research topics. For example, effective semi-structured interviews that have lasted one and a half hours and longer have been conducted with teachers, school leaders and local policy representatives where the research topics have been salient to their situation (for example, MacBeath et al., 2009).

Concluding the interview and post interview feedback

- Final questions can include opportunities for summarising and reflecting to ensure that you have accurately understood and noted what is being said.
- You should also provide an opportunity for the interviewee to add any other information they feel is relevant but has not been covered by your questions.
- It can be useful to provide the interviewee with an interview summary or transcript. This helps check your interpretation of what was said and can help interviewees in their own practice. Feedback of this type also helps us clarify any ambiguous emerging themes.
- However, it is possible that some interviewees might, on reflection, feel uncertain about allowing what they have said to be included in your research. Even with assurances of confidentiality they might feel vulnerable or anxious about the impact of their comments.
- You should thank interviewees, by letter or email, for their participation.
- The findings of the research should also be fed back in an appropriate form and language to the research participants at the end of the study.

Dealing with the interview information

An individual qualitative interview can produce a substantial volume of information and even conducting a modest number of interviews results in the daunting task of processing and analysing all of the qualitative information gathered. We deal with the analysis of qualitative data more fully in Chapter 13. Here we briefly describe the main stages in processing interview information.

Pre-analysis

Assuming that you have recorded the interview information using a combination of written notes (including any research diary insights) and audio recordings of the discussion, you first have to sort and organise this material. At the planning stage of your research you should have decided whether the research objectives required full transcripts to be produced from the audio recordings or detailed summary notes that draw on the recordings for quotes. Transcripts are necessary when you are interested in the precise details of what people have said and how they have said it. Importantly, transcripts also allow for what people have said to be kept in context and this is particularly important when others are involved in the analysis. The first level of analysis, therefore, starts as you write up your notes, transcribe and read through this material.

Main analysis

Qualitative analysis is the process of working with non-numeric information to reach an understanding, explanation or interpretation that takes into account perceptions, interactions, processes, meanings and context, for example:

Why do people think an education initiative has or has not worked?
What do people think about their role in an education initiative?
How have certain challenges been addressed when implementing such an initiative?

Qualitative analysis is based on an interpretative philosophy rather than one that seeks to generalise. Typically, but not always, this type of analysis involves identifying themes in qualitative information. The qualitative information that interviewing usually generates includes notes and transcripts from your audio and possibly video recordings. This information will provide descriptive accounts of what was said or happened and you might also begin to write up your developing analytic ideas concerning this information informed by your supporting material from observations, reflective field notes and documents provided by interviewees. Indeed, Wengraf (2001) writes quite technical yet still very useful chapters on processing and analysing interview information once collected. Wengraf highlights the benefits of reflecting on notes and drawing on insights and memories of the interview experience to help build up 'theoretical memos' that will inform your analysis (Wengraf, 2001: 209) a process first described by Glaser (1978: 83).

When you need to elicit themes which are related to your research questions and objectives you can usually code or label parts of your notes and transcript text (or images and so on) so that these can be associated with a particular theme. Ideally, when you have time, this process is repeated as you gather new information. This process of reflection on initial themes should occur as you go through the information and if necessary refine, add to these themes or even abandon them. Much qualitative analysis reflects if not adopts the *Grounded Theory* approach developed by Glasser and Strauss (1967). The process can be seen as working from the descriptive through to more complex themes and associations that can address the research objectives and even contribute to theoretical understanding.

The analysis of your interview information, therefore, will usually follow a sequence similar to this:

- *Codes* – producing labels that allow the key points of the information to be highlighted.
- *Concepts* – collections of codes of similar content that allow the data to be grouped and compared and contrasted.
- *Categories* – broad groups of similar concepts that are used to generate a theory.
- *Theory* – a collection of explanations that explain the subject of the research.

This approach includes the concept that little is assumed about the research topics, and generates concepts/theory from the data (*inductive*). Seidel (1998) developed a model to explain the qualitative data analysis process, which is similar to solving a jigsaw:

- *Noticing* and coding
- *Collecting* and sorting into themes
- *Thinking* and analysing.

Usually, however, you will have some idea of what you are looking for. If you are seeking to explore and test theories (*deductive*) your initial codes will reflect your research objectives, questions and related concepts. These codes can, of course, be modified as you progress with the analysis. Qualitative analysis can often include both inductive and deductive elements.

Organising qualitative information

In order to do qualitative analysis you need to organise the information and make it manageable. Ideally, researchers will read and reread the transcripts/notes and use highlighter pens or other graphic means to code and annotate the material. Some researchers will physically cut up the material to help sort it into themes. It is important, however, that your annotating allows you to trace back the highlighted selections of text to their source so you do not lose sight of the context.

Increasingly, various computer packages (for example, NVivo, Ethnograph and NUD*IST) have become available to assist with coding, summarising and categorising tasks. However, you still need to be familiar with the material to apply sensible codes and, while the software helps the sorting and categorising to be particularly systematic, it cannot actually do the analysis for you.

The analysis process in the real world of practitioner research

Qualitative methods such as interviews might involve relatively few individuals, carefully chosen to allow us to gather insights relevant to your research foci. However, the volume of information produced from even a modest number of interviews and focus groups can be considerable.

It is unlikely that full transcripts can be produced so detailed notes are made instead. These notes can be summarised using research questions as an analytical framework. You will still need to be alert to new, unforeseen yet relevant information in the material. Also, under ideal circumstances material would be analysed intensively, coding reflecting, recoding and generating themes, which takes up a lot of time. Few practitioners (and arguably full-time researchers) have this luxury. Often, the analysis process has to be adapted to fit constraints while preserving as much rigour as possible.

What does this mean for the majority of practitioners who want to analyse interview information within tight constraints of time and resources but still have to maintain rigour? The process can be summarised as follows:

- The initial reading through the material and coding will produce descriptive labels that help you summarise the information.
- As you become more familiar with the information, after reading other transcripts/notes, you can elaborate these to categorise and begin to analyse.
- You move towards interpretations that reflect informants' views and meanings, triangulating emerging findings with other evidence sources and maintaining an awareness of context as you develop a deeper understanding of *why* things have happened, what factors and processes have been important and reasons underpinning informants' views.
- Where practitioners are using qualitative approaches in their own schools and organisations they have the advantage of familiarity with context which can assist interpretation. However, you still need validity checks, for example, asking colleagues for their interpretation of the same material and feeding back findings to informants for comment. If you make your analysis transparent, involve others in this process and feed back emerging findings, you can provide checks on the interpretive process.

The analysis process is, therefore, 'streamlined' but not compromised. This is particularly important when the findings supplement other types of data/ evidence and feed into the planning and self-evaluation process of schools and organisations.

Summary ▢

Qualitative interviewing is an extremely flexible method and enables the gathering of non-numeric information from people to help researchers better understand, explain and interpret the social world. When used in association with other methods, interviews are usually key to obtaining a comprehensive understanding of the focus of a study.

Effective use of interviewing requires skill but teachers should have most of the communication skills to conduct interviews. Interestingly, many teachers often overlook their skills that transfer to research and think that external 'experts' are always required to conduct meaningful research in their school. There can, however, be issues in training and building capacity among staff and young people to conduct interviews as part of school-based practitioner research, but these are not insurmountable.

Interviewing usually produces a considerable volume of information to analyse and you need to plan ahead to ensure you have sufficient time and resources to analyse the evidence collected. However, with adequate safeguards and checks, robust and meaningful analysis can be conducted without full transcripts and extensive qualitative software-assisted procedures that large-scale, well funded research might deploy.

Further reading

Coffey, A., Holbrook, B. and Atkinson, P. (1996) 'Qualitative data analysis: technologies and representations', *Sociological Research Online*, 1(1). Available at: http://www.socresonline.org.uk/1/1/4.html.

Gibbs, G.R. (2002) *Qualitative Data Analysis: Explorations with NVivo*. Buckingham: Open University Press.

Miles, M.B. and Huberman, A.M. (1984) *Qualitative Data Analysis: A Sourcebook of New Methods*. Beverly Hills, CA: Sage.

Using Focus Groups

This chapter introduces the use of focus groups in education research. We summarise its advantages and limitations and emphasise the gathering of information from young people, including researching sensitive topics. The chapter also includes the main stages of planning and conducting a focus group. We discuss what can influence the effectiveness of focus groups. The examples are from research conducted by the SCRE Centre and reflect practical issues researchers face when gathering information in educational settings.

What are focus groups?

A focus group can be broadly defined as a small group of people with similar characteristics selected from a wider population (for example, parents, pupils within a year group, headteachers, non-teaching staff, and so on) that is convened to elicit, via moderated discussion, members' views, attitudes and experiences relating to particular topics that are relevant to the research being conducted. A key feature of the method is the interaction and discussion between participants which provides detailed insights on a limited range of topics.

> Focus groups provide an excellent opportunity to listen to the voices of students, explore issues in depth, and obtain insights that might not occur without the discussion they provide. (Palomba and Banta, 1999: 196)

Focus groups ideally:

- use small groups (usually between 4 and 12) of carefully selected individuals
- use discussion and group interaction to elicit detailed information, particularly participants' perceptions, on research topics
- use a skilled moderator/facilitator who not only asks questions but engineers or guides the group interaction to promote the provision of information and

insights not normally available using other methods. In an ideal focus group the moderator actually says very little but ensures the group actively discuss the range of topics of relevance to the study

- have a scribe in attendance to make notes to supplement the recording and allow the moderator to concentrate on facilitating the group
- foster a non-judgemental and relaxed environment which is conducive to open discussion.

Focus groups were once methods associated more with market research but they have been increasingly used to gather information in social and educational research. With origins in post-Second World War American market research, focus groups were developed to address certain shortcomings of marketing surveys, that is, to help explain why people decided to buy certain products, to explore views on how to improve goods and what consumers wanted. Soon after this, political researchers adopted the method to better understand voting behaviour and, eventually, academics began to use it. It is arguable that, unlike quantitative methods, the development of qualitative methods in social research and focus groups in particular has taken longer to establish recognised procedures and good practice.

As Hoppe et al. (1995) have noted, focus group methods are relatively new to social science research and, therefore, guidelines for conducting groups and dealing with the information gathered are still developing. One example where this is particularly the case is where focus groups are used to gather information from young people and school children.

Benefits and limitations of focus groups

As with every research method, focus groups have benefits and limitations. Focus groups are particularly well suited to exploratory and illuminative work when there is little research on a topic or when we want to ask 'why' questions. For example, focus groups can help formulate hypotheses or refine relevant survey questions and their language and terminology. Clarification of language, terminology and frames of reference of the people being researched is especially important not only in formulating closed-category quantitative research instruments, but also in allowing researchers to sensitise themselves to the 'natural language' of those being researched and so increase their credibility with a particular group. This credibility can promote more detailed and/or accurate responses from those being researched. This has been found to be particularly evident in research looking at young people's perceptions of health issues, particularly drugs and sexual health (for example, Connell et al., 2004; Lowden and Powney, 1996). In focus groups, participants are allowed to express themselves in their own words and this can provide insights on their understanding of topics and the level of feeling associated with them.

Focus groups can also be used to explore further and clarify themes which have emerged from quantitative research so that we can better understand why people report certain views or behaviours. The information provided in this way can 'fill in the gaps' in survey data when ambiguities arise, when it is clear that a particular question did not fully work in eliciting meaningful data.

Obtaining information using groups can elicit information which would be difficult or impossible to obtain using other methods. As Hoppe et al. (1995: 102–3) note, 'one participant's responses may provoke responses from others in the group, resulting in a synergistic effect not achieved in the usual interview situation'. In groups, people will say things which will provoke responses from others which, in turn, can illuminate more about the research foci (Basch, 1987; Folch-Lyon and Trost, 1981; McDonald and Topper, 1989). This effect is impossible to obtain in a one-to-one interview. Some research has indicated that participants feel more relaxed in groups because there is less direct focus, and therefore pressure, on any one individual. Participants who are more at ease will usually provide more detailed responses (Festervand, 1984–85; Mariampolski, 1989).

Focus groups, however, do have limitations. First, the findings are not generalisable in the sense that the findings from a robust quantitative survey are. This is because of the limited numbers of groups that can be conducted in most research projects. However, one could argue that this is a false limitation in that these methods are qualitative and are not meant to be generalisable in the sense of quantitative-based work. An analogy would be to say a screwdriver is no good for cutting wood. However, it was never intended for this purpose. Used together these tools can be complementary. Perhaps a more significant limitation is that focus groups are resource and personnel intensive and therefore, expensive. For these approaches to work well, they require skilled facilitators/moderators and these can be expensive. Given the costs of these approaches, one has to decide whether they are appropriate methods to address the aims of the research (Krueger, 1994). On the other hand, in small-scale practitioner research you yourself are likely to be the facilitator/moderator and so no real 'extra' expense is actually incurred.

Focus groups should never be used purely to increase the number of respondents, as Drever (1995) stresses: 'If you interview 150 people in groups of ten, your sample is fifteen groups, not 150 individuals.' Use of focus groups can present particular challenges. For example, it can be difficult to record what is being said in a group, or certain individuals can monopolise the time while others may feel reticent about speaking out, especially if their views differ from the apparent consensus in their group or from the views of an opinion leader. However, there are strategies that can address these issues and these are covered elsewhere in this chapter.

There is some uncertainty over whether social inhibitions are reduced when talking in a group (Mariampolski, 1989). Hoppe et al. (1995) found that the amount of information provided on sensitive topics varied from group to group. This suggests that the actual personalities, participants and interviewers involved may influence the dynamic of the group. Research for the SCRE Centre (Lowden and Powney, 1996) on sexual health education, that used focus groups to gather information, has shown that different personalities have less of an impact on group dynamics when a skilled interviewer moderates the group. A more important factor appears to be the gender of participants.

When focus groups are judged to be the most appropriate method to use there can still be certain issues to address, particularly when the participants are young people or school pupils and the research foci include sensitive topics. The next part of this chapter looks at issues arising from using focus groups in education research and strategies that you can adopt to address these.

Gathering information from young people using focus groups

As Hoppe et al. (1995) have reported, numerous authors have suggested that modifications are needed when using focus groups to obtain information from young people rather than from adults (Folch-Lyon and Trost, 1981; Greenbaum, 1990; McDonald and Topper, 1989; Stewart and Shamdasani, 1990; Worden et al. 1988). Additional effort and time will usually have to be spent establishing ground rules, clarifying the reasons for the research and the role of the moderator. Indeed, it could be justifiably argued that focus groups should always be 'fine-tuned' to suit the needs and nature of any group of participants (for example, adults who have low self-esteem and those with difficulties with their learning skills).

Numerous research projects conducted by the SCRE Centre have used focus groups to gather information from adults including policy-makers, teachers and other educational professionals, health education professionals, adult learners, students and school pupils. For example, this method has been used extensively in SCRE Centre projects researching the impact of health education on young people's sexual health and drug-related knowledge and behaviour. This experience has shown that using group methods with young people and children means that certain special considerations have to be taken into account. When such methods are used to gather information on sensitive topics, particular issues arise which can further affect the quality and amount of information gathered as well as the well-being of the participants.

Regardless of whether the research is seen as sensitive or not, the planning of focus groups, as with all research methods, must consider ethical issues and appropriate protocols. For example, what are the implications for those individuals who take part in our study and the wider ramifications of our research? As we highlighted in Chapter 4, adequately addressing the potential ethical issues of your research is not simply an additional administrative task but rather a core consideration that must shape the overall design, implementation and reporting of your research project.

Identifying participants

Unlike quantitative methods, the selection of participants for focus groups is usually purposive rather than random. However, the demographic character-istics of the people we are interested in will usually inform selection. As Hoppe et al. suggest: 'We recommend determining the salient demographic factors for conducting the focus group research and then sampling based on those factors' (1995: 106). For example, an evaluation of a secondary school sexual health programme might well require gathering illuminative informa-tion to complement data from pupil questionnaires. The groups, therefore, could be selected from the project participants and reflect school year group, levels of ability and, in this case, separate groups for males and females.

This sampling approach might not be generalisable but it is purposive in order to provide detailed insights and information from those groups we are interested in. The findings emerging from focus groups can thus be used to inform related quantitative studies with respondents possessing the same char-acteristics.

Composition and size of groups

The actual composition of the focus group is important in affecting the inter-personal dynamics and the willingness to provide useful information. Factors such as group size, gender, age, status and peer relationships all play a part in influencing the effectiveness of group methods.

Size of group

Ideally, focus groups that involve children should consist of between five and eight participants. Smaller groups can mean that children feel uncomfortable because of the more obvious attention of the moderator. Smaller groups also mean that there is a possibility that, by chance, all children might be quiet while a group of five or eight will have a better mix of personalities, some of whom will be better able to start the group talking. Experience from SCRE Centre research has shown that discussion can be promoted when all the children are friends or when the group has spent longer building up a rapport with each other and with the moderator. Friendship groups can be particu-larly good for gathering information on sensitive topics because there is often an already established trust between participants and they are used to discuss-ing personal topics. Participants who are used to discussing sensitive topics as part of their personal, social and health education (PSHE) classes can be brought together for focus groups as they have already established a certain level of trust and adhere to certain established 'ground rules' on disclosure and respect of others' views.

Larger groups might seem attractive in that we are getting information from more people. However, larger groups (that is, those over ten in number) can pose problems in terms of managing the group and recording information. Even when all participants in a large group are very active and willing to provide information, the moderator can have difficulties hearing and taking in what is being said. In such cases, recording becomes almost useless as responses combine to become unintelligible when the recording is played back. Turn-taking, where children are encouraged to put their hands in the air to contribute, can help add some order to large groups but often the enthusiasm of participants means this is often short-lived and limited. In adult focus groups, turn-taking protocols can be more successful, with participants providing their first name to assist transcription, but again this can sometimes inhibit the interaction and group dynamic.

Age

The age of participants is another important factor in the composition of groups. Too large an age discrepancy might mean that younger children feel intimidated by older participants, often because they are not used to interacting and communicating in a group context with older children. There can be exceptions when pupils of differing ages have been working together, for example on a pupil council or confidence-building event. However, pupils of different ages might also have quite different ways of perceiving their world based on different experiences, and this can pose problems in group discussions, particularly where maturity is important (such as in sexual health and other health-related behaviours).

Gender

There can be a gender dimension to the issue of group interaction and willingness to talk. Evaluation research conducted by the SCRE Centre of a secondary school sexual health programme (Lowden and Powney, 1996) involving 11- to 18-year-olds found that even when friendship groups comprising same-sex participants are used, female groups seemed to be culturally more disposed to discuss sensitive and personal topics. In male focus groups, participants were less willing to discuss sensitive issues from a personal perspective. When they do, there is a tendency to hide behind machismo posturing and statements. Hoppe et al. (1995) advocate using same-sex groups for all focus group work involving sensitive issues. In SCRE Centre research, however, this has usually been found to be the case with sexual health topics, but is less true of other so-called sensitive issues research such as drug education. In SCRE Centre studies of drug education (Lowden and Powney, 2000) researchers have found that mixed-sex groups were very effective in promoting conducive group dynamics and eliciting illuminative information. In such mixed-sex groups with equal numbers of girls and boys, the girls will often challenge the boys' bravado statements and encourage openness. Often it is the girls who are the catalysts to active group discussion on topics. This applies to all age groups and contrasts with the experience reported by Hoppe et al. (1995) and by Stewart and Shamdasani (1990), who state that older children may be so interested in the opposite sex that mixed groups are too distracting for them. In the aforementioned SCRE Centre sexual health education research, with the focus groups with older pupils (15 years to 17 years), pupils usually decided that they wanted single-sex groups, not because the opposite sex were distracting but usually because the girls found the males were immature and distrusted their ability to maintain confidentiality on sexual subjects.

Young males often seem eager to try to impress peers, both male and female, and may also be interested sexually in others, but when they are used to being taught in mixed classes these effects are controllable in most focus groups where a skilled moderator is present. There will, of course, be exceptions, for example, where the ethos in a school or class has promoted respect and maturity that is reflected in peer interaction. It is up to you as the researcher, often in consultation with others, to assess the ability of the target groups to conduct equitable and mature discussions.

Moderator skills and characteristics

Your skills as a researcher are always important in any kind of interview work, but this is especially true for gathering information from groups, particularly those which are based on sensitive topics. For example, a skilled focus group moderator can carefully challenge machismo statements to probe underlying tensions and issues relating to the research foci. There may be times when you decide it is better to approach a colleague or someone else to act as the facilitator in your focus groups.

Building rapport is a complex process which can vary from individual to individual and from group to group. Focus group moderators can learn skills which facilitate rapport building but the perceptions of individuals and groups can mean that even a skilled moderator might have difficulty engaging the cooperation of all informants. For example, younger moderators can be more readily accepted and trusted than an older person who is perceived as being more like a 'teacher' or authority figure. Young people when discussing drugs or sex often perceive, rightly or wrongly, that teachers and older adults are more likely to make value judgements about their actions. This affects the nature and amount of information young people will disclose.

However, there is a balance to be struck. If the moderator is seen as a direct peer then certain focus group participants may modify or restrain their responses because they want to be seen in a certain 'positive' or credible light to 'manufacture' their image in front of peers. This can include displaying bravado, macho behaviour and views or adopting an overly critical stance on something which is developed by teachers. Again, the researcher has to be sensitive to these possibilities when gathering and analysing focus group information. Debate in a group, even when quite heated but controlled, can be effective in illuminating issues and topics of relevance to the research. Again, the skills of the moderator are important in managing the group to the extent that open hostility is avoided.

Interviewers/moderators have to be alert to any stress or discomfort among participants and alter the questioning or format of the session, while at the same time working to meet the objectives set for the group. Skilled interviewers are therefore essential especially when groups consist of children. Pupils may be reticent about providing accurate details on sensitive topics and expressing their views because they feel they might be identified. The researcher must make every effort to keep such details confidential and stress the steps he or she is taking to those they wish to gather information from in the hope of encouraging participation in the research. If others are involved in the processing of this information (such as secretarial staff and other researchers) then they should sign declarations of confidentiality and follow the relevant ethical protocols. The Scottish Education Research Association has a clear set of ethical standards that are relevant for research in schools and educational settings (www.sera.ac.uk/docs/.../ SERA%20Ethical%20GuidelinesWeb.PDF).

How do focus group moderators acquire the skills necessary to facilitate effective focus groups? Can they be trained or are there 'innate' personality attributes that are important? Researchers certainly can acquire many skills from experience and in working with other, more experienced colleagues. Experiential learning is important in gaining the relevant skills to conduct focus groups but training also has an important role. As Hoppe et al. (1995: 107) point out, recruiting people with substantial experience of working with children and focus groups is important but so is training, which should include 'advanced interviewing techniques such as using non-directive probes and working from scripts, as well as role-plays of problematic interview situations and practice sessions with children'. Other broader skills which relate to all forms of qualitative interviewing are also helpful and include the ability to conduct the focus group in a flexible way, to accommodate unexpected but relevant emerging issues or to encourage discussion while at the same time achieving the aims of the research.

In addition to the methodological and research skills, training should include how to avoid creating stress or discomfort for participants when gathering information on sensitive topics. Related to this, is a responsibility to support interviewers and moderators who might have to gather information which could create stress for the interviewer. Such requisites place a responsibility on research organisations or those organising the research to ensure that professional development and training are provided for those who conduct interviews and focus groups.

Even the way focus group moderators dress can affect their credibility with participants and this seems especially true when the participants are young people and children. Dressing formally can be associated with authority figures and might limit openness in discussion of topics that have legal implications such as drug behaviours. Dressing smartly but casually might be preferable for some groups; on the other hand, if the participants are policy-makers then one would have to consider other appropriate, and perhaps more formal attire. This emphasises the chameleon-like aspects of successful social research interviewing.

In some cases, the age and sex of the interviewer/moderator can also affect the information collected in group methods. When interviewing children on certain topics such as sexual health, a younger interviewer of the same sex as the group can promote rapport and discussion because such characteristics are perceived by the participants as indicative of credibility and empathy. For example, in SCRE health-related research, a female moderator in her twenties was seen by pupils as being particularly able to relate to and understand the situation of older secondary school girls in focus groups discussing sexual health education. These focus groups were particularly effective in generating relevant and detailed information on the research topics.

The questions

As with most research methods, the development of focus group questions should usually relate to the main research foci, previous knowledge and literature on the research area. The numbers of questions and associated sub-probes will reflect how much we know about the research topics and wish to follow these up. The attention span of participants will also affect the numbers of questions and how the session is structured. Many school-age children may get bored after 30 minutes on a specific topic unless there are specific activities to break up the session. However, adults may well tolerate focus group sessions of up to an hour and, in some cases, sessions of three hours can be conducted if there are various breaks for refreshments and different activities are involved.

Activities can be used to supplement or replace questions to promote opportunities for participants to contribute. For example, you can ask the group to break into subgroups in order to review a particular topic, with each subgroup writing their thoughts on a flipchart to be shared and compared in a plenary. This might include subgroups discussing and summarising on paper the main reasons participants feel something has worked well or less well, or their ideas on how a programme or course could be improved. Such activities promote participation and encourage discussion.

The actual wording of questions and appropriate probes and the structuring of the topic guides/schedules will also be affected by more practical concerns such as the time allowed for the group session. Gathering information using focus groups in schools can present particular challenges. Given the intensity and complexity of many school timetables it may be difficult to arrange sessions of the duration you would prefer, especially if they are not with your own students. Multiple visits to discuss topics with the same groups will allow a better rapport to be built with the group and more detailed information to be obtained. However, this is usually a luxury for researchers who are constrained by resources, funds and time and a wish to minimise disruption to pupils' lessons. Teachers and other educators, however, are more likely to have this opportunity.

In the case of conducting interviews and focus groups, particularly where sensitive topics are involved, the actual question order should move from the less sensitive and complex to the more sensitive and complex questions (Stewart and Shamdasani, 1990). Hoppe et al. (1995) found that focus group work with children should avoid abstract questions as they can be 'potential conversation stoppers'. If abstract questions are really necessary, then they should follow questions on the topic which allow children to draw on their own experiences to make sense of, and relate to, the questions.

Often in educational practitioner research we are looking to evaluate courses and focus groups can play an important part in exploring pupils' experiences and views on their provision. In such cases, topic guides can be quite structured and detailed, because pupils can refer to their recent experience of the course.

In cases where topics are potentially sensitive and address issues that might incur sanctions, some care will have to be given to how questions are phrased in order to elicit openness yet avoiding informants feeling they have to disclose information that will make them vulnerable to negative attitudes or actions from peers or others. For example, when discussing whether a drug education programme has been effective, we would ideally want to know whether the behaviours of young people using drugs had been positively influenced. The lack of anonymity of a focus group or face-to-face interview will usually make direct questioning on this topic undesirable. An anonymous survey with some additional open-ended questions for elaboration might be best suited to gather basic information on changes in any drug use. However, focus groups can still be very useful in probing whether and why such programmes have been useful.

Such focus groups would stress at the beginning of the session clear guidelines and ground rules on avoiding disclosing details of personal behaviours or those of *named* peers. Thereafter, questions would explore whether informants

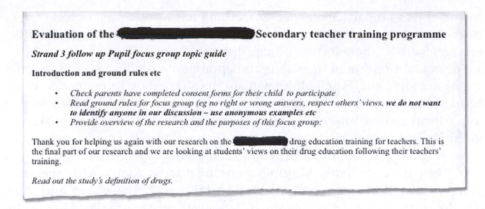

Evaluation of the ▮▮▮▮▮▮▮▮▮▮▮▮▮▮▮**Secondary teacher training programme**

Strand 3 follow up Pupil focus group topic guide

Introduction and ground rules etc

- *Check parents have completed consent forms for their child to participate*
- *Read ground rules for focus group (eg no right or wrong answers, respect others' views, **we do not want to identify anyone in our discussion – use anonymous examples etc***
- *Provide overview of the research and the purposes of this focus group:*

Thank you for helping us again with our research on the ▮▮▮▮▮▮▮▮ drug education training for teachers. This is the final part of our research and we are looking at students' views on their drug education following their teachers' training.

Read out the study's definition of drugs.

Figure 9.1 Extract 1: Focus group introduction and ground rules

believe the programme has been effective in terms of its aims, the reasons underpinning informants' views and how the programme might be improved.

The following extracts from an actual focus group topic guide for upper secondary pupils provide examples of questions used to explore the views of pupils on their drug education. This focus group was used to explore whether pupils thought their drug education lessons had improved, following a teacher training programme aimed at increasing the capacity of staff to deliver lessons to secondary pupils. The particular questions and probes were intended to illuminate whether pupils thought the teaching approaches and lessons had changed (in line with the aims of the training) since the programme. It also then explored the potential impact of the revised teaching approaches.

The first extract (Figure 9.1) provides an example of how a topic guide sets out key introductory steps the facilitator will use to ensure participants understand the ground rules and aims of the study, and so on.

The next extract (Figure 9.2) provides parts of the topic guide designed to get pupils talking about their drug education, with probes to help them remember and explore the research topics relating to whether the teacher training had influenced the lesson content and methods, and so on. Note how questions move from pupils' general views on their drug education and then probe for descriptions and views on teaching approaches, materials and content.

The focus group also aimed to address whether pupils believed this type of drug education would make a difference in terms of shaping attitudes and behaviours. Note that the following focus group questions avoid directly asking whether the participating pupils have altered their behaviour following their teacher's drug education training but rather explore whether the lessons have the potential to influence the decisions pupils make concerning substances (Figure 9.3). Hopefully, within the parameters of the ground rules, this type of questioning means informants are able to provide generalised, anonymous or hypothetical examples to illustrate their responses on the efficacy of the training.

Since we last spoke, have you been enjoying the drug education that you have been taught by your teacher?

Probe: Reasons

- Was the drug education interesting
- Did it cover *relevant content/topics?*
- Were the *teaching approaches* interesting – Does your teacher now use different approaches to teach drug education?
- Do you think that the *teaching materials* now being used are interesting and relevant?

Was there much discussion among students in these drug education lessons?

Probe:
- Did all students in the class feel comfortable discussing the drug education topics that arose during your lessons?

- Did the teacher seem comfortable with drug education topics that arose during your lessons?

Figure 9.2 Extract 2: Questions exploring the impact of the teacher training on drug education

What do you think have been the main benefits from the drug education taught by your teacher?

- Has it improved pupils' knowledge about drug facts (effects, legal consequences etc) that they can use to help make choices/decisions?

  - What information do they think is particularly relevant? Is there consensus in the group?

- Will the drug education taught by your teacher make a difference to the decisions pupils make about drugs and other substances? If so How?

  - Reasons for answers

Figure 9.3 Extract 3: Questions exploring the impact of a teacher drug education training programme on pupils

This particular focus group concluded by asking pupils what characterised 'good' and 'effective' drug education, and invited pupils to outline what they would include in a training programme for teachers of drug education. Finally, pupils were asked whether they had anything else to add.

Conducting the focus group

Participation in a focus group, as with all research participation, must be voluntary. In some cases, researchers might encounter school children or people in an organisation who have been nominated or 'volunteered' to participate.

This has to be avoided. Such individuals may not only be inappropriate for the purposes of the research; they can also inhibit productive group interaction as they may also be more reticent in providing information than a volunteer. Most importantly, coerced participation is unethical.

The environment in which the focus group is conducted is another major influence on the quantity and quality of information one can obtain. As with adults, the setting for children should be comfortable and convey a sense of a secure and private place to talk. You should try to ensure that there are no interruptions.

If the group has no set activities to complete, such as looking at materials or writing down comments, then a semicircular seating arrangement works well with the interviewer/moderator seated in clear view. If tasks are to be carried out, then seating participants around a table with the moderator again in a position to be clearly seen and heard is desirable.

In researching sensitive topics in schools, SCRE Centre research (Lowden and Powney, 2000) has found that the presence of a teacher can inhibit detailed discussion about issues relevant to the children, so you may wish to consider bringing someone else in to conduct the focus group. The experience of SCRE researchers, who are external to the institutions where the research is taking place, has been that most teachers are aware of this and will agree to leave the room during the focus group. In recent years, the introduction of disclosure checks on researchers working with children and vulnerable groups should also mean that teachers and other professionals can be assured that researchers are cleared to work in such contexts. However, researchers will also have to liaise with teachers and others to acquaint themselves with relevant child protection protocols.

Where teachers and educators are conducting focus groups, they will already have clearance but the question of their presence inhibiting open discussion among young people or their colleagues in focus groups might still be an issue. However, this is not inevitable. SCRE Centre researchers have found that where those working with young people on a day-to-day basis have developed rapport and a sense of trust with the group, they can be particularly well suited to conduct focus groups. In some cases, it is possible and desirable to consider training pupils to be focus group moderators. For example, in recent years as pupil leadership initiatives have increased in schools there have been more opportunities to find pupils willing to be facilitators and a greater likelihood of their peers accepting the pupil-led focus groups. Where it is seen as a potentially useful approach to have pupil facilitating focus groups, it is particularly important to ensure the young person and the group understand issues such as ground rules for the session and those concerning disclosure.

The aim in a focus group is to create an atmosphere of trust and appropriate rapport and the establishment of clear ground rules can assist in this. In addition to establishing how participants will provide information, for example, whether turn-taking is required, rules on respecting others' opinions and avoiding derogatory statements are helpful. Stressing that the research is interested in people's views and that there are no right or wrong answers also builds participants' confidence and facilitates contributions. What is particularly important in developing a good rapport is stressing to the participants that their responses are confidential and the findings will be reported anonymously. If, for whatever reason, there are exceptions to this, the participants must be made aware of the limitations of confidentiality at the very start of the session or earlier when groups are being recruited. For example, most schools have guidelines for teachers on the disclosure of facts which relate to a child's well-being and safety. Teachers have to act upon disclosure of illegal drug use or physical and/or sexual abuse. If in the course of gathering information for research purposes such disclosures are made and if assurances of confidentiality have been given to the participating children, the moderator will usually find him or herself in an ambiguous position unless the ground rules for such disclosures have been made explicit at the outset.

Recording information from group methods

Audio recording of focus groups allows a general record of what was discussed and, along with the interviewer's notes, provides the necessary material for analysis. However, recordings can be prone to missing information if more than one person is speaking at any one time. Also, if the acoustics of a room are poor the recording can be impaired, a fact that is sometimes only evident after the event. It is worth testing the playback during the introduction with the group. Given the vagaries of acoustics in different settings, a high-quality recorder is worth the investment. Digital voice recorders are now relatively inexpensive and of sufficient quality to replace tape-recorders and therefore, allow much greater audio clarity and versatility in terms of storing and manipulation of recordings.

Audio recording is usually unobtrusive and not disruptive as participants soon forget about the presence of the recorder. However, younger pupils can sometimes view the recorder as a novelty and want to play with it, thus disrupting the session. Again, the interviewer's skills are important in maintaining the pupils' focus on the interview topics and away from the equipment.

The use of video-recording is a relatively new approach to recording focus groups but it has the benefit of collecting additional information on who is talking and the context of the session. The context can be helpful in assessing whether all participants seem interested or whether some are being excluded by more assertive individuals. The processes involved in the group can, therefore, be observed again and again during playback to better assess the quality of the information gathered.

You should always seek permission from participants and from their parents if the participants are younger than 16 years, before recording. If assurances about confidentiality and anonymity have been given then most participants, including children, will agree to be recorded even when the topics to be covered are sensitive.

Conclusion

Focus group approaches have the potential to obtain information which would be impossible to gather using other methods. The method can be demanding in terms of ensuring we have appropriately skilled moderators and the time and skills to deal with the considerable amount of information focus groups can elicit. Nevertheless, the method is a key part of a researcher's repertoire which makes developing the skills required to effectively use focus groups worth the effort. You will find guidance on how to analyse the data you derive from focus groups in Chapter 13.

10

Observation

This chapter considers observation as a research method, with a particular interest in how you might use it as a practitioner researcher. The main focus is on qualitative observation approaches, particularly participant observation. We cover the different types of observation, the strengths and weaknesses of the method, ethical issues and the main considerations when planning observation. We also consider issues you will need to address when preparing observational information and data for analysis.

Observation as a research method

Observation is a flexible research method that can be used to gather quantitative or qualitative information in various contexts and settings. Visual and aural information are used to describe a particular context, detail what is happening and who is involved. Observation can also draw on secondary evidence such as photographs and videos taken by others.

As with all research methods, you will wish to ask whether observation is a suitable research method to address your research objectives and questions or to contribute to developing a particular theory. More often than not, observation can be used to provide useful but arguably partial insights on research foci. The other insights and evidence that are required are provided by complementary methods that will allow a more comprehensive analysis. Indeed, interpretation of what is observed, even the everyday and commonplace, cannot be taken for granted. People's underlying meanings and intentions can be quite different to that which might be inferred from their behaviour; this stresses the need for other corroborating research methods.

Observation is therefore often used to complement other research methods to 'triangulate' and strengthen interpretation of emerging findings. Regardless of the type of data and information collected, rather than just watching, observation needs to be systematic and open to scrutiny. Given the nature of the method, the activities or settings that are being observed might be transient and make it difficult for others to conduct repeat observations that might verify the findings. Therefore, recoding of what is observed and the analysis and reporting must include all relevant details to allow others to see how you have arrived at the conclusions.

Different kinds of observation

Observation can be adapted to suit various types of research approaches and objectives. For example, it can be used as a quantitative method, when there is a need to collect data on the number of times particular interactions or social 'events' occur within a setting. Alternatively, it can be used within a qualitative study to observe in a largely unstructured way when there is a need to learn more about a social context and the various dynamics that are present. The rationale for the type of observation you will use will be informed by the research objectives. As Hannan (2006: n.p.) states:

> One of the points at issue here is whether it is best for observers to immerse themselves in 'the field' first and then generate categories to order their at first unstructured observations, or whether it is best to walk in with research 'instruments' designed by other researchers which can then be applied in a seemingly unproblematic manner. Which is the best technique depends on the nature of the research undertaken, the former method being better for exploratory case studies and the latter for large-scale surveys, or as a means of providing wider reference points for more qualitative small-scale enquiry.

The focus of the observation will, therefore, be informed by the research objectives and how explicit these are. For example, if your research focuses on understanding what makes for effective continual professional development (CPD) for science teachers, you will likely attend CPD sessions to observe the methods adopted by trainers and the responses of participants. You will want to ensure that you observe a range of the various types of sessions provided and cover the various groups of teachers involved in the CPD programme. In observing these sessions you would aim to collect sufficient information to allow identification of the key features of CPD which are valued by staff. Ideally, such a study would extend the observation by following the participating teachers and observing whether their practice adopted what they had learned during their CPD.

Quantitative and systematic observation

Where the research requires a focus on the frequency of certain occurrences or behaviours, for example, the number of times primary pupils access education technology in their classroom, or the number of times pupils share ideas in group work, then observation can be used to record this type of data. Usually, this quantitative approach will use an observation proforma that allows the researcher to systematically record the frequency of different types of behaviour and activity of interest to the study over a period of time using previously specified categories. Croll (1986) provides discussion and examples of structured observation schedules used in education research.

Such observations are also likely to record and code who is involved in the activities and any other variables of interest such as location and time at which the activity took place. This type of observation might select intervals to observe, for example, time sampling where you monitor and observe for short periods, say 10 minutes with a break of 10 minutes over a 60-minute period. Alternatively, you may observe over a period of time but only record details of particular events of interest to your research, such as every time examples of active learning are used within a teacher's lesson. Observed activities can also be given a rating or numerical code to signify frequency and other descriptive details such as who is involved, or use a scale to denote the type of discourse between teacher and pupils in a lesson. The data can then be treated using basic statistical techniques to summarise and to explore simple relationships across variables. This 'event' recording can be useful when supported by other information such as interviews to help understand why the recorded events took place.

The type of schedule used to systematically record observations will typically focus on a relatively limited number of events or activities that are of interest. Attempting to systematically record numerous events can be impractical and overwhelm most people's ability and thus be counterproductive. The systematic observation schedule might facilitate a simple tallying of events or behaviours from a pre-defined list. This process will also note details such as time and location of event, duration and who is involved. For example, such a systematic observation schedule that is used in a study of the teaching of religious education (RE) might look something like Figure 10.1.

Here, the observer is able to maintain a note of the frequency of the various activities of interest that have been highlighted by previous visits to the school in studying this particular subject. Such a system, if adopted over time and across teachers in a school or even across schools, would provide an indication of the relative emphasis given to, say, preparing for examinations or the frequency of instances where the teacher responded to pupils' questions. However, this approach does not provide details or description for each of the categories, some of which might be key to your research topics. If, for example, the researcher involved in the example study above wanted to monitor the types of topics that teachers introduced as part of their RE lessons, then the observation schedule might just focus on this one activity but maintain a record using codes for the type of topics raised and whether there was active discussion. Such a schedule might look like Figure 10.2.

Religious education study observation schedule				
Teacher name: Mrs Smith **School:** Green Oaks High School **Class:** S4 j	**Date:** 4 March 2010 **Time of lesson:** 11:00 – 12:00	**Date:** 8 March 2010 **Time of lesson:** 15:00 – 15:50	**Date:** 12 March 2010 **Time of lesson:** 11:00 – 12:00	**Date:** 16 March 2010 **Time of lesson:** 15:00 – 15:50
Use of textbooks	IIIV II	IIII	II	III
Use of religious artefacts	III	I	II	II
Reference to examination questions	IIIV IIIV I	IIIV	IIIV IIIV IIIV II	IIII
Answering pupils' questions	IIIV IIIV IIIV II	IIIV IIIV IIIV III	IIIV IIIV II	IIIV IIIV IIIV IIII
Use of worksheets	IIIV IIIV II	IIIV IIIV IIIV II	IIIV	IIII
Abstract discourse	II	I	III	II
Use of video	I	–	II	–
Use of ICT	IIIV	II	IIII	I
External speaker	–	–	–	–
Instances of disruptive behaviour	III	IIII	III	IIIV

Figure 10.1 Systematic observation schedule

Religious education study observation schedule: classroom interaction	
Time:	**Focus and nature of interaction:**
9:00 a.m.	WF/AC
9:02	WF/AC
9:04	Mu/P
9:06	WF/Mu
9:08	Un
9:10	ME/AP
9:12	ME/AC
Key: *Focus of discussion:* WF = World Faiths ME = Moral and Ethical E = Existential, Nature of existence Mu = Multicultural Un = Unrelated to subject	*Interaction:* P = Passive AP = Active involving one pupil AC = Active involving the Class

Figure 10.2 Specific event recording

As Simpson and Tuson (1995) stress, using such an observation guide will require using a digital clock or watch to keep track of the 2-minute time intervals. Clearly such a system still does provide much detail about the nature of the questions and the interaction this might have stimulated. Where such questions are important, qualitative approaches are required.

Qualitative observation approaches

Where the research requires information to help to explore and understand why people behave in certain ways, what values they hold and how they perceive their situation, then qualitative approaches are appropriate. Observation has a well-established history within qualitative research, particularly ethnographic approaches. For example, research that is based on symbolic interactionist and ethnomethodological theory assumes that human action is meaningful and intentional, and that interaction is based on shared social understandings, values and norms. The research based on such theories will typically use participant observation alongside qualitative interviewing.

Non-participant observation

Non-participant observation is a common form of observation in education research and the researcher attempts to observe and record what is happening in a particular site but does not actively participate in the activities being observed. For example, sitting at the back of a meeting or lesson and observing without disturbing the situation. This approach can draw on visual information note taking and video evidence. An adaptation of this role involves the researcher getting involved occasionally in order to better see and understand what is happening and to ask questions of those being observed without actually being a full participant.

Participant observation

In ethnographic research the researcher will usually rely heavily on collecting extensive field notes which are supplemented by interviews. As Hannan (2006) notes, 'In ethnographic observation the researcher is the research instrument and he/she must make decisions about how and what to sample and about issues which currently require attention'. The notes will record detailed accounts of what happens, what is being said, who is speaking, what roles and activities are being demonstrated. In addition, the notes will include the researcher's reflective insights, memos and developing ideas concerning the research objectives (for example, see Woods, 1986). This approach is effective when relatively little is known about the research objective. It allows the salient issues, findings and theories to emerge as the information accumulates. As Hannan (2006) states, the findings are grounded in observed experience. This 'inductive' approach was developed by Glaser and Strauss (1967). Using this approach, the observer has to work through the accumulated information and draw on the different sources to gradually prioritise and develop the findings. This process has to be made explicit to others in that key material and evidence are available or presented to illustrate how the researcher has come to his or her conclusions.

The participant observer then, watches and records what happens in the research site using detailed field notes and research diaries, and can supplement this with interviews and discussions with those in that setting. Participant observation can also involve shadowing individuals, for example, accompanying a member of staff in a school during a typical day to observe what their duties are, how they and others interact and respond to everyday challenges.

In participant observation the researcher will, to a greater or lesser extent, gather information about the research site through their own interaction and participation. In ethnographic research the researcher will typically participate in the everyday life of those being studied over a period of time to better understand people and their behaviour through experiencing aspects of their lives. The extent to which the researcher shares in the experiences of those being studied will be influenced by whether the research objectives are best addressed by spending time embedded in a group or setting. Participant observation can be seen as a spectrum with the researcher fully living the life of those being studied at one extreme (similar to some anthropology) through to the researcher sharing the space and experiences of those studied and interacting with them but having a clear demarcation between their role and lifestyle and that of those being studied. The latter extreme may not lend itself very well to practitioner research where you tend to be fully immersed in the site of study.

Practical concerns such as available time and resources for the research will influence the time that can be spent doing this type of observation. Other factors that can facilitate or limit the level of participation can include cultural, gender or generational differences. Depending on the focus of the research, such differences might present challenges to accessing or being sufficiently accepted into a group or setting in order to observe 'authentic' behaviours. For example, an adult researcher is unlikely to easily gain access to youth peer groups to conduct observations of underage drinking as part of a study into health behaviours and the efficacy of health programmes. In such situations it might be desirable to consider involving and training young people to act as participant observers. However, the ethical issues and safeguards facing such an approach would be considerable. Observation of some sensitive and less visible phenomena, for example, peer group power dynamics in schools, presents challenges but can still be achieved if the researcher is in a position to gain the trust of those being observed.

Strengths and limitations of qualitative observation

The strengths and limitations of observation will vary by type of observation method adopted, and many of the limitations of observation can be addressed through the skill and experience of the researcher and good planning. In qualitative approaches the researcher is seeking to be as unobtrusive as possible and avoid distorting that which is being studied.

Strengths of qualitative observation

- It allows detailed information to be gathered in a natural context which provides a deeper understanding of issues, practices, problems and people, when triangulated with other evidence, such as interviews.
- The researcher is more likely to see important behaviours and activities that would be undetectable using other methods. It also allows observation of phenomena that people in the study might not raise in interviews, either because they are sensitive issues or they are taken for granted.
- The above points mean that observation is a very useful corroborating approach to supplement other approaches such as interviewing.
- Through their experience and participation in the research context, the researcher obtains a greater awareness of salient issues which assists in their interpretation and analysis of their data and information.

Limitations of qualitative observation

- If the researcher is a member of the organisation or setting being studied – as is often the case in practitioner research – this will afford useful insights, however they might find it difficult to distance themselves sufficiently to observe analytically and critically to overcome taken-for-granted assumptions. The research diary and discussions with others who are external to the setting but aware of the research issues can help enhance this critical awareness.
- Again, if the participant researcher is a member of the organisation being studied there might be a range of problematic issues such as role conflict, ensuring confidentiality and power dynamics that might influence opportunities to observe.
- Qualitative observation approaches require time to collect and analyse information. Practitioner researchers will have to consider how they can build this approach into their work life.
- Evidence of sensitive issues is less likely to be observable. For example, if you are exploring people's attitudes and beliefs, particularly if these are on sensitive topics, you might first think that these are not observable. However, you can observe behaviours that might reflect people's attitudes. The information gathered from the observation can then be compared with that from interviews that explore people's views and attitudes, which might highlight the complexities and contrasts between stated attitudes and behaviours.
- There is a danger that your presence will influence and distort what you are seeking to observe. This can be addressed by spending time in the research setting and conducting observation over periods of time so that participants become accustomed to the researcher and even build rapport.
- However, spending relatively long periods of time in the research setting and developing rapport with participants might leave you open to criticism

that your analytic distance and objectivity have been compromised. This can be addressed by sharing emerging research findings and themes with a colleague who can act as a 'critical friend'. Triangulation with other research methods will also help reduce possible observer bias.

- Unless the observations are conducted over a period of time there is a danger that they will be only a snapshot of the activities being studied. Therefore, it is important that the duration of the study is sufficient to provide coverage of a 'typical' period where a range of behaviours, events and activities are likely to occur. If observations can be conducted at different days and times of the day this can also help promote more 'natural' observation.

Observation and ethics

Conducting observational research can present particular ethical challenges mainly because this approach allows the researcher to record the actions and behaviours of those being studied and not just their spoken words. Those being observed might not be aware of the presence of you as an observer, even when the observation is open and not covert. This might well mean you are observing more natural behaviour and this can enhance your research. However, those being observed might believe that this constitutes a breach of their privacy.

Even when the observer adopts a neutral or non-interventionist position there might be situations when this stance is challenged when serious ethical issues emerge. There are particular ethical issues when observation is conducted as part of practitioner enquiry and research because of the existing relationships, responsibilities and power/status dynamics between the observer and those he or she works with and teaches. For example, there can be certain ethical implications if a teacher conducting an observation sees pupil behaviour that seriously contravenes school regulations or even breaks the law. The practitioner researcher might also observe teaching practices of colleagues that fall short of required standards and, again, while this is valuable research material, there might well be consequences for those observed if the researcher cannot ensure anonymity.

The researcher should, therefore, aim to ensure anonymity as far as is practicable and if there is any likelihood that anonymity cannot be guaranteed then this must be made clear to those in the study. As we emphasised in Chapter 4, all social research has to adhere to an appropriate ethical code and the Scottish Educational Research Association (SERA, 2005) provides clear and useful ethical guidance for research in educational settings. Usually, ethical protocols require that you obtain informed consent from all involved in the research setting. However, this can be difficult if the observation setting is a whole school. Ideally, in such a situation all staff, pupils and parents should be informed about the research and the methods to be used via a letter and information leaflet that provides details of who to contact if people have concerns about the conduct of the research.

Observing in practice?

The process and initial stages of conducting an observation will follow similar procedures to that conducted when setting up and negotiating access for other field research. Chapter 8 on interviewing details this process, but the key actions will include:

- Identifying and contacting participants to arrange access.
- Providing participants with details of your research approach including the purpose of the study, what is required of participants and the level of anonymity and confidentiality that will be assured.
- Obtaining formal consent from participants. Some ground-breaking socio-logical studies have involved observation where those being studied were unaware that they were being covertly observed by the researcher (see Chapter 4); this is unacceptable in practitioner research and arguably difficult to defend in any circumstance.
- During the observation, your actions will usually be informed by the research aims. For example, if your research is interested in the status and role of a particular subject you will want to observe examples of how that subject is taught, what the interactions, roles and relationships are in the classroom, but also across the wider school.
- You will want to ensure that you are positioned in the research site so that you can effectively observe but without disrupting the everyday activities of those being studied. If your observation involves your active participation then you have to think about how you will record and take notes. Is it feasible to make mental notes during your participation and then write these up as soon as you get an opportunity?
- If you are using video recording in your observation then you have to ensure that you have consent and place your equipment so that it does not distract participants.

Rather than using a schedule with pre-defined categories, the recording of qualitative observations will typically involve writing a running narrative as field notes. Delamont (2002) states that notes should include verbatim quotes, summaries of key discussions and other text that can remind you at a later stage about certain interactions. She and others, such as Clancey (2001), stress that observational notes should be frequently reviewed to help keep the task of analysis manageable. This process also highlights emerging themes and informs the focus of the ongoing observation. Clancey (2001) recommends that these emerging draft concepts can be shared with colleagues for their views on interpretation.

In most observations, particularly those which are qualitative, there will be some common aspects of the setting which will need to be recorded. These include:

- The physical setting. You will want to summarise the features of the setting that are relevant to your study. For example, in school-based research, you would document the layout of rooms, facilities available, equipment present, décor and even your impressions of the ambience and ethos of the school. If your research is ethnographic in nature the observation might also extend to gathering observational information about the whole school and local community to better understand wider factors and processes salient to your study.
- Key informants involved in the research setting and their behaviours and interactions. Here you would be interested in recording who is involved in the various interactions, their status, role and relevant characteristics as well as documenting accounts of what types of verbal and non-verbal interaction take place. You will also want to note the nature of power relations and discourse between people. It is important to also note any inaction and missing features that you might have expected to see. For example, if you were observing schools where you have been told that there have been developments and progress in pupil leadership and confidence but you actually see groups of young people who appear reluctant to be involved in activities and the life of the school, then it is important to record this and any other inconsistencies.
- The observation ideally will happen over a period of time to allow you to build up rapport with those around him or her and to increase awareness of the social processes involved. This also helps counter claims that the observation is a 'snapshot' of the activity or behaviours being researched, and allows the researcher to be come 'sensitised' to less obvious interactions and behaviours. This increased understanding can help improve interpretation and analysis. As an observer you are also a part of that which is being studied and, even when trying to be unobtrusive, this can potentially influence the interactions around you and so alter that which is being studied. This can be addressed to some extent by the usual pattern being that the longer you spend observing a particular group or site, then the more likely those around you are to accept your presence and to 'normalise' their behaviour.
- Many practitioners conducting observational research might be able to spend prolonged periods of time in the research setting if it is their own workplace such as a school or organisation. However, they might have to think how they will find the time to maintain detailed notes and be able to focus on what is happening around them in an analytical way.

Observation tools

When observing, you will need to consider how to gather and record information. Commonly used tools and information gathering aids will include:

- Weather-resistant notebook, which can be easily accessed to record your observations which will usually include:

  - date, location, duration of observation, details about those being observed including numbers, gender, names or pseudonyms (if necessary), roles, and so on
  - narrative description of what happened including interaction and discourse, quotes from key informants but also details of your reactions, feelings, reflections.

- Laptop with word processing and ideally, qualitative analysis software (such as NVivo). This will help order and eventually analyse the information. Analytical software can help sort and label text, photographs and video and assist categorisation and prioritising of key themes.
- Camera (ideally digital). Photographs can help document environment layout (for example, classroom seating arrangements) artefacts of interest (for example, pupils' work) and provide valuable contextual information to help interpret the other observational evidence you gather.
- Video camera. Video recording helps record interaction and its context and allows you to study and reflect on what happened in more detail after the observation. You can also share with other researchers, colleagues and participants to check your interpretation. Clancey (2001) draws on his ethnographic observation in demanding field conditions to summarise some 'lessons learned' concerning the use of video, most of which are valuable for observers in almost any situation. An adapted version of Clancey's list is provided below:

  - Ask yourself what you are trying to observe and video relevant types of events, particular places and interactions between people.
  - If the camera is handheld, follow someone; do not jump around.
  - The most difficult aspects of video documentation are good sound and a proper mixture of close-ups, focused shots on speakers, and group/contextual shots.
  - Use a wind microphone on all outside shots if there is any wind at all; aim at the speaker; monitor the sound, and in general keep recordings short if the conversations cannot be heard clearly.
  - Use two wireless microphones if two people are together.
  - Include voiceover narration when starting a scene if the location is new.
  - Always ask people on camera what they are doing, why they are stopping, where they are going, and so on.
  - If people are working or sitting in one place, use a tripod to hold the camera unobtrusively to the side.
  - Log all videos in the field (dates and participants).
  - Time lapse video can provide valuable information that highlights overlooked patterns in behaviour and this can be used to inform interview questions to seek clarification and interpretation.

Managing and processing your data

Qualitative observation usually generates a great deal of detailed information that will include text (field notes, recalled information, initial thoughts on interpretation and various other impressions), photographs and possibly video. Analysis of qualitative observation information usually attempts to provide a narrative that draws on diverse and complex source material to illustrate and illuminate findings.

Analysis of qualitative information is addressed more fully in Chapter 13 but in this section we summarise the key stages and processes that are typically followed to analyse collected observation information. As noted previously in this chapter, it is recommended that the analysis of the material is an ongoing periodic process. This means that your understanding of the material develops and informs your ongoing research. This helps avoid being overwhelmed by the volume of information you have collected.

The material must first be sorted and categorised. If your research has existing research questions, these can provide an initial framework. However, with much observation the important themes and issues will emerge from the information as you begin to analyse it. Your field notes are read chronologically and summarised to identify emerging and recurring themes arranged and categorised by themes.

You will then look across the information to see whether other parts of your text, recordings, photographs, and so on fit within these themes. If new but relevant themes or sub-themes emerge, these are added to the analysis framework. As the analysis proceeds, you might find that the collected evidence does not support some of your original ideas and themes and these can then be modified or discarded. This process of identifying and refining useful themes continues until all of the observation information is able to be organised according to these themes.

The qualitative analysis process and analysis of observation information in particular, requires that the researcher makes explicit the process and thinking underpinning the analysis. You will have to provide clear evidence for your conclusions. For example, Hannan (2006) suggests that the reporting of qualitative observation findings can include, in the text or in appendices, key excerpts from your field notes and observation evidence with accompanying notes to demonstrate and justify how you have reached your conclusions and interpreted the material.

Summary ☐

We have seen how observation is one of the key methods in practitioner research, that facilitates the generation of data on actual behaviour and activity, rather than on views and experiences. However, what is observable is not always readily understandable and so it is important to complement observational data with other forms. We have also seen that there may be a range of particular ethical issues involved and that when you are researching in your own setting, as is very common – indeed normal – in practitioner research, there are many questions about how to make sense of the data that has been gathered.

Further reading

Croll, P. (1986) *Systematic Classroom Observation*. London: Falmer Press.

Delamont, S. (2002) *Fieldwork in Educational Settings*.

Hannan, A. (2006) 'Observation techniques', Faculty of Education, University of Plymouth. Available at: http://www.edu.plymouth.ac.uk/resined/observation/obshome.htm.

Scottish Education Research Association (2005) *Ethical Guidelines for Educational Research*. Available at: http://www.sera.ac.uk/docs/00current/SERA%20Ethical%20GuidelinesWeb. PDF.

Simpson, M. and Tuson, J. (1995) *Using Observations in Small-Scale Research*. Glasgow: Scottish Council for Research Education, University of Glasgow.

11

Other Methods

In earlier chapters of Part 4 we examined the principles and techniques associated with conventional ways of undertaking a research study. This chapter shows some non-conventional research methods used in educational research and discusses practical examples.

What are the 'other methods'?

Novel and creative approaches are increasingly employed in educational research and school evaluations for a number of reasons:

1 The data acquired can significantly enrich the overall research process and the credibility of its findings.
2 They are instrumental in overcoming challenges associated with accessing participants' views (see Elliot et al., 2007; Moore et al., 2008).
3 They effectively serve as a springboard or 'prompts for discussion' for getting the primary data (Bailey et al., 2009; Bryman, 2004: 312).
4 They are a useful means for triangulating research evidence using a variety of methods (Cross et al., 2009).
5 Capturing data using non-conventional methods can be challenging and fun.

You should only resort to the *other methods* available if doing so, in conjunction with traditional research methods, enables you to bring added value to the overall research study. While using non-conventional methods may offer considerable advantages, you will need to take the practical or technical challenges as well as the required ethical protocols into account.

In this chapter, the discussion of other methods will be restricted to the three archetypes that we ourselves have had practical experience of using and are more likely to be employed in practitioners' small-scale research studies. Such methods may involve visual representations as well as imaginative means of getting textual data. Therefore, the discussion will focus on the following: (1) use of photographs, (2) use of drawings, and (3) use of diaries.

One may argue that none of these methods strictly falls under either the quantitative or the qualitative paradigm since it is equally possible to obtain either numerical or textual data using them. Even if the type of data capture is likely to lend itself to qualitative analysis, especially if the data are accompanied by narratives, there is nevertheless scope for categorising and quantifying the data (for example, images and drawings) and subsequently presenting them in numerical form. It is worth bearing in mind that the question(s) that your research is/are aiming to address will inform the nature, focus and extent of your analysis.

Use of photographs

The growth of interest in the use of visual images in recent years has been widely acknowledged (Bryman, 2004), even at a global level (Prosser and Loxley, 2007). Although visual methods in qualitative studies have been utilised in both sociology and social anthropology for many decades, where photography acted as the anthropologist's 'visual notebook' in documenting the culture of a particular society, the number of books written on this subject since 2000 is an indication of a renewed interest in the role of visual methodology in social research (for example, Banks, 2001; 2007; Prosser, 1998; Thomson, 2008).

Of films, photographs and video recordings, photographs have received the most attention (Bryman, 2004), and so they are the main focus in this section. The use of photographs in research presents its own strengths and challenges at the same time. As Poser (2006, cited in Tinkler, 2008: 256) argued, the images created by the participants are not 'records of reality' but 'investigatory landscapes' in which the person taking the photographs uses this as a mode for carefully and powerfully presenting oneself, one's identity, views, and innermost thoughts. Yet, researchers in the field also express the view that sole reliance on photographs as research evidence has its own challenges. Just like the classic cognitive optical illusion called Rubin's vase – named after its promulgator, a Danish psychologist, Edgar Rubin – an image can offer two different mental interpretations that are equally valid depending on the figure/ground differentiation (see http://en.wikipedia.org/wiki/Rubin_vase for an example).

Since photographs can potentially portray multiple and misleading depictions of reality (Bryman, 2004), it is advisable that you use them with other non-visual ways of investigation (for example, interviews, focus groups or questionnaires) since each research medium helps validate the other. Some of the studies we conducted in the educational setting incorporated and at times made use of photographs as the core for data collection and analysis (see Bailey et al., 2009; Elliot et al., 2007) but we always endeavoured to

Table 11.1   Guide questions for using photographs in research

• Were the photographs taken before or during the research?	**Yes**	**No**
	Go to 1A	*Go to 1B*
• Were the photographs taken exclusively for the purpose of the research?	**Yes**	**No**
	Go to 1B	*Go to 1A*
• Will the photographs themselves be treated as evidence?	**Yes**	**No**
	Go to 1C & 1E	*Go to 1D*
• Are the photographs participant-driven?	**Yes**	**No**
	Go to 1c, 1d & 1e	*Go to 1a*
• Are the photographs accompanied by participants' narratives?	**Yes**	**No**
	Go to 1e	*Go to 1a, 1b & 1c*
• Are the photographs as research data meant to bring about change?	**Yes**	**No**
	Go to 1e	*Go to 1c & 1d*

supplement our data from other sources to seek consensus and 'confirmability' of findings.

There are a number of ways in which photographs can be employed in research. Being convinced that the use of photographs will enhance and add value to your research is always a good starting point. We have devised a series of questions in Table 11.1 to guide you in deciding how you would like to use photographs in your study.

What are the potential sources of photographs in research?
1A – Extant
These are photographs that are found rather than created for the research; they already existed, perhaps even before the research had been conceived. They belong either to the investigator or to the research participants and were probably used earlier for a different purpose. If these photographs are contextually appropriate for the research topic in question and are instrumental in illustrating and supporting the points raised in the research then they can powerfully support and validate other research data (see Bryman, 2004).

In a sense, the use of extant photographs is similar to the use of secondary data discussed in Chapter 5. The visual materials were originally utilised for another purpose that was not necessarily related to the current research. There are countless examples of how extant photographs can be used. Here are a few possible scenarios:

1 *Photographs taken at a school event.* Existing photographs taken at a school open-day event, during an educational trip or at a parents' evening may reveal something about the school's ethos and the relationship between school staff, pupils, and parents.

2 *Family photos.* Photographs from the family album can assist research discussions on family matters or studies that have children and young people's relationships with their parents or carers at their core.

3 *Archived photos.* Archived photographs of a town, for example, can be utilised in setting the research context where the historical background of the place provides informative and useful insight into the study. There might even be scope for evaluating the changes that took place in the town over several years or decades.

1B – Research driven

As the name implies, research-driven photographs are created specifically for research purposes. These photographs are intended to capture visual information from one-off visits, rare events, and special fieldwork by using a camera to aid in recording of what transpired.

At times, photos themselves are treated as research evidence. On other occasions and in conjunction with other forms of non-visual data, they are useful instruments in further eliciting participants' views through their responses to visual stimuli.

What are the ways of using photographs in research?

In order to avoid the 'Rubin's vase effect' or the implicit misrepresentation that photographs alone can bring, combining the use of photographs with other means of collecting data appears to be a sensible option. There are several ways by which photographs can be integrated into the research and we will discuss each of them in greater detail.

1C – Photographic display

It can be argued that this is the simplest way of using photographs in a research context. Photographs taken either prior to or during the course of the study may be presented as either primary or secondary evidence to other forms of data (for example, interviews, focus groups, questionnaire data) while presenting a clear link between them.

This way of using photographs was a common feature for a number of Scottish schools when they narrated their schools' journeys in the Schools of Ambition (SoA) programme. A specific example was in relation to a secondary school's evaluation of their intervention for raising both staff and pupil cohorts' 'enterprising attitude'. Apart from the conventional questionnaires administered to both groups, photographs taken during the 'enterprise day' were included in the presentation of the key findings. Similarly, the photographs of a high-profile fashion show organised by another school participating in SoA were brought into play in the discussion of how taking part in a fashion show stimulated the pupils' creative thinking, and instilled a sense of responsibility and genuine self-confidence.

Through the use of photographs, another SoA school explained the steps (that is, creating a special logo, wearing a distinctive necktie) taken by a group of students (referred to as peer mediators) in an effort to raise the whole school's awareness of the service that they provide to fellow students. A single photograph of the logo is arguably a much more succinct way of conveying the point as opposed to describing all the characteristics (for example, shape, colour, size) of the logo. Likewise, a complementary photograph instantaneously validated a statement describing how the necktie made the peer mediators stand out.

1D – Photo-elicitation

In this approach, which originated from early anthropological research (Hurworth, 2003), interviewing is combined with the use of photographs. During the interviews, photographs act as a trigger or stimulus inviting a response. Either extant visual images or photographs purposely created for the interview are potential photo-elicitation research materials.

As a researcher, you may select existing photographs that are linked to the topic under investigation and use them as prompts for getting the participants' in-depth views. Photographs could also be a researcher's personal collection; they could be personally acquired or purchased, and are either in a private collection or publicly available. Such a collection could be a combination of digital and paper photographs.

Visual prompts for research may also be obtained from websites that provide stock photos as part of their service (for example see http://www.shutterstock.com). Likened to the use of vignettes (short hypothetical scenarios) or actual objects to provoke responses in qualitative research, participants are invited to respond to photographs as a means of exploring further their ideas, judgements and attitudes (especially with personal and sensitive topics).

In another research study that we conducted, we sought the assistance of Primary 6 pupils in taking photographs of their school's playgrounds and play areas. These photographs proved to be a very useful 'aide memoire' as they were effectively used as a basis for group discussions in which they highlighted the things that they enjoyed most as well as the things that they would have liked to see improved in their school playground (see Bailey et al., 2009). Interestingly, the fact that the children were very familiar with the images in the photographs gave the research process a personal slant. This also encouraged the children to be more open and keen to share their views during the interview.

Hurworth (2003) strongly argued that using photographs for interviewing could be a very powerful tool for researchers. They can be used to 'challenge participants, provide nuances, trigger memories and lead to new perspectives and explanations, and help to avoid researcher misinterpretation'. Additionally, this technique can:

- be used at any stage of the research
- provide a means of 'getting inside' a programme and its context
- bridge psychological and physical realities
- allow the combination of visual and verbal language
- assist with building trust and rapport
- produce unpredictable information
- promote longer, more detailed interviews in comparison with purely verbal interviews
- provide a component of multi-methods triangulation to improve rigour
- form a core technique to enhance collaborative/participatory research and needs assessments
- be preferable to conventional interviews for many participants.

1E – Photographic essay

This technique bears some resemblance to photo-elicitation in the way that photographs are combined with participants' stories or narratives. In photographic essays, participants are often given the freedom to take photographs with minimal guidance from the researcher, select a few meaningful photographs and then offer their reflective commentaries.

Wang and Burris (1997), who initially used a technique called 'photo novella' (meaning 'picture stories') as a means of encouraging informants to talk about their day-to-day experiences, later used the term 'photovoice'. Photovoice is a specific type of participatory action research that starts with a direct and open dialogue with the participants guided by the photographs that the participants themselves took. The discussions aim to explore participants' needs, their views of the issues affecting them and their perceptions of how current circumstances can be improved. An inherent goal to improve current conditions for the benefit of the research participants is a vital aspect of this type of research and makes the photovoice approach different from other uses of visual data. Research dissemination entails negotiation with the policy-makers based on the findings obtained to bring about the changes raised by the study participants themselves.

Because of photovoice's creative, non-threatening and empowering nature, it is particularly suitable for using with vulnerable groups of people and those who have been marginalised in society (Elliot et al., 2008). Through participants' own photographs and stories, they offer a 'lens' that enables the researchers to view impressions of the participants' lives and experiences more closely. Graziano (2007) aptly describes the photovoice process: 'By entrusting cameras into the hands of oppressed individuals to act as recorders of their own community, Photovoice enables people to define for themselves and others, including policymakers, what is worth remembering and what needs to be changed.' Participants have the tendency to capture images of what appear to be mundane objects and activities. Yet, these very ordinary photographs often contain metaphors of how people view themselves and their day-to-day experiences and also powerfully reveal even their most inner-most thoughts – joys, struggles and fears.

In the photovoice-based research that we undertook, the study participants (who consisted of vulnerable young college learners) selected buildings, doors, gates and entrances as objects of interest. At first glance, their photo-graphs seemed trivial but the accompanying stories that prompted the par-ticipants to take the photographs revealed that these objects were, in fact, metaphors of what they perceived to be psychological barriers preventing them from pursuing further education.

For example, a young female learner took a photograph of the college building (see Figure 11.1) and said: 'This is a picture of the front of the college. When I first came here and looked at the building I felt small. It made me feel a bit scared, compared to the building, I felt small.' In the discussion that fol-lowed, she stressed the stark contrast between the old building and the new and highlighted the significance of the contrast, which was an allegory of her emotional and psychological readiness at the time. After revisiting the photo-graph, she reflectively added, 'I didn't think of it when I took the picture, but

Figure 11.1   Old and new college buildings – Adam Smith College

now I can see that you've got the old building and the new building, like my old life at school and my new life at college'.

Through the photographs combined with discussions with other college learners, the findings unravelled their stories and highlighted the psychological hurdles commonly experienced by vulnerable young people as they took the first steps in their college education. Perceived obstacles were a combined result of being in an unfamiliar environment, feelings of insecurity and a deep need for belonging.

At the end of the study, college decision-makers responded to the issues raised by the findings. For example, social events have been incorporated into the induction events to make the college more welcoming to new students. The college also increasingly acknowledged how critical it is for new learners to see a friendly face the moment they come to college and so newcomers are reassuringly greeted by friendly and helpful staff. Furthermore, they made an effort to communicate to students that college provides opportunities for learners to make friends quickly and, thus, lessen their fears of being alone. Such practical examples illustrate how a photovoice-based study is designed to produce actual changes and improvements for the participants of the research.

Use of drawings

Drawing reflects children's knowledge and understanding of the world and provides a means by which they express their thoughts and feelings. Although it is not a language-based activity, children's drawings are communication channels as they articulate their views and perceptions of the world to other people. Apart from the content of the drawing, one could argue that children's drawings also enable people around them to have a glimpse of their motor coordination, self-concepts and social attitudes.

In the past, children's drawings have been widely utilised in developmental psychology as projective tests and ways of analysing traits, behaviours and personalities. More recently, they have been deemed key in conducting research with young children. This is due to the fact that researching young children can be challenging for various reasons. Literacy and language development can be a hindrance for some, making questionnaire surveys a less than ideal method of gathering children's views. Inadequate language and vocabulary development can also pose a challenge to the questions asked by the researcher, often resulting in short or even monosyllabic responses. Drawing, on the other hand, is an enjoyable activity for children, which is easily likened to playing games. In addition, it is suggested that drawing is an early form of writing for children and it is regarded as an excellent technique with which to listen to children (Roberts-Holmes, 2005).

Since children's drawings are a reflection of their views, it is not surprising that this method is increasingly used in research with very young children.

Young children's drawings are acknowledged by researchers to be a door to understanding their thoughts, feelings, likes and dislikes, and experiences. It has also been suggested that these drawings are the 'child's attempts to make sense of their experiences on at least three levels: cognitive, affective and linguistic' (Hawkins, 2002, cited in Roberts-Holmes, 2005: 136). It was proposed that using drawings by children and young people as research data characterises a child-centred approach; asking children to convey their thoughts through drawings relays the message that their views are considered important. As children realise that their views play a vital role in the search for meaning, this leads to both a motivating and an empowering experience for them (Bailey et al., 2009).

In one of the studies that we conducted, a theoretical concept called the 'Mosaic approach' informed the use of young children's drawings as research evidence.

> A mosaic is an image made up of many small pieces, which need to be brought together in order to make sense of the whole. The Mosaic approach gives young children the opportunity to demonstrate their perspectives in a variety of ways, calling on their 'hundred languages'. (Edwards et al., 1998 cited in Clark and Moss, 2005: 13–14)

Children's drawings used as research evidence is just one of the ways through which young children can communicate their ideas, thoughts and feelings. Therefore, it is worth arguing that in the same way that a picture may have several interpretations, it is equally important that children are given the opportunity to discuss their drawings with the researcher to ensure that a valid interpretation of the drawing is achieved.

This is precisely the approach that we took when we involved young children in a research study. We asked primary schoolchildren to represent their experiences and views about their playground visually. This was followed by a short conversation between the researcher and the children to decode the meaning conveyed in their drawings. While the drawing per se is an important source of information, clarity is achieved through the follow-up discussion with the 'authors' of the drawings. See Figure 11.2 for an example.

Another activity, which is close to a drawing activity, is when researchers engage pupils in various forms of 'art project'. In a study that explored the extent of pupil participation in various school and community activities 'to have their voice heard and valued', a workshop was organised to encourage pupils to express themselves and their views creatively using different media (see Cross et al., 2009: 103). Examples of such activities included:

- depicting in a comic strip how respect did or did not happen in their school setting
- illustrating the different decisions pupils are making in school
- illustrating what a school would look like if they were headteacher
- depicting what is best and/or worst about participation.

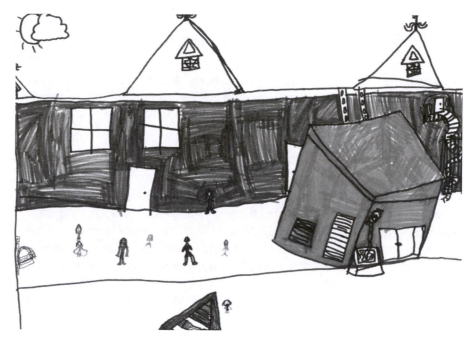

Figure 11.2 A child's drawing of her school playground

In the same way as data generated through 'other methods', data arising from these activities are often analysed and interpreted in conjunction with other forms of data.

Use of diaries

> Diary. A term that in the context of social research methods can mean different things. Three types of diary can be distinguished: diaries written or completed at the behest of a researcher; personal diaries that can be analyzed as a personal document, but that were produced spontaneously; and diaries written by social researchers as a log of their activities and reflections. (Bryman, 2004: 538–9)

As Bryman explained, a research diary can be understood in three different ways. The first two definitions regard a diary as a potential source of research data whereas the third describes the diary (also referred to as a research journal or field notes) as a researcher's tool to record different stages of the research process for future planning, development, and reflection. Blaxter et al. (2001) explained further that this diary is a record of the researcher's progress, feelings, thoughts, insecurities and insights, on a day-to-day basis until the completion of the research.

It is therefore important to have a sound understanding of the diary method that you would like to employ in your own research. In this regard, this section will primarily focus on the first two definitions of a diary as examples of 'other methods' in educational research.

Diary – a method of data collection. The researcher devises a structure for collecting either quantitative or qualitative data for completion by the participants more or less at the same time as when other research activities are undertaken.

Elliott (1997) regarded this way of collecting data as a 'researcher-driven diary' due to the fact that the diary is devised for the purpose of gathering research data in the same fashion that a questionnaire, an interview schedule or an observation schedule are specifically created for research purposes.

There are two types of researcher-driven diary: *structured diaries* and *free text diaries*. *Structured diaries* can be likened to the format of a questionnaire where activities are pre-categorised, whereas *free text diaries* have an open format to give people an opportunity to record activities and events using their own words (Corti, 1993). In general, the researcher-driven diary functions like a self-completion questionnaire but it is also considered to be the 'equivalent of structured observation' (Bryman, 2004: 140). A 'time-use' diary is an example of the type of diary that comprises closed-ended questions and is often used to investigate the way in which people spend their time as well as the amount of time that participants are engaged in certain activities (for example, a teachers' time-use diary would cover teaching contact, teaching preparation, non-contact time) (see Menter et al., 2006).

Here are some very specific guidelines when designing a diary. It is also advisable that the diary is piloted as it helps to refine the instrument.

1 An A4 booklet of about 5 to 20 pages is desirable, depending on the nature of the diary.
2 The inside cover page should contain a clear set of instructions on how to complete the diary. This should stress the importance of recording events as soon as possible after they occur and how the respondent should try not to let keeping the diary influence their behaviour.
3 A model example of a correctly completed diary should feature on the second page.
4 Depending on how long a period the diary will cover, each page should denote either a week, a day of the week or a 24-hour period or shorter. Pages should be clearly ruled up as a calendar with prominent headings and enough space to enter all the desired information (such as what the respondent was doing, at what time, where, with whom and how they felt at the time, and so on).
5 Checklists of the items, events or behaviour to help jog the diary keeper's memory should be printed somewhere fairly prominent. Very long lists should be avoided since they may be off-putting and confusing to

respondents. For a structured time budget diary, an exhaustive list of all possible relevant activities should be made together with the appropriate codes. Where more than one type of activity is to be entered, that is, primary and secondary (or background) activities, guidance should be given on how to deal with 'competing' or multiple activities.

6 There should be an explanation of what is meant by the unit of observation, such as a 'session', an 'event' or a 'fixed time block'. Where respondents are given more freedom in naming their activities and the activities are to be coded later, it is important to give strict guidelines on what type of behaviour to include, what definitely to exclude and the level of detail required. Time budget diaries without fixed time blocks should include columns for start and finish times for activities.

7 Appropriate terminology or lists of activities should be designed to meet the needs of the sample under study, and if necessary, different versions of the diary should be used for different groups.

8 Following the diary pages, it is useful to include a simple set of questions for the respondent to complete, asking, among other things, whether the diary keeping period was atypical in any way compared to usual daily life. It is also good practice to include a page at the end asking for the respondents' own comments and clarifications of any peculiarities relating to their entries. Even if these remarks will not be systematically analysed, they may prove helpful at the editing or coding stage (adapted from Corti, 1993).

Depending on the data collected, both quantitative and qualitative research software can be used in the analysis of the data. Similarly, the same flexibility for using quantitative and qualitative findings can be employed during the presentation of the findings and writing the report.

Diary – a document. These are written accounts of the diarists, which are not prompted by the researcher. They are regarded as personal documents, which are used in the analysis of both historical and contemporary contexts.

Diaries, in this sense, are treated in the same way as letters, biographies and autobiographies and have been mostly used by historians rather than social researchers (Bryman, 2004). It is important to emphasise the type of data considered, as these diaries are those that are not kept at the request of the researcher.

A practical example could be a group of pupils keeping a self-initiated record of their activities and experiences during their educational trip abroad. If these pupils are willing to disclose their diaries to a school staff member who wants to conduct a small study about the impact of the pupils' educational experience, their diaries can serve as informative sources of evidence for the study.

Other considerations for using 'other methods'

First and foremost, it is worth asking yourself the question whether or not using a less conventional method for gathering data will enable you to get useful data that cannot be easily obtained using other means. Secondly, it is equally important to consider the suitability of using 'other methods' with the target study participants. Previous experience shows that innovative and creative research methods are found to be of most benefit in studies involving specific cohorts (for example, very young children, vulnerable learners).

Ethics

When using visual images in research, the protocols involved in the use of photographs as a means of collecting data during the reporting or dissemination process need to be carefully considered. You need to seek out and pay careful attention to ethical guidelines prior to undertaking research that involves either the researcher(s) or the participants taking photographs, to ensure that informed consent is obtained and that confidentiality and anonymity are carefully safeguarded. (For further discussion of ethical issues and considerations, see Chapter 4.)

Summary ▢

There has been growing recent interest in the use of non-conventional methods in educational research. In practitioner research you may choose to use these as a way of generating data that would be difficult to obtain through conventional methods. This may either be because the topics that you are addressing are not easily represented through normal 'discourse' or because the subjects of your research have some difficulty in expressing themselves in conventional ways.

Checklist: Using 'other methods' as sources of evidence

Finally, here are some questions to reflect on as you consider using 'other methods' in your research. A positive answer to most of these questions will give you some assurance that your decision to adopt a less conventional research approach is worth pursuing.

Checklist for considering the use of *other methods* in research

---

- Are the data generated through *other methods* relevant to the purpose of your research? ☐

- Can the data generated through *other methods* be systematically collected and analysed in conjunction with other forms of evidence? ☐

- Can you fulfil the requirements of the ethical protocols that need to be in place prior to collection of data and during dissemination of the findings? (This may involve seeking permission from participants, their parents/ guardians, schools or educational authorities.) ☐

- Are you familiar with the Data Protection Act to guide you in making decisions that affect participants' right to privacy (presenting and storing non-conventional data, for example, images)? ☐

- Will you be able to receive technical support and practical assistance in using special equipment and administering the research and/or analysis? ☐

- Will the timescale allow you to incorporate the collection, analysis and writing up of the data acquired through *other methods* into your study? ☐

- Do you have the budget for the extra resources (for example, disposable cameras) needed for this type of research? ☐

- Is using a non-conventional research methods the only way to obtain high-quality research data? ☐

Further reading

Banks, M. (2007) *Using Visual Data in Qualitative Research*. London: Sage.

Blaxter, L., Hughes, C. and Tight, M. (2001) *How to Research*. 2nd edn. Buckingham: Open University Press.

Bryman, A. (2004) *Social Research Methods*. 2nd edn. New York: Oxford University Press.

Corti, L. (1993) 'Using diaries in social research', *Social Research Update*, no. 2. Available at: http://sru.soc.surrey.ac.uk/SRU2.html.

Elliott, H. (1997) 'The use of diaries in sociological research on health experience', *Sociological Research Online*, 2(2). Available at: http://www.socresonline.org.uk/2/2/7.html.

Prosser, J. (ed.) (1998) *Image-based Research: A Sourcebook for Qualitative Researchers*. London: RoutledgeFalmer.

Part 5

What Does It Mean?

12

Quantitative Data Analysis

Doing your data analysis can be daunting. You know that an orderly sifting of information will be required in order to find the nuggets from the mass of accumulated data. Like any other stage of the research process, data analysis needs to be undertaken systematically. Your role as a researcher is to find answers to your research questions.

If you are a teaching practitioner, you may have distributed a questionnaire to some pupils in your school as part of a small-scale study. Now, all the questionnaires have been completed and returned to you. And your question is 'What should I do now?'

This section is all about how to approach, manage and analyse your quantitative data. If you have taken a quantitative approach and have worked methodically in the preliminary aspects of your research (for example, defining the research problem, implementing a sampling plan, developing a workable research design), then potential errors (for example, sampling errors, sampling-related errors and data collection errors) can be avoided. As a result, you will be rewarded with a more straightforward data analysis (Bryman, 2004). In the following sections, we will provide a more detailed discussion of the steps involved in quantitative data analysis, namely *data preparation*, *descriptive statistics* and *inferential statistics*, but there will be a greater focus on the first two as they are what are commonly required when undertaking small-scale research studies.

Data preparation

Both researchers and non-researchers alike can expect that research frequently ends up being messy and complicated. Prior to the actual data analysis, it is advisable for you to ensure that the data you gathered are reliable and error-free. Failure to do so can easily cause serious implications for the validity of the research findings. In research, a type of error called 'data processing error' (Bryman, 2004: 105) can occur by which the data is wrongly coded or keyed-in, but with the use of systematic data cleansing and organising, a number of errors arising from 'faulty management of data' can be remedied.

Data preparation refers to the first stage of the data analysis that involves

- comprehensive record-keeping
- data checking for accuracy
- constructing a database
- data cleansing
- transforming the data. (Blaxter et al., 2001; Trochim, 2006)

Comprehensive record-keeping

Strictly speaking, comprehensive record-keeping begins the moment you start collecting your research data. Quantitative data are data expressed in numerical form (also called hard data) and are analysed statistically. They are normally obtained through questionnaire surveys, existing school databases, pre-test or post-test data, and/or structured observational data.

Whether you have one or more than one source of quantitative data, a system for archiving the questionnaire data is always good practice. There are at least three good reasons for keeping a questionnaire archive.

1 Keeping the originally completed questionnaires, for example, will allow you to trace the research findings to the raw data themselves, which will be useful should you or others have any doubt about the accuracy of the findings.
2 Your archive will enable you to reconstruct your database in the unfortunate event of computer file corruption.
3 If another party were to challenge the claims made by your study, the whole data-set can be re-analysed and the whole research process can even be replicated with the use of the collected archived data.

Having an efficient procedure for recording all the incoming sources of data is a preliminary stage for data management and a critical component in conducting good research. Record-keeping is particularly important whether you expect to collect one type or many different forms of data-sets.

Checking your records can also be a useful reminder, for example, that so far, less than 20 per cent of the respondents have returned your questionnaire, and therefore, sending a reminder letter with a new deadline might boost the response rate.

Data checking for accuracy

As Trochim (2006) explained, initial screening of the data for accuracy needs to be done as soon as practicable. Data checking detects if the responses are not easily readable or if some important questions have been accidentally missed out because of a 'data collection error', for example, there are missing pages in the questionnaire. It is to your advantage if you have direct access to your study participants especially if you need to seek clarification on any vague responses.

Data checking for accuracy is a 'quality assurance' procedure whereby removal of inaccuracies increases the quality of the actual data for analysis. If you choose to administer your questionnaire through online questionnaire survey software (for example, Zoomerang, SurveyMonkey) however, this step will not be necessary since all the data will be collated automatically and, thus, errors arising from faulty data management will be avoided.

Constructing a database

A numerical database that corresponds to the responses from the question-naire survey is indispensable in quantitative data analysis. First, you will need to code all the responses for each of the questions in the questionnaire (except for those where long textual responses were given in order to explain and/or provide an example and therefore, no numerical comparison of responses is required). In essence, coding means that you attribute a number to a piece of data to enable it to be analysed in quantitative terms (Denscombe, 1998). See examples of coding in Table 12.1 based on the sample question-naire in Figure 12.1. Either a coded questionnaire or a list of legends will help with the organisation and interpretation of the findings at a later stage.

Based on some of the data obtained and analysed by one of the participat-ing schools in the Schools of Ambition initiative, we will present an abridged questionnaire in order to show you how to create a coding list and an abridged database (which we will revisit later in the discussion of data analy-sis using a PivotTable).

In discussing how to use a PivotTable in analysing your data, we con-structed an example of a database (see Table 12.2) based on the questionnaire in Figure 12.1 and the coding sample or legend in Table 12.1.

As a starting point, you can use a more common spreadsheet program such as Excel to construct a database. It is also worth noting that different types of questions need to be entered differently in a database. As you can see in Table 12.1, the questions from the questionnaire are coded in a different way.

- For a basic question 'Are you?' answerable with either 'Male' or 'Female', one column will be allocated for this question where it is conventional to use 1 for 'Male' and 2 for 'Female'.
- Questions that require more than one response (ie these questions are often followed by an additional instruction 'Please tick all that apply') require one column for each option provided.
- With scale questions, it is advisable to allocate the highest number to the most positive response (ie 4 for 'Always', 3 for 'Sometimes', and so on).

Our Lady and St. Patrick High School:

Creativity Questionnaire for Pupils

Introduction

Our Lady and St Patrick High School aims to understand the concept of creativity through the development of creative thinking. Your views are important and we would appreciate you taking the time to complete this questionnaire. It should not take long to complete since many of the questions require only that you tick boxes or write a few lines of text.

Section I – About you

1   Are you...? *(Please tick one box)*   ☐ Male   ☐ Female

2   What year group are you in?   ☐ S1   ☐ S2

    (Please tick one box)

Section 2 – Your views on creativity

5   What does *creative thinking* mean to you? (Please tick all that apply)

    Creative thinking is ...

☐ expressing myself in an interesting way
☐ using my imagination productively
☐ writing stories, poems, songs, etc.
☐ finding different ways of solving problems
☐ thinking of new ways of looking at issues and topics
☐ designing things well
☐ capacity to make something ordinary into something special
☐ performing in public confidently

6   How would you rate yourself with regard to *thinking creatively*? *(Please tick one box per line)*

Ways of thinking creatively	Always	Sometimes	Rarely	Never
a I express myself in an interesting way	☐	☐	☐	☐
b I use my imagination productively	☐	☐	☐	☐
c I write stories, poems, songs, etc.	☐	☐	☐	☐
d I find different ways of solving problems skilfully	☐	☐	☐	☐
e I think of new ways of looking at issues and topics	☐	☐	☐	☐
f I design things well	☐	☐	☐	☐
g I have the capacity to make something ordinary into something special	☐	☐	☐	☐

(Continued)

(Continued)

---

7   Give the best example of when you used *creative thinking* at school.

```
[                                                            ]
```

Section 4 – Promoting creativity

10.   Can *creative thinking* be developed?

☐ No   ☐ Yes, if so, how?

```
[                                                            ]
```

Figure 12.1   A sample of an abridged questionnaire

- Questions that allow participants to provide an example should allocate additional columns for the extra (textual) data (see columns for questions 10a and 10b in Table 12.2).
- Likewise, for open-ended questions where textual data have been obtained, an additional column can be added should you want to categorise numerically the responses according to themes.

Table 12.1   A coding sample/list of legends for the sample questionnaire

Question	Value	Value label
Question 2 (Gender)	1	Male
	2	Female
Question 3 (Year level)	1	S1
	2	S2
Questions 5a to 5h (Views on creativity)	1	Ticked
	2	Unticked
Questions 6a to 6g (Rating one's creative thinking)	4	Always
	3	Sometimes
	2	Rarely
	1	Never
Question 10 (Views on the development of creative thinking)	1	Yes
	2	No

Table 12.2 A sample of a database

ID	Q1	Q2	Q5a	Q5b	Q5c	Q5d	Q5e	Q5f	Q5g	Q5h	Q6a	Q6b	Q6c	Q6d	Q6e	Q6f	Q6g	Q7a	Q7b	Q10a	Q10b
1	1	2	2	1	2	1	1	2	1	2	4	3	2	2	1	3	3	text	9	2	text
2	1	2	1	2	1	1	2	1	2	2	2	2	4	2	1	1	2	text	1	1	text
3	1	2	1	1	1	1	1	1	1	1	3	2	2	2	2	2	2	text	12	2	text
4	2	1	1	1	2	1	2	2	2	2	3	2	2	2	3	3	2	text	1	2	text
5	2	1	1	1	2	1	2	1	2	2	2	3	2	2	2	1	1	text	18	1	text
6	2	1	2	1	1	2	2	1	2	2	2	2	4	1	3	2	3	text	20	2	text
7	2	1	2	2	2	2	1	2	2	2	2	2	4	3	2	2	3	text	8	1	text
8	2	1	1	1	1	2	1	2	1	1	2	1	1	2	2	2		text	8	1	text
9	2	1	2	1	2	2	2	1	2	2	2	1	1	2	2	1	1	text	8	1	text

In Table 12.1, Question 7 originally was not coded because a textual response was expected. In the database sample (see Table 12.2), however, the responses were analysed further according to relevant subject areas, and coding was added as a result by inserting a column for 'Q7b' and referring to the column for the textual response as 'Q7a'.

In the questionnaire (see Figure 12.1), question 10 required stating the 'No' before the 'Yes' option but when it comes to coding, it is important that we employ the conventional codes: 1 for yes and 2 for no to ensure consistency and to avoid any confusion.

Clearly, an appropriate database layout is crucial for subsequent analysis. Cohen et al. (2000: 77) cautioned that 'inappropriate layout may obstruct data entry and subsequent analysis by computer'. For example, if questions 5a to 5h (Views on creativity) were not keyed in individually as illustrated in Table 12.2, then data analysis would be erratic, if not impossible, even with the use of special statistical software. Further to this, consistent data entry is of utmost importance; unnecessary spaces or the irregular use of upper/lower case letters can make the database unanalysable! If the constructed database needs to be exported later for a more sophisticated statistical analysis (for example, PASW/SPSS, Minitab), it is crucial that options are entered as numbers rather than as text (for example, '1' for 'Yes' and '2' for 'No').

You can do data entry as the main researcher, or it can be done by any member of the team if you are working in collaboration with colleagues or any person carefully recording the responses obtained from the paper questionnaire into an appropriately laid out database. Again as canons of good practice dictate, a random re-checking of a sample of the data entered immediately after keying them in will also help increase the overall accuracy, and thus, quality of the content of the database.

Data cleansing

Before data analysis can get under way, data cleansing needs to take place. This is another quality assurance step that improves the accuracy of the data entered by identifying any potential errors in data sets.

If you are working on a small database, a careful 'sweep' of the database is sufficient to identify erroneous entries (for example, '22' instead of '2'). If, however, you have a larger database, either getting a summary of data or sums of each column will help ascertain if there is any existing 'outlier' or ambiguity with the data entries that need to be amended. You will need to decide whether or not outliers are to be removed as these unusually high or low values will distort the results when calculating the mean or the range, for example.

Transforming the data

Transforming the data is perhaps the last important step in data preparation that you will need to consider in order to make the research data manageable, usable and ready for analysis. This step is very necessary if the study uses a response scale with mixed positive and negative statements that are eventually to be summed, and/or where addressing the research questions will require data to be aggregated or combined. Whereas negatively stated questions should have the responses for the scores reversed to reflect correct answers, calculating the total score for two or more questions may also be needed in the analysis. This can be done manually by adding additional columns, re-calculating the data as well as indicating that they are 'transformed data'. For example, you can call a reversely calculated Q4 column 'RQ4' or the total score for Q5 and Q6 column 'TQ5_6'.

Very often, however, transforming the data is employed if sophisticated statistical analysis beyond an ordinary 'count' or 'percentage' is required. Therefore, access to suitable statistical programs when transforming the data would be ideal. Trochim (2006) suggested several ways of transforming the data with regard to:

- missing values – applying '9' or '99' to indicate that the value is missing
- item reversals – changing the scores given to a response scale for negatively expressed statements to conform with what the questionnaire aims to measure
- scale totals – getting the individual's total score for each subscale in the questionnaire
- categories – collapsing two or three entries into a single category (for example, grouping the 'Strongly agree' and 'Agree' responses as well as the 'disagree' and 'Strongly disagree' responses).

Descriptive statistics

In quantitative research, numbers are used as the unit of analysis. However, as Denscombe (1998: 177) asserted, you do not need to be an expert in statistics in order to perform quantitative data analysis: 'Provided the researcher has a vision of the pros and cons, and appreciates the limitations to what can be concluded on the basis of the data collected, good quantitative research need not require advanced statistical knowledge.' Generally, small-scale research does not need to go beyond the use of frequencies and percentages in presenting findings. Descriptive statistics aims to describe and provide summaries about the data. Very often, analysis is geared towards reducing lots of data into a synopsis of key information.

Before delving into the different ways in which descriptive data can be presented in a report, let us have a short look at the different types of data. Understanding the type of data that we are using is important as it informs the way we code, manage, analyse, interpret and present the data.

Nominal data
Categorisation, in this case, is merely based on names, hence, nominal. As previously noted, '1' may stand for male and '2' for female but '2' does not

imply a higher value than '1'. These numbers can be easily replaced by letters (for example, A, B) or names (for example, men, women). Other examples could be year level, job, race and political party. These data are regarded as the 'lowest' level of quantitative data in the sense that only basic mathematical operations can be conducted with nominal data, not even rank ordering.

Ordinal data

With ordinal data, it can be observed that the categorisation is in a certain order or ranking. A Likert scale, which is often used in questionnaire design to measure the respondents' level of agreement by selecting an answer out of a multi-point scale (for example, *Strongly agree, Agree, Neutral, Disagree, Strongly disagree*) is a case in point. A clear order or direction is embedded through the response, that is, a 'Strongly agree' response indicates a more positive view than an 'Agree' option. As a convention, the highest number should be given to the most positive response; this proves useful if the participants' overall score is to be obtained as part of the analysis.

Despite ranked categorisation with ordinal data that enables a distinction between higher and lower values, its main limitation remains: it can never ascertain the true or exact 'difference' between each response in the scale. In essence, there is no way of knowing the actual difference between your participants agreeing and strongly agreeing to a given statement.

Interval data

Interval data are ordinal data at an advanced level because the difference between the responses is a known factor. As a result, it allows for different types of analysis to be made. With interval data, it is possible to compare and contrast the data directly. Furthermore, interval data having an arbitrary zero allows for such simple mathematical operations as addition and subtraction but not multiplication or division (Denscombe, 1998). Examples for interval data include calendar years and temperature.

The lack of true zero is best explained by considering that whereas in the Gregorian calendar – which is the internationally accepted calendar – it is now 2010, it does not mean to say that time did not exist 2,010 years ago. It is also worth mentioning that in other cultures, the years count start at different times; in the Thai calendar for example, 2010 is equal to 2553. Despite exact difference between variables, the lack of a true zero poses some challenges when it comes to analysis.

Ratio data

Finally, the highest level of the data in the continuum is ratio data. Unlike interval data, the categories for ratio data are on a scale, which has a 'true zero' as an absolute reference point. A good example of this is speed. In order to answer the question: 'What was the car's speed when the accident took

Table 12.3 Types of quantitative data

Types of Quantitative Data	Qualities	Examples	Ways of presenting the data
Nominal data	Categories are based on names; there is no underlying order to the names	• male/female • pupil/teacher, parent • schools 1, 2, 3, 4	• table (frequency, %) • chart (pie, bar)
Ordinal data	Categories are in some clear, ordered, ranked relationship	• Likert scale • good, medium, bad	• table (frequency, %) • chart (stacked bar)
Interval data	They are like ordinal data but the categories are a known factor	• calendar years • temperature • IQ results and personality tests	• table (frequency, %) • chart (histogram)
Ratio data	They are like interval data, except that the categories exist on a scale which has an absolute reference point – a 'true zero'	• speed • height • weight • salary • word count	• table (frequency, %) • chart (bar)

place?', the response will be in a form of ratio data (for example, 30 miles per hour, 60 miles per hour) because 0 miles per hour means something precise – that the car is not moving at all. Similarly, in answering the question 'How many pupils are absent today?', a zero answer means that everybody has come to class.

A summary of the types of data, their characteristics, examples and suggested ways of presenting data in a descriptive manner (as opposed to using and presenting inferential statistics) are provided in Table 12.3.

Discrete and continuous data

Data can also be either 'discrete' or 'continuous'. If the numerical data come in chunks, whole units or exact numbers, then they are considered discrete. Common examples for this include the number of pupils in the classroom; the number of correct test answers, or the number of A-level passes. Continuous data, on the other hand, although measurable, will need to be approximated or expressed to the nearest fraction. Your age is an excellent example; age is a continuous variable and the question 'How old are you?' is answerable in different ways depending on the categorisation used (for example, years, months or days or, most commonly, age at last birthday). This has obvious implications for analysis. Denscombe (1998: 180) suggests that '[t]he accuracy of statistics based on continuous data depends on knowing the boundaries and mid-point to the categories of the data'.

Table 12.4 Sample table for pupils' average scores in mathematics

Average score in mathematics	Male	Female
S1	84%	80%
S2	89%	92%
S3	82%	81%
S4	95%	93%

Analysis and data presentation

It is worth noting that you may use either a table or a diagram to present your data. Denscombe (1998) explains that using tables or charts is essential in 'transforming' and 'making sense' of a large amount of numerical data. Transformation of data, in this respect, entails 'moulding, extracting and refining the raw data, so that the meaning and significance can be grasped' by the readers (Denscombe, 1998: 183). Tables or charts will contain summaries about the characteristics of the sample in terms of various criteria or specific variables used in the study (for example, gender, year level). For instance, a table that contains a comparison of secondary school pupils' average scores in a mathematics examination according to year levels and gender is one way that you can organise data into a readable summary (see Table 12.4 for an example).

Essentially, in the same way that the Table 12.4 summary can be converted into two smaller tables, it can also be translated into two separate diagrams (that is, according to gender or year level), but depending on the research question it may be more meaningful to present all the information together in a stacked bar chart (see Figure 12.2) where a direct comparison between both year levels and gender is possible. There are various

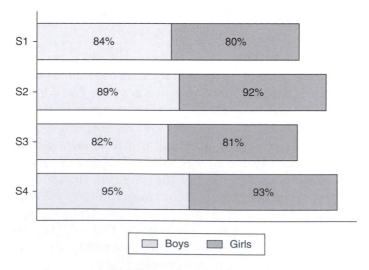

Figure 12.2 Sample chart for average score in mathematics

possibilities for creating diagrams and it may be a matter of trial and error to find out the best way of presenting your data.

Summaries such as these presented in either a table or a chart are adequate for most of the studies undertaken by school practitioners. They provide a helpful synopsis of a large amount of data that are difficult to read in their 'raw' form.

In the discussion relating to table and chart presentation, Denscombe's (1998: 183–4) advice is worth heeding:

- *Present enough information* without 'drowning' the reader with information overload.
- Help the reader to interpret the table or chart through *visual clues and appropriate presentation.*
- Use an *appropriate type of table or chart* for the purpose at hand.

Table and diagram presentations are some of the most frequent, but not the sole, means of reporting descriptive data. In descriptive statistics, describing means merely reporting what the data show but does not imply reaching a conclusion that can be generalised for a larger population, which is largely a function of inferential statistics. Basically, the three most common ways of using descriptive statistics are:

- frequency distribution table – as the name implies, this contains the distribution of the frequency across cases for the same variable
- central tendency – refers to the estimate of the 'centre' of the values distribution through the use of mean, median or mode
- dispersion – gives an indication of how the values are spread out around the mean.

As previously noted, the use of a frequency distribution is very common, and is a good way of capturing in summary form how the participants are represented according to a selected variable. Either a table or a graph (for example, a pie chart, bar graph or line chart) can depict a frequency distribution. With a diagrammatic representation of a frequency distribution, key segments are accompanied by percentages. The advantage of diagrams over tables is that they are relatively easier to interpret and understand. Figure 12.3 shows some examples of different types of diagrams that can easily be created using Excel.

The distinction between discrete and continuous data will also inform the way you visually present your data. Whereas an ordinary bar chart can be used for discrete or nominal data, a histogram is more appropriate for presenting continuous data (see Figure 12.3E). The lack of gaps between bars in a histogram gives the impression of continuity rather than a sense of distinction and separation portrayed by each bar in the bar graph, and thus reflects the nature of continuous data.

The use of central tendency is useful when getting the middle value of the data. The decision whether to use the mean, median or mode depends on the type of data that you are working on (for example, mode for nominal; median for ordinal, mean or median for interval and ratio). As a measure of dispersion, standard deviation is the most common. This measure examines the dispersion of a set of values and its relationship with the mean of the sample. If you require further reading on the subject, Trochim (2006) in his book *Research Methods Knowledge Base* has presented a reader-friendly discussion to illuminate these concepts. Both the use of central tendency and a measure of dispersion are better presented in a table.

Making sense of the data using an Excel PivotTable

Let us suppose that all the data preparation has been accomplished: data have been recorded systematically, checked and cleansed for accuracy. We will discuss in this section how you can proceed with your data analysis by showing how you can use a PivotTable to make sense and/or summarise a large amount of numerical data.

In our discussion, we will again refer to the abridged questionnaire that contains different examples of question types (see Figure 12.1). After learning the different types of quantitative data (see Table 12.3), you can probably surmise that responses to questions 1, 2 and 5 are regarded as nominal data, and ordinal data for question 6. Question 10, on the other hand, requires textual data. As stressed earlier, each type of data needs to be recorded properly. We reproduce Table 12.2 but this time a shaded table is presented (Table 12.5) to assist with the analysis by making a clear distinction between questions. At this stage, you may also prefer to use the actual words for the more commonly used variables (for example, 'Gender' instead of Q1 and 'Year' instead of Q2).

A   A pie chart showing the composition of participating schools

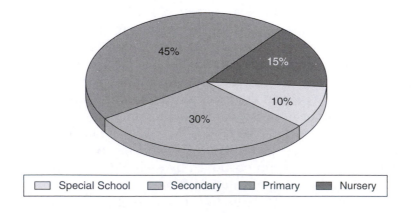

B   A bar graph showing priority given to students' creativity and artistry

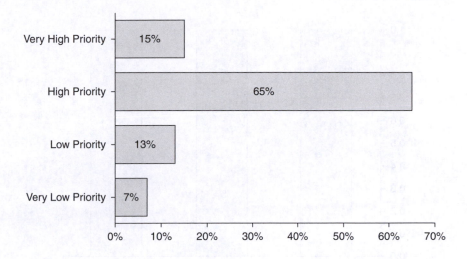

C   A line graph showing a record of the students' attendance for six consecutive months

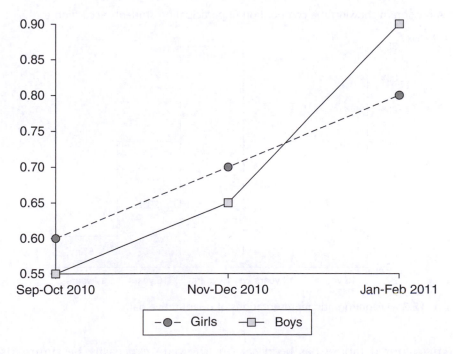

(Continued)

(Continued)

D　A stacked graph showing a record of the after-school club composition for three consecutive years

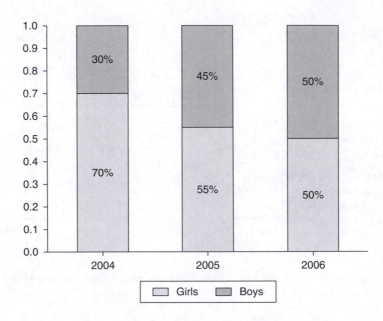

E　A histogram showing the composition of participating students according to their age

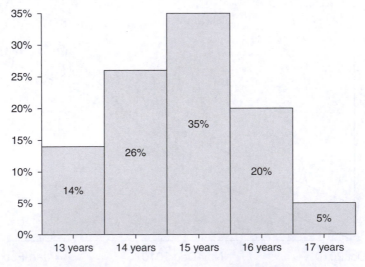

Figure 12.3　Diagrammatic representations of quantitative data

Once your database has been set up, the data can easily be summarised using the PivotTable function in Excel. You will need to ensure that when using a PivotTable:

Table 12.5 A sample of a database

ID	Gender	Year	Q5a	Q5b	Q5c	Q5d	Q5e	Q5f	Q5g	Q5h	Q6a	Q6b	Q6c	Q6d	Q6e	Q6f	Q6g	Q7a	Q7b	Q10a	Q10b
1	1	2	2	1	2	1	1	2	1	2	4	3	2	2	1	3	3	text	9	2	text
2	2	2	1	2	1	1	2	1	2	2	2	2	4	2	1	1	2	text	1	1	text
3	1	2	1	1	1	1	1	1	1	1	3	2	2	2	2	2	2	text	12	2	text
4	2	1	1	1	2	1	2	2	2	2	3	2	2	2	3	3	2	text	1	2	text
5	2	1	1	1	2	1	2	1	2	2	2	3	2	2	2	1	1	text	18	1	text
6	2	1	2	2	1	2	2	1	2	2	2	2	4	1	3	2	3	text	20	2	text
7	2	2	2	2	2	2	1	2	2	2	2	2	4	3	2	2	3	text	8	1	text
8	2	1	1	1	1	2	1	2	1	1	2	1	1	2	2	2	3	text	8	1	text
9	2	2	2	1	2	2	2	1	2	2	2	1	1	2	2	1	1	text	8	1	text

Setting up your PivotTable

1 Click a cell in the source data.
2 On the Data menu, select PivotTable Report.
3 Follow the instructions in steps 1 through 3 of the wizard.

Note: You can lay out the PivotTable report by clicking the Layout button in step 3 of the wizard, or you can lay out the report directly on the worksheet.

Choosing a 'new sheet' for your PivotTable analysis is preferable as it will give you a clean spreadsheet to work on for your analysis.

There are four elements to your data:

* a ***data field***, where the data field is the variable you want to summarise
* a ***row*** and/or ***column field*** where the row and/or column fields are the variables that will 'control' the data summary
* a ***page field*** – optional!

Figure 12.4   Setting up a PivotTable

* There should be a heading for each of the columns (for example, Q1, Q2, Q3) that is clearly distinguishable from other headings.
* There should not be any blank columns or rows within the database. (The PivotTable will automatically exclude the rows or columns beyond the blank ones during analysis.)
* Missing cells are allowed within the database so long as no entire row or column is empty.

Figure 12.4 and 12.5 contain simple instructions on how to set up your PivotTable using the Excel database that you created for your questionnaire responses.

Now, you will see a template that looks like the one in Figure 12.5 if you are using Excel. (You can expect slight variations between different versions of Excel.) This template will guide you in what you would like to summarise from your data, more specifically, what you want to be in the 'column fields' and 'row fields' and what data you want to analyse. This type of data analysis where two variables are considered is referred to as cross-tabulation. The PivotTable Toolbar that appears (see Figures 12.6 and 12.7) contains not only the special functions of a PivotTable but also the variables (represented by the column headings) for you to use in your analysis.

When using a PivotTable,

* you may want to choose variables with fewer classifications for your 'column fields' (for example, gender) and variables with more classifications for the 'row fields' (year levels). Doing so will help create a vertically orientated rather than a horizontally orientated table.
* the largest box 'Drop Data Items Here' is designated for the actual data that you would like to summarise, in this case, according to gender and year level.

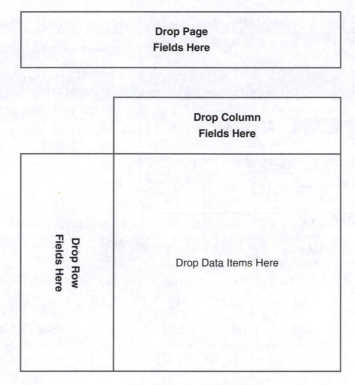

Figure 12.5   Template for the PivotTable

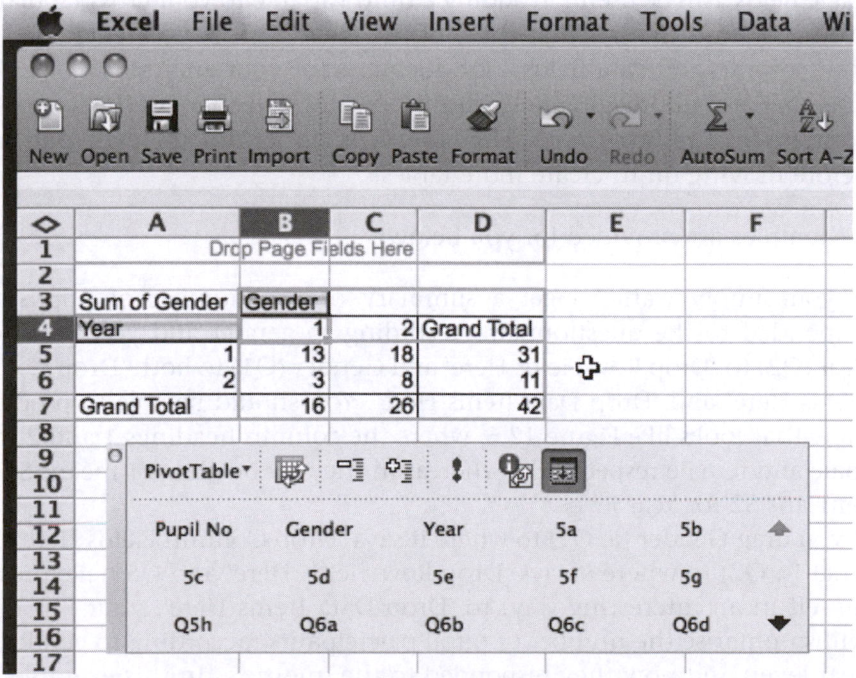

Figure 12.6   Table created using a PivotTable – Example 1

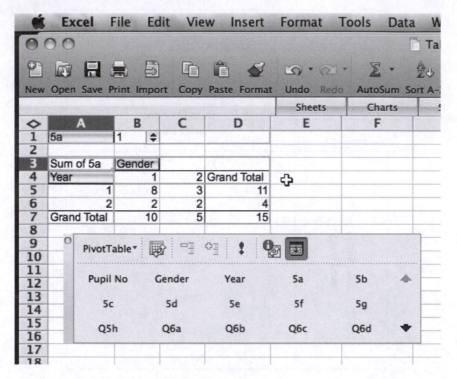

Figure 12.7   Table created using a PivotTable – Example 2

- 'page fields' can be useful in adding a third variable to your cross-tabulation. (You may find though that three of the elements of the PivotTable – the row, column and data fields – are adequate for your analysis.)
- dragging and undragging field buttons creates and changes the format and contents of the PivotTable. Therefore it is important to save your tables before moving on to create more tables.

Two examples are provided for you below:

- If you simply want to get a summary of the number of pupils who responded to the questionnaire according to gender and year level, drag Year (Q2) to 'Drop Row Fields Here' and Gender (Q1) to both 'Drop Column Fields Here' and 'Drop Data Items Here'. You should be able to produce a table that looks like Figure 12.6, where the column headings 1 and 2 mean male and female respectively, whereas in the row headings 1 means S1 and 2 means S2 for Year level.
- If you drag Gender (ie Q1) to where it says 'Drop Column Fields Here', Year (that is, Q2) to where it says 'Drop Row Fields Here' and Q5 (ie expressing myself in an interesting way) to 'Drop Data Items Here', your PivotTable will summarise the number of pupil participants (according to gender and year level) and how they responded to the question. In this example, it is essential for you to use the 'Drop Page Fields Here' by dragging Q5 to it as

well; this will give you an option to view the summary of the respondents' answers for 'ticked' (1) or 'unticked' (2) options. Your PivotTable result for the 'ticked' responses may look like Figure 12.7.

The steps to follow to create and save a PivotTable are summarised in Figure 12.8. There is a lot of flexibility in using PivotTables, but you have to ensure that you save your table before revising it or creating another one, otherwise you might end up losing what you previously created.

There are a few ways that you can revise or change the content of your PivotTable (Figure 12.9). You may also want to try experimenting with the different field buttons and functions in the PivotTable toolbar.

Once you have managed to summarise the data with the help of a PivotTable, you can then decide how to present your data – sticking to the table you created or transform your table data into a diagram.

Inferential statistics

Inferential statistics is the type of statistics that professional statisticians employ. There are certain conditions that the data need to meet before they

---

Creating your PivotTable

1 Bearing in mind your research questions, you will need to decide how you want to summarise the data and/or what variables you require for cross-tabulation.
2 Select and drag field buttons (representing variables from the list) from the PivotTable toolbar to the layout diagram. You will not need to use all the field buttons!
3 Save each table after constructing it. It is advisable for you to create a new sheet for your created PivotTables. When saving, you will need to highlight the table from one line below. Then, copy and paste special. Click 'values'. While the new table is still highlighted, do the paste special again, but this time select 'format' to ensure that the new table has the same formatting as the original PivotTable.

Then, being sure that you have a saved copy of your created table, you can revise your PivotTable!

Figure 12.8 Creating and saving a PivotTable

Revising your PivotTable

In modifying your PivotTable, two of the buttons on the PivotTable toolbar are key.

- Field settings – allows you to change the number count to percentages.
- PivotTable Wizard – helps you to return to the Wizard layout view and modify the table from there.
- Alternatively, you can drag and drop items onto and off the PivotTable and move them around in the layout just by using the mouse.

Figure 12.9 Revising a PivotTable

can be used in such a way that the findings can be used to make inferences from the data to more general conditions and a larger population. These include:

- generating the right type of data (ie interval or ratio data)
- giving each potential participant a chance to take part through random sampling
- obtaining an adequate amount of data to enable the statistical analysis to be carried out.

Conclusions acquired through inferential statistics can be used beyond the data sample for the larger population. Hence, 'inferential', because the statistics are used for drawing inferences about the population by studying the sample (that is, a subset of a population) and its characteristics (Salkind, 2008). Using inferential statistics, findings based on how a group of boys and girls differ in their performance on computer-related subjects can be extended to other boys and girls from the same year level and from the same school.

Preliminary analysis of the data may produce a trend or a pattern on how variables are associated with each other. Through the use of 'statistical tests of significance', you will be able to determine whether this apparent relationship is genuine or not; whether or not the findings are based on chance. Whereas in medical research, the statistical significance is based on the probability that less than 1 in 100 ($p < 0.01$) or 1 per cent that the results are based on chance, in social science the probability commonly used is less than 1 in 20 ($p < 0.05$) or 5 per cent that the results are the product of pure chance.

However as Denscombe (1998: 199) asserted '[s]tatistical significance does not necessarily imply social significance'. Your knowledge of the research context will help inform if the findings indeed have significant implications in educational terms.

The most commonly employed statistical tests in inferential statistics include t-test, Analysis of Variance (ANOVA), and Analysis of Covariance, regression analysis, factor analysis, multidimensional scaling, cluster analysis and discriminant function analysis, to name just a few (Trochim, 2006). With inferential statistics, it is advisable to use computer programs such as Predictive Analytics Software (PASW) (previously called SPSS) as it contains more sophisticated ways of analysis using statistical tests.

Summary

We have seen that it is possible to use simple numerical techniques to analyse quantitative data in a way that will enhance even a small-scale study. In most practitioner studies any quantitative data and its analysis is likely to be complemented by other qualitative data and by a careful account of the context in which the quantitative data have been gathered. Numbers on their own do not tell us very much but they certainly can reveal very interesting patterns of response or behaviour.

If you do enjoy manipulating numbers then you can certainly take this further by learning statistical techniques that begin to enable you to consider the wider significance of your research.

Checklist: Conducting quantitative analysis

Here are some questions to reflect on when undertaking your statistical analysis. A positive answer to these questions will help to give you confidence with your data, your analysis and your study conclusions.

Checklist for considering data analysis using quantitative means	
Can your research questions be addressed through the use of quantitative analysis?	☐
Do you understand what type(s) of data you have gathered (for example, nominal, ordinal)?	☐
Have you taken the basic steps in data preparation (for example, data checking, data cleansing) to ensure that your analysis will be based on accurate data?	☐
Keying-in the data is a time-consuming task. Do you have anyone who can assist you in data preparation?	☐
Have you considered the most appropriate way(s) of presenting your findings (for example, tables, diagrams)?	☐
Do you understand the extent to which your findings are generalisable?	☐

Going further with statistics

If you are seriously considering using inferential statistics as tools for your research, it would be helpful to read the following resources:

Pallant, J. (2007) *SPSS Survival Manual*. 3rd edn. Maidenhead: Open University Press.

Salkind, N. (2008) *Statistics for People Who (Think They) Hate Statistics*. Los Angeles, CA: Sage.

Trochim, W. (2006) *Research Methods Knowledge Base*. 3rd edn.

http://www.socialresearchmethods.net/kb/.

Further reading 📖

Blaxter, L., Hughes, C. and Tight, M. (2001) *How to Research*. 2nd edn. Buckingham: Open University Press.

Bryman, A. (2004) *Social Research Methods*. 2nd edn. New York: Oxford University Press.

Denscombe, M. (1998) *The Good Research Guide: For Small-scale Social Research Projects*. Buckingham: Open University Press.

13

Qualitative Data Analysis

We turn now to the questions concerning qualitative data – that is, mainly, words. In earlier chapters we discussed research techniques which lead to the generation of qualitative data, especially interviews (Chapter 8) and focus groups (Chapter 9). But other methods discussed, such as observation or visual methods, may also generate forms of qualitative data.

We discuss how to prepare the data, how to sort and code it, before you develop your analysis, and then how to prepare the report. Computers can assist your analysis, and we touch on these, but it is also possible to have very rigorous use of qualitative data in practitioner research where the analysis is predominantly done 'manually'.

Preparing the data

If we assume that you have recorded the interviews or focus group discussions that you have undertaken, then the first step towards analysis is to create a transcript. If you are doing this yourself then bear in mind that for every hour of recording you have made it is likely to take at least six hours to make a transcript – unless that is you are a superfast audiotypist. So, the first things to consider are whether you need to transcribe everything on the recording and/or whether you can get some help with this.

The first point, whether to make a complete transcription, can be a difficult decision. Rigour and completeness would tend to suggest that the whole recording should be transcribed. However, practicality and realism may mean that this is unwise. It is very common for some sections of an interview or focus group to have strayed away from the main focus of the research. It is a good idea to listen to the recording as soon as possible after you have made it and take notes, using the timing or reference number on the recorder, to create a list of the sections which seem to be most important and then to prioritise those for transcription. However, do be careful not to close down opportunities to identify unexpected responses by taking relevance merely at face value.

If you are working in a school or college where there is administrative support that might be deployed to help you in the transcription, then that can be a great help. However, it is most important that you consider the ethical aspects of this. You will need to have made it clear to your respondents at the time of the interview that the recording may be listened to by someone in addition to you, someone who in this example, may well be known to the respondents. This is an important factor to take into account when you are planning your data gathering.

If you are doing the transcription yourself then do try to use the best equipment, which may well be a set of headphones and a foot pedal operated playback device. Digital audio files can be easily loaded on to computer and free software such as Express Scribe can be used with the foot pedal to control audio playback and assist the transcription of recordings. This set up allows you to easily stop and start the digital recording on your computer, enabling you to listen to short sections, type them and then go on.

You may wish to anonymise the respondents at the earliest opportunity, as you transcribe, so that if you do need to show the transcript to anyone else, there is greater chance of maintaining anonymity. Also, it is a very good idea to number the lines on the page so that you are ready to do your first set of notes on the transcript. It can often be helpful to type the words into a half-page width left-hand column so that you can then annotate it with your own notes in the adjacent right-hand column – either by hand or by typing in your comments.

Sorting and coding the data

Focus groups and interviews do tend to generate a large volume of information. Rabiee (2004) provides a useful overview of the underlying analytical concepts for dealing with qualitative focus group information and gives some clear guidance on how to analyse such material.

The particular way in which you now deal with the data will depend partly on the nature of your study and partly on the particular purpose of the interview or focus group that you have conducted. Whatever the particularities of the case, however, it is a good idea to reread your own research questions as a preliminary. What is it that you have been trying to find out through your study? Once reminded of the real focus for the analysis then read through the transcript and either highlight what seem to be the most relevant sections or use your right-hand column to make some annotations. These can be 'analytic memos', that provide the starting point for your examination of what was said.

As you read the data, however, you should also be applying a critical perspective – always asking yourself what the respondent meant by what he or she said, whether they appeared to be confident in what they were saying or were struggling very hard to answer the question you had asked them. In other words you will not necessarily be taking what you now read at face value (and if you made field notes at the time of the data gathering, you will need to refer back to those as well, at this stage).

So, if you start to make notes on the transcript then you are likely to be identifying particular responses that seem significant. These might be particular words that seem to relate closely to some of your research questions. It may be that through gathering up these words or phrases, you start to identify themes that emerge from the transcript.

Assuming that you are dealing with several transcripts, it will be important to go through this process with all of them. As you do so, you may find themes recurring and you may identify new themes as well. Again, it is important that you keep your mind open to what may emerge. Do not always assume that the first transcripts you read will provide you with all of the important insights you are hoping for and then all you are effectively doing when you read the later ones is looking for confirmation. Indeed, it is good to be looking for countervailing evidence that seems to contradict your previous judgement or at least represents a very different experience or perspective.

Once you have worked through all of your material, it will be helpful to write a list of the key categories, codes or themes that have emerged. If certain words seem to be of particular significance then you can easily apply a search function in your word-processing package that will identify all of the uses of this term throughout all of your transcripts. This is a speedy way of finding further examples that you may have missed on your initial reading.

Let us now look at a couple of examples. In a study of ten secondary schools which were implementing school development plans, in the City of Glasgow, the following four research questions had been agreed upon:

1 What is the nature of the social and educational challenges faced by the schools?
2 How have the schools and their communities responded to these challenges in developing their plans for transformation and improvement and for the evaluation of the implementation of these plans?
3 What lessons have been learned through this work about the management of change (including management style and capacity) and about internal and external communication processes, including the involvement of parents and a range of external partners?
4 What opportunities have emerged for teachers and other staff in relation to the development of their professional skills and expertise, including the capacity to manage change and to engage with other agencies in service delivery?

In each school a range of interviews and focus group discussions were held. These were transcribed (professionally) and the data were then analysed very much along the lines that we have suggested here.

Let us look at an extract from a focus group discussion with four parents at one of the schools (Figure 13.1). Interviews had already been conducted with the headteacher and with a number of teachers. No school students had yet been interviewed (although they were subsequently).

1	*Int: Does the school have parents' evenings of some sort you're invited to? What's your impression of how many parents tend to turn up to that?*	
6	**Mother 1** A fair amount turn up. I think they are fairly well attended.	
11	**Father 1** The school has been very, very good at listening. Because of the parent council a lot of us were actually discussing the fact that there's been sometimes problems trying, not so much I think too many parents were turning up	Earlier problems with parents' evenings
16	and we couldn't actually see the teachers we wanted to see, so the school's been trying all sorts of different avenues to try and get parents in, so we've went from having an open night to	
21	having an appointment time and then it's back up for discussion again because I think the parents group isn't too happy with it.	Cycle of discussion between parents and staff
26	**Father 2** We're kind of split I think of how we want to see it.	Not all parents have the same view
31	**Mother 2** 10 minutes with a teacher that doesn't even have your child for a class. She's a registration teacher but she doesn't teach your child and she's just telling you wee notes the teachers are giving, and it's not really letting you know, and	
36	I think when your child is maybe in 4th Year when they're sitting all these exams, you need to see the different teachers to really find out how they're doing and what you can do to	Anxiety about children's performance in exams?
41	encourage and help them and what work they're doing so you can look at that yourself and help her with it.	
46	*Int: It does become more important when they're taking their public exams.*	
	Mother 1 Yes, most definitely.	
51	**Father 2** To be fair we kind of slated the old system as well because it was taking two or three hours to get round, but on balance we would probably prefer the old system, rather tire	Confirmed
56	yourself out meeting all the teachers.	
	Mother 1 You don't necessarily get to see all of them because	
61	of the time constraint really, but it's better than 10 minutes with a registration teacher who the first time round when we asked questions never, ever got back and couldn't get back because lots of other parents had asked questions and she had all	
66	these notes written down and she said "I've got a full-time class myself and I don't know how I'm going to get back to	
71	everybody" and you felt if you had met a teacher you could ask the teacher and that would have been it.	Father 1 is very strongly supportive of the school – are the others as certain as him?
	Father 1 It was pushed by us in a certain extent, tried. They are definitely listening.	

Key terms – 'listening' and 'discussion' have been highlighted and notes in the right-hand column have been added as the researcher read through the transcript.

Figure 13.1   Transcript – four parents in a focus group at a Glasgow secondary school

In asking questions of the parents there was clearly an interest in exploring dimensions of the third research question above but that did not mean that the other three questions were not relevant – they were. So, in analysing the transcription, because these are parents, we were particularly interested to see whether what we had been told by the headteacher and some of the teachers about the importance of parents and communication with them, was confirmed, or not, by this particular group. And of course it was important to remember that the sample had been identified for us by some of the teachers we had interviewed. What these parents said to us therefore did not necessarily represent what the wider parental body would have said if we had been able to elicit views from all of them.

Analysing the data

In a sense you have already started the process of analysis when you have been sorting and coding the data. As we mentioned above, professional researchers now often use qualitative analysis software such as NVivo to assist the managing, sorting, indexing, arranging and rearranging data of qualitative information. Once the material is coded using the steps summarised above, the software allows the researcher to conduct very systematic sorting of the material to ensure all relevant indexed pieces of text are included in the analysis process and minimise overlooking relevant information. However, such software can be expensive. Practitioner researchers and students might not have access to such resources and therefore, the main analytical stages can be conducted using paper printouts of the transcripts, as suggested above. Again Raibee provides a clear example of how this manual approach is conducted (see Raibee, 2004: 658). Generally, manual qualitative analysis procedures will use copies of transcripts. So, to summarise again, on each transcript you would:

1 number each line of each transcript
2 print transcripts on different coloured paper to represent types of participant or group
3 use coloured highlighter pens to identify key text and quotes with the colours of the pens indicating thematic areas
4 cut out the text associated with the main analytical themes and arrange under the existing and/or developing main thematic areas.

When conducting stages (3) and (4) above, the main stages of qualitative analysis involve examining, categorising and tabulating and recombining the evidence to address the initial goal of a study (Rabiee, 2004; Yin, 2003). Indeed, Kruger and Casey (2000) stress that the research objectives provide the main focus for analysis.

With all analysis, not just qualitative research, there is an interpretative selection process with a degree of subjectivity as the researcher examines and highlights themes of interest to the study. Therefore, we need to make our analysis as systematic and as transparent as possible to allow scrutiny from others, which provides a 'trail of evidence' (Kruger and Casey, 2000). As Rabiee states: 'The first step in establishing a trail of evidence is a clear procedure of data analysis, so that the process is clearly documented and understood. This step would allow another researcher to verify the findings; it safeguards against selective perception and increases the rigour of the study' (2004: 657).

Rabiee (2004) draws on Kruger's (1994) qualitative approaches as well as incorporating stages of that proposed by Ritchie and Spencer (1994). These 'Framework analysis' approaches are characterised by a focus on developing themes from the narrative accounts gathered by the researcher which are initially guided by the main research objectives and questions. Unlike quantitative analysis, the analysis process occurs as the information is being gathered and is not linear. This means that important analytical themes can also be generated during the focus groups or interview interaction.

Kruger (1994) sees the process as moving from the raw data to generating descriptive statements and then on to interpretation. Ritchie and Spencer (1994) elaborate and describe the analytical process as involving distinct but interconnected stages:

- *Familiarization.* Listening to recordings, reading transcripts, checking our notes and research diaries. This sensitises the researcher to relevant content and key issues within their context.
- *Identifying a thematic framework.* Using the research questions the researcher initially develops a framework to work through the accounts to look for related material. The framework is also informed by the researcher's notes and developing ideas and concepts that form during the information gathering and reading through the accounts.
- *Indexing.* Using the thematic framework the researcher then explores the qualitative accounts looking for associated segments of text, recurring patterns and concepts. Key pieces of text and quotes are highlighted that relate to the themes. The emerging themes and related key points can then be checked within the individual accounts and comparisons made across other accounts (for example, the key issues arising from other focus groups' accounts).
- *Charting.* Taking the process further, the relevant pieces of indexed text and quotes are extracted from the narrative context and placed within the thematic groupings.

Rabiee (2004) summarises Kruger and Casey's (2000) advice for charting text into themes. They recommend reading each quote and addressing the following four questions:

1 Did the participant answer the question that was asked? If yes, go to question 3; if no, go to question 2; if do not know, set it aside and review it later.
2 Does the comment answer a different question in the focus group? If yes, move it to the appropriate question; if no, go to question 3.
3 Does the comment say something of importance about the topic? If yes, put it under the appropriate question; if no, set it aside.
4 Is it something that has been said earlier? If yes, start grouping like quotes together; if no, start a separate pile.

Those quotes and text that have been sorted into the 'not so relevant' category can be then examined to see if they tell us about the focus group participants' views and attitudes on related issues and themes that we might have overlooked as relevant but which the participants see as important.

- *Mapping and interpretation.* The final stage involves any associated researcher notation rearranging them under the newly developed thematic content. As Rabiee (2004: 658) says, 'one of the tasks here is not only to make sense of the individual quotes, but also to be imaginative and analytical enough to see the relationship between the quotes, and the links between the data as a whole'.

Reporting the data

Writing the report is very often an important stage within the analysis – when using qualitative data it is not something that is necessarily separate, as Thomson and Kamler (2010) have pointed out. How you report and 'write up' will depend on a lot of factors, not least, who your audience is. As a practitioner researcher, you yourself will be a key recipient of the findings, but you will be hoping to share the research more widely with colleagues or a professional gathering of your peers.

Very often, if your research has been primarily qualitative in nature you will have a huge amount of data which your task in writing is to present only your summary analysis. Taking the example we used above, we had at least 50 pages of data for each of the ten schools in which we were working. The report to come from that study presented each of the ten schools as cases, typically eight to ten pages long (see http://www.scotland.gov.uk/Publications/2010/05/11135358/0). But we were also required to provide a short report of some 25 pages in total and in this report each school case was presented as a one page summary (see http://www.scotland.gov.uk/Publications/2010/05/11135304/0). Here we include the summary for the school where the parental focus group was held:

Springburn Academy

Springburn Academy has a new building, opened in 2002, and replaced two former secondary schools, Albert and Colston. The roll has been steadily increasing from about 300 at the time of its creation and is now over 1000.

The original Transformational Plan contained four strands for development

- teaching and learning
- young people
- staff development and leadership
- parents.

A key element of the cultural change has been to do with the relationships between staff and pupils.

I think the senior management team have been really key to the success in Springburn because one thing is they speak to you like you're on the same wavelength. It's not in a bad way, but they're speaking to you as if you deserve respect. They're not speaking to you as if you will do this and you'll do that and I just think that's a better way to learn because if somebody's offensive towards you you're going to be defensive towards them and you're not going to do that. (Undergraduate student, former pupil)

The opportunity created by the additional funding provided by the *Schools of Ambition* project came at a very good time in the development of the school. The headteacher had been in post for three years and had developed a clear vision of what was possible and used the *SoA* project as a vehicle for accelerating the process of change and development.

Managing changes you need to have a vision and a plan. I think having the funding ... is important because [it helps to make] staff feel good about themselves. 'We are a School of Ambition, we've been chosen,' and there is that little bit of extra funding and if you do get it wrong it's not the end of the world. That's part of it as well – that you kind of looked at things and experimented with things. (Head Teacher)

Springburn Academy has gone through a considerable transformation over recent years. There is no doubt that the *SoA* project has been a key facilitator of this transformation. However as acknowledged by many of the respondents, the leadership and vision provided by the head and her management team would undoubtedly have led to some significant change whether or not the particular status of *SoA* had been achieved. Nevertheless, the additional funds were acknowledged by staff and students as helping to drive change at an increased rate. While some pupils had concerns about maintaining the changes that had taken place in the school, teaching staff were more hopeful that elements of the initiative had become self perpetuating. Parents involved in the study suggested that the initiative had had a positive influence on the ethos of the school.

Can you actually see any evidence of the data presented above in this summary? It is quite sobering to reread such a summary and to think how it was arrived at from a process of analysis of the huge amount of original raw data!

But if we assume that you are writing a somewhat lengthier report using your qualitative data, then among the questions you will need to decide upon as you write are these:

- How should you organise the main part of your report? Should it be around the original research questions or around the themes that have emerged from your analysis – or a combination of both?
- How much of the actual data are you going to include in your writing? Might you put some of the data in an appendix to your main report? If so, why?

- Are the data that you include being used to illustrate the themes or theories that have emerged from your research?
- Or, are you including the data in order to give your respondents their 'voice' in your report?
- Will the reader have confidence that you have not selected the data in a partial way, simply to suit your argument and that you have avoided examples of contradictory evidence?
- Will you attribute any quotations you use, in some way, perhaps through fictitious names or through use of a code of some kind (for example, Teacher 1, Teacher 2, and so on).

Very often, writing up qualitative data is strongly influenced by narrative forms of writing – you are in some respects, 'telling a tale' and there is every reason to make your writing enjoyable for the reader. What makes it research rather than a novel or short story is essentially the rigour and system that you have used in developing the story from your original research design, through the data collection and through the analytical process.

Taking qualitative data analysis further

If you do wish to explore the use of computer software in your analysis of qualitative data then these two texts will guide you – the first covers a range of applications, the second focuses on NVivo. Do check that you are using the latest edition of such books, so that it will refer to the current version of the software.

Bazeley, P. (2007) *Qualitative Data Analysis with NVivo*. London: Sage.

Lewins, A. and Silver, C. (2007) *Using Software in Qualitative Research, A Step by Step Guide*. London: Sage.

Online Qualitative Data Analysis (OQDA) website hosted by Huddersfield University: http://onlineqda.hud.ac.uk/Intro_QDA/how_what_to_code.php.

Further reading

Saldana, J. (2009) *The Coding Manual for Qualitative Researchers*. London: Sage.

Silverman, D. (2009) *Doing Qualitative Research – A Practical Handbook*. 3rd edition. London: Sage.

Walford, G. (2001) *Doing Qualitative Educational Research*. London: Continuum.

Part 6

How Will We Tell Everyone?

14

How Do I Write Up My Research?

In this chapter we present a case for teachers 'going public' with their enquiries (Hatch et al., 2005; Stenhouse, 1985). We discuss reservations expressed by critics and advocates of the teacher research movement. We then outline ways in which teacher researchers share their work in oral, print and digital media. We consider factors which influence the products of teacher research and offer guidance and examples to support the development of conference papers and poster presentations. We look at common components of the teacher research report and suggest strategies to help you initiate and sustain your writing for different audiences through research reports, articles for professional magazines and scholarly journals.

Key writers	Key terms
Lawrence Stenhouse	Dissemination and knowledge exchange
Marilyn Cochran-Smith and Susan Lytle	Conference paper and poster presentations
Thomas Hatch	Online multimedia presentations
Thomas Newkirk	Components of a research report
Ann Lieberman	Editorial review process
Desiree Pointer-Mace	Audience
	Identity and voice (self-representation)

Why write?

Private research for our purpose does not count as research. Partly, this is because unpublished research does not profit by criticism. Partly, it is because we see research as a community effort and unpublished research is of little use to others. (Stenhouse, 1985: 17)

Teachers frequently express considerable unease at the prospect of writing for publication, which is seen as a potentially high-risk and demanding activity with many obstacles to negotiate. Many teachers lack confidence and are unsure of their entitlement to participate in published conversations about professional practice. Accomplished teachers who engage in practice-based research often do not perceive themselves to be legitimate members of the publication community. Common refrains include:

- Other people write 'academic' pieces for publication.
- No one would be interested in what I have to say.
- I don't have time to write for publication. I am a practitioner first and foremost.
- I wouldn't know where to start.
- I am a capable teacher but I have no experience of formal report writing.
- I am unfamiliar with the language and conventions of scholarly writing.
- I'm not sure that I should 'go public' with our classroom stories.
- I don't want to expose myself to critical scrutiny by strangers, who know more.

We start this chapter by offering seven reasons why we feel it is important for teachers (and those who work with teachers) to strive to share what is learned from high quality practice-based enquiry.

1 Teachers are under-represented as producers of knowledge about teaching

Teachers are often positioned as 'consumers' to be helped to take up research findings in their practice or as 'user reviewers' to aid transferability of lessons learned from intervention studies conducted elsewhere (Rickinson et al., 2004). Indeed, teachers' failure to engage with the research of others is often stated as a 'problem' characteristic of the profession in knowledge 'transfer' models of professional learning. When intervention research is 'scaled up' teachers are provided with scripts to follow with details about 'what works'. 'Fidelity' is expected to prevent implementation failure. It is paradoxical that transmission models that are routinely challenged in regard to children's learning continue to be regarded as a source of enhancement of teachers' expertise.

2 Writing a research and enquiry summary is in itself educative

The write–reflect–revise process can enhance professional growth, especially where ideas are shaped in collaboration with peers, co-enquirers and critical friends (Robbins et al., 2006). Smiles and Short (2006: 133) have argued that, 'the process of preparing and presenting understandings to others transforms and deepens our understandings as well as influences the transformation of others'. Teacher researchers have reported that writing for publication is in itself developmental and educative, contributing to the 'transformative' process. The act of moving from 'writing up' to 'writing about' deepens reflection on practice and may support additional insights (see Badley, 2009; Holly, 2009).

Writing to learn in the Schools of Ambition programme – an illustrative example

It was through the process of writing that I managed to achieve clarity. This was something that I had said to my own pupils frequently enough, but having to do it myself was quite daunting. It actually gave me lots of new insights into what it must be like being a pupil. I would begin by writing a small section and I would feel quite satisfied with it. Later I would look back over it and discover more needed to be added, a certain point needed to be explained or something just simply had to go.

I felt shy about sharing what I had written, but it was really important to let others read what had been said in order to see where the gaps were and where I had laboured a certain point. It was by sharing and discussing what I had already put down on paper that I was able to move towards a deeper understanding of what I was really trying to say.

I would look back over fragments or whole sections after I had spoken to a colleague or my mentor or after having read something new and think no, that's not right at all. At first I felt as though I just kept getting it all wrong, but I realised that the process of writing, reading, thinking was more important than the amount of words I had got down so far. Without having something there in front of me it was impossible to think critically about the actual issue. The process of thinking, writing, thinking again and writing again was how I achieved the clarity I sought and escaped the confusion that was so frustrating, but nevertheless, an essential part of the process. (Jane Carson, Wallace Hall Academy)

---

3 Writing for publication can help to counter teacher privacy and isolation

It enables teachers as researchers to participate in research communities where argumentation and deliberation are professional norms. While willing to engage with others in research, novice teacher researchers often find this challenging at an organisational and interpersonal level. Where teacher researchers are working in isolation from their peers with restricted opportunities for professional dialogue, it is less likely that new ideas and challenges to support further learning will be generated. Despite an initial high-profile launch of school-based research initiatives, teachers' accounts often indicate that awareness among the wider school community dissipates quickly. A culture of 'privacy' (Nias et al., 1989) and the enduring realities of teacher isolation and subject-based territoriality are well documented barriers to collaborative enquiry, especially in secondary schools (Cochran-Smith and Lytle, 1993). Teacher researchers often question the wider relevance of their enquiries beyond their own classrooms. This hesitancy contributes to a sense of *individual* rather than collective responsibility; wherein separate time-bound 'projects' are seen through to their private conclusion.

Barriers to collaborative enquiry and professional learning in the secondary school. Views of Best Practice Research Scholarship award holders

'I think it is difficult to mix in a small department. I have given the information to Mr Smith but he is such a traditional teacher he doesn't want to deviate. It is going to be really hard work for me to get him involved. The rest of the school? I don't even think they know what I am doing really'.

'I don't know if it has had as high a profile in the school as it could have had because people were working on so many different topics and for the most part individually. It kind of gets swept away into individual classrooms to a certain extent. I sent a copy off to [the university] and I gave a copy to the head if he wants to read it. I don't think my study was really relevant outside the English Department.'

'Everybody seemed to be quite detached. There wasn't a strong connection. In secondary schools there is generally not a strong connection between different subjects. When we went to do the research it was, 'I'm doing mine in geography'. I'm dong mine here. I'm doing mine there. Nobody really connected the research together'.

Creating opportunities to share the experiences and outcomes of enquiry and to plan collaborative enquiries is consistent with collegial models of professional learning. It is through such exchange that the quality of practitioner research is enhanced and professional problems are identified for further cycles of enquiry. Sharing writing with a teacher audience can help teachers to problematise their practice by exposing it to critical deliberation. Cultivating a research orientation to change may encourage a move away from decontextualised 'best practice show cases', towards more finely grained investigations that consider what is hardest is change and the limits of models borrowed from elsewhere. In 'Silences in our teaching stories', Thomas Newkirk (1992) draws attention to the value of writing in overcoming the myth of the 'super teacher'. Participation by teachers in *writing groups* is founded on an acknowledgement of the significant contribution of *social* processes to the writing development of experienced practitioners who may be novice writers (Heron and Murray, 2004). This is not to deny the considerable challenge of writing *for* and *about* one's peers, which commonly evokes feelings of exposure and risk. In the construction of an emerging professional identity as an enquiring teacher, novice teacher researchers juggle the multiple roles of teacher, scholar, co-enquirer, writer, co-author and presenter (Pearson-Casanave and Vandrick, 2003).

Writing as a 'community product' in the Schools of Ambition programme – an illustrative example

As an English teacher I write all the time. I write to correct, to advise, to warn, to cajole, to encourage and to demonstrate. I had written to pupils, parents, to bosses, to colleagues ... but had never written about my colleagues and our work. It was difficult to know where to begin and how to start. Writing research was an exploratory journey. I was writing about myself and my colleagues and our shared purpose. I found it quite hard to know how to explain sensitive points and express the views of others without colouring their words with my own ideas and thoughts. They were bound to creep in though. After all, this was me writing for them, about us.

Because I had invested so much energy and time in the project and writing the report, I felt that in some way it was mine. It belonged to me. I was reluctant at first to share it. I was going to have to hold myself up to critical examination by my colleagues, friends and strangers.

But the whole point of the report was that it would be shared. It would open up the private world of our classrooms, not to expose our weaknesses and inadequacies, but to explore what was happening in there and to share what we were doing in order to improve the way we were working and how we were working together.

The report wasn't mine. Everybody who had contributed to it, been a part of it or made even the smallest suggestion had a stake in it. This was a public piece of writing with a clearly defined purpose. There was absolutely no point in having done all of the work without sharing what *we* had learned. (Jane Carson, Wallace Hall Academy)

---

4 Dissemination helps teachers connect with audiences that extend beyond the local and/or professional

The potential audience for teacher research can be wide, embracing a wide range of stakeholders, service users and other interested parties:

- teachers in other schools and regions
- parents (of pupils involved and parent interest groups)
- pupils (participants and pupil forums such as pupil councils and pupil parliaments)
- local community (through community groups and local media)
- practitioners in education-related areas (inter-agency work in children's services)
- local authority personnel (continuing professional development coordinators)

- education decision-makers
- university schools of education (teacher education faculty).

5 Openness to critical peer review helps to bridge the theory–practice divide

MacLure (1996: 274), among others, has written of the well rehearsed 'opposi-
tional dilemmas' between 'theory and practice, between the personal and the
professional; between the organisational cultures of schools and the academy;
between 'insider' and 'outsider' perspectives; between the sacred languages of
science, scholarship or research, and the mundane dialects of practice and
everyday experience' (see also Sikes and Potts, 2008). In contrast, Cochran-
Smith and Lytle (2009) describe collaborative practitioner research as 'working
the dialectic', wherein theory is both generated *from* and *in* practice.

> Inquiry and practice are understood to have a reciprocal, recursive and symbi-
> otic relationship and it is assumed that it is not only possible but indeed ben-
> eficial to take on simultaneously the roles of both researcher and practitioner.
> (Cochran-Smith and Lytle, 2009: 94)

6 Dissemination of teacher research goes some way to address the deficit of studies that connect strongly with teachers' classroom practice

Concern has been expressed about the relevance, accessibility and usability of
educational research to teachers. Research utilisation is impaired by perceptions
of research as abstract, requiring high levels of skill in analysing and using data
about interventions that were conducted elsewhere with different student and
teacher populations. Teachers frequently call for nuanced or 'personalised'
research and analyses of data that connect more closely to the experiences of
their pupils, fellow teachers and local school setting. Much teacher research uses
vivid, rich descriptions of classroom practice. Accounts of action research draw
on fieldnotes, classroom vignettes and artefacts including pupil work samples,
learning logs, teacher-designed assessments and observation records. However
while valuing the persuasiveness of 'thick description', we acknowledge that
teacher research – if it is to be regarded as 'research' – should write from 'a position
of tension' that exceeds description (Smiles and Short, 2006).

> Practitioner research is about valuing the real-time, knowledge-in-action,
> context-specific understandings which people use to solve old and new
> problems ... it is probably not quite accurate to talk in terms of the 'applica-
> tion' of 'evidence' to teaching; it is altogether a much more interesting and
> dynamic process, with teachers' structured learning – collective as well as indi-
> vidual – at the core. The knowledge created in this way is not so much accumu-
> lated as 'caught', like fire or laughter. *Above all, the knowledge is meaningful
> because it is being created in the places and contexts where it will be used, challenged
> and further developed.* (Saunders, 2007: n.p., added emphases)

7 Research engagement helps professionals 'talk back' to decision-makers

Engagement *in* and *with* research may enhance the capacity of teachers to influence local policy and provide support for evidence-informed change at school, cluster, local authority and national levels. The Teachers' Network Policy Institute (TNPI) in the USA aims to give teachers an active voice in education policy-making so that policies for schools might be informed by the realities of classroom life. Fellows of the TNPI conduct action research in classrooms and schools to support informed dialogue with decision makers. Similarly, a small group of US National Board Certified Teachers (who have achieved advanced certification) have undertaken research reviews of the impact of Board certification on students, practice and the profession (see Teacher Solutions National Board Certificate Team (TSNBCT), 2008). Participation in research communities may encourage 'principled infidelity' (Wallace, 2008) where 'ecologies of practice' (informed by professional values) are acknowledged to conflict with externally imposed 'economies of performance' (Stronach et al., 2002).

> In the current climate of increased scripting of curriculum and reliance on high stakes tests as mirrors of children's aptitudes, small stories from classrooms are emblems of resistance. Close accounts of experience of teaching illuminate the specificity of the work in a way that belies the notion that standardisation of the work is desirable to even tenable ... *I publish my writing in order to change reductive thinking about classrooms.* (Maimon, 2009: 217)

How is teacher research shared?

In the previous section, we made a case for teachers 'going public' with their enquiries. In the following section, we outline the diverse ways in which teacher researchers can and do share their work. In his account of 'teaching as community property', Shulman (1993: 7) points out that 'scholarship entails an artefact, a product, some form of community property that can be shared, discussed, critiqued, exchanged, built upon'. How teacher research is shared reflects the motivation and purposes for engaging in enquiry for the participant, the agendas of those who sponsor and support teacher research, and the intended audience.

A range of factors influences the final products of teacher research. These include:

- the assessment criteria/rubrics of taught courses
- requirements attached to funding, for example, the provision of templates and models for dissemination outputs
- expectations of local supporters, for example, school management and local authority facilitators
- the available resource in terms of time, technology, capacity in writing for and presenting to different audiences.

Research reports do *not* need to be written to be of value. Outside the formal dissertation or other coursework for award bearing programmes ('writing for grades'), the types of dissemination activity teachers engage in reflect the pragmatic concerns of local communities of practice and include:

- conference presentations (paper sessions, symposia, roundtables and posters)
- invited presentations for local authority personnel and teacher education programmes
- seminars and workshops (professional development sessions for other teachers).

Dissemination may take the form of *oral*, *print* and *digital* media including:

- the production of school documents (briefings, newsletters, formal reports)
- regional bulletins (local authority and ITE partnership newletters)
- poster presentations
- multimedia representations through digital online portfolios (see Pointer Mace, 2009)
- postings within virtual research environments including Wikis (for example, the Schools of Ambition virtual research environment and the Carnegie Gallery of Teaching and Learning[1])
- visual and arts-based approaches (see Mitchell et al., 2005)
- articles and reports of work in progress in professional association magazines such as *Teaching Scotland* (a publication of the General Teaching Council for Scotland)[2] and subject association journals
- scholarly (peer reviewed) journals (for example, *Educational Action Research*).

Opportunities for teachers who seek to share their work most frequently arise from participation in existing *networks* such as funded school–university partnerships (such as the Schools of Ambition programme or the Scottish Teachers for a New Era[3] programme at Aberdeen University), university research projects that recruit teacher fellows (see for example Smith et al., 2009), teacher research networks (such as TeacherNet[4]) or local authority professional development initiatives (for example, teacher learning communities to support *Assessment for Learning* or *Teaching for Understanding*).

Conference papers and poster presentations

Professional conferences provide excellent opportunities to report and discuss the findings of practitioner enquiry. Unlike writing for publication (which can entail lengthy processes of peer review), conferences offer opportunities for quick dissemination of pilot studies and work in progress, as well as opportunities to deliberate on completed studies. There is a range of local, national and international conferences that address or include practitioner research.

It is useful to consider the following factors when selecting a conference:

- Does your proposal fit the conference theme?
- Does this conference attract the audience you want to communicate with?
- Is this an age/stage/curriculum area/discipline specific or cross-sector/ cross-disciplinary conference?
- Will the session formats provide sufficient opportunities for dialogue?
- What opportunities are there for networking and future collaborations?
- Accessible location and convenient time of year/duration for your schedule and commitments?
- Is bursary support available for replacement teaching costs, if required?
- How will travel, registration and accommodation fees be met?
- What sources of funding are available to you? (Information on grants)
- What institutional permissions and advance arrangements are needed to support attendance? (Headteacher/local authority and cover arrangements, if required.)

Conference presentations include paper sessions, symposia, roundtables and poster presentations. *Paper sessions* are typically clusters of three or four papers on loosely related topics in a 60- to 90-minute session (see also Figure 14.1).

Schools of Ambition Evaluation Conference
Information for Presenters

All the break-out rooms have a *data projector and screen*. A laptop will be provided. If you intend to use your own laptop, please ensure that this is set up in advance of your session. If you intend to use a DVD, please ensure that you bring PC speakers. You may also wish to bring along a cordless remote control presenter/mouse for your presentation.

Internet access You will be able to access the internet via a WIFI enabled laptop. *If you require internet access in your session, please let us know* so that this can be booked in advance. You will need to enter a *log-in code* available from the venue when you open internet explorer.

If you intend to use a PowerPoint presentation, please ensure that you take the time to upload your presentation well in *advance of your session*. It is advisable to email a copy of your presentation to the conference organisers before the event.

The Schools of Ambition presentations are organised in parallel sessions throughout the day: session one (10:45–12:00), session two (12:45–14:00) and session three (14:15–15:30). Please note the timings and location of your session.

Each presentation in the *leading change and teacher-led evaluation* sessions will be 15 minutes, followed by five minutes for questions. The *evaluation workshops* are extended sessions of 30 minutes, followed by discussion. *Poster presentations* are 5 minute presentations. A chairperson in each session will assist with timekeeping by showing a yellow card when you have 2 minutes remaining. The remaining time in each session will be used for general discussion.

Each break-out room has a *maximum capacity of 30 persons* and delegates will be asked to sign up to sessions on arrival and over lunch. This will ensure an even distribution of delegates between sessions. If you are bringing *handouts*, please prepare sufficient copies for the maximum attendance.

Figure 14.1 Example of advice for presenters at paper sessions at a professional conference

The papers are grouped by the conference organisers on the basis of a short (approx 200-word) abstract (or sometimes a lengthier proposal) submitted by the applicant. The session and speakers are introduced by a *chairperson*, who also ensures timekeeping and moderates the discussion. Each presenter speaks for up to 15 minutes (depending on the number of papers and length of the session), with time for questions at the end of the presentation. *Symposia* are themed sessions of three to four explicitly linked papers, with a chair and discussant. The *discussant* is an invited speaker who receives and reads symposium papers in advance of the conference. Their role is to synthesise the collection of papers, identify key points, pose questions and offer balanced feedback to the speakers. *Roundtables* provide opportunities for informal discussion of work by groups of colleagues. Delegates are issued with a seating plan and visit the signposted tables of colleagues whose work they are interested in hearing more about. Roundtable discussions offer informal opportunities to ask questions in a less structured environment.

Example of abstracts submitted for a professional conference

'Evaluation of distributive leadership' by Fiona Malcolm, Lossiemouth High School
   This presentation outlines the evaluation of one aspect of the transformational plan: leadership. The evaluation strategy is adapted from the Hay Group's questionnaire for educators. It asks the question, 'What impact has distributive leadership had in terms of your own experience within Lossiemouth High School'? The questionnaire is separated into four sections: departmental level, whole school, pupils at departmental level and pupils at whole school level. The session reports preliminary analysis of questionnaire results.

'The impact of residential experiences on leadership development' by Neil Blance, Orkney Secondary Sector
   This presentation considers the impact of the Hoy residential course on the development of leadership skills among pupil participants. It considers: (a) how the pupils perceived themselves at the start of the course compared with their perceptions on course completion; (b) the incidental effects of course participation on the pupils' return to their related schools; and (c) how pupils felt their leadership skills had been put to use in the schools and the impact of training on the pupils. The presentation draws on analysis of pupils' journals, questionnaires and focus groups.

Checklist for conference paper presentations

☑ Length of time allotted for the presentation (Run through timings completed)?
☑ Likely number of attendees at the session?

(Continued)

(Continued)

☑ Copies of handouts and any other materials (copies of slides or written report)?

☑ Access to data projector and computer (booked in advance)?

☑ Is a microphone provided for the speaker (book in advance, if needed)?

☑ Eight slide presentation prepared; spelling and grammar checked.

☑ Do not overload slides with text – restrict to key points only.

☑ Remove distracting slide transitions and animation schemes.

☑ Title slide with contact details of contributors.

☑ Overview slide – structure of the presentation and the questions to be addressed.

☑ Context slide – research site, rationale and professional literature.

☑ Methodology slide – research design, tools of enquiry and approach to data analysis.

☑ Data sets and analysis, linked to questions and methods.

☑ Findings and conclusions slide.

☑ Final slide – future implications and areas for further work.

☑ Email the slideshow to the conference organiser, if required?

☑ Back up copies of the presentation (saved on a memory stick)?

☑ Slideshow compatible with PC software available at the conference (for example, Mac format)?

☑ Access needed to a DVD player or speakers (book in advance)?

☑ Web access needed (check and test WIFI/Internet availability in the meeting rooms in advance; test any hyperlinks embedded in the slide show)?

☑ Contingency plan in event of technological problems (for example, screen shots on slides, copies of web material on DVD, OHP transparencies, data slides on handouts)?

☑ Networking – business cards to hand?

Source: Adapted from Craig, 2009: 212

Poster presentations are a useful way to introduce ideas and evaluations of interventions quickly in a less formal setting. Conferences can offer *structured poster presentations* in scheduled sessions or display posters in an exhibition area at the venue throughout the conference. In structured sessions, several poster presentations are each accompanied by a 5-minute oral presentation. In conference *poster displays* each exhibitor is allocated a display area. Presenters display their posters at the start of the event and are available to answer questions posed by visitors at a set time during the day. Posters can be displayed on free-standing boards or mounted on table-top boards (see Figure 14.3). Exhibited posters are larger than those expected in

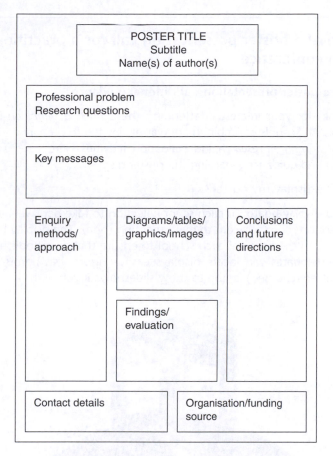

Figure 14.2 *Sample poster presentation layout*

structured poster presentations, as all the information to be communicated is presented in visual form.

Posters need to be easily read from a distance of 1.5 metres. Select an appropriate type size (for example, 18 or 20 pt) and avoid overloading the poster with text. Twenty per cent text, 40 per cent graphics/tables, 40 per cent empty space is a useful general guide. Place the title at the top and your contact details at the bottom (Figure 14.2). PowerPoint can be used to generate a poster and then enlarged. Alternatively poster displays can comprise separate A4 sheets for each section, with a title sheet. If a budget is available, professional reprographic services can be used to enlarge and laminate larger posters. Designs can be saved to a data stick or emailed to a company providing colour poster printing services. Poster displays can be a maximum of 1 metre wide by 1.5 metres long. The display can be supported by leaflets to be distributed to the audience at the event.

Example of a poster presentation call for a practitioner research conference

Conference poster presentations: additional guidance

Many thanks for your interest in attending the *Schools of Ambition* Evaluation Conference. All Schools of Ambition are warmly invited to prepare and display a poster illustrating their research and evaluation activities. Here is some additional information and guidance regarding the poster display.

Where will I display my poster?

A table and display board for each school electing to take part will be available in the reception room adjacent to main meeting room. The display boards will be headed with the name of each school to ensure that all schools have equal space and delegates can locate displays easily (Figure 14.3). You can bring along a (battery-charged) laptop to show slideshows if you wish.

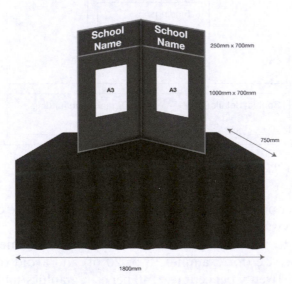

Figure 14.3 Conference poster presentation and display board

What size should the poster be?

Each display board has space for two A3 posters. This size of poster can be produced in school without the need to incur the costs of professional reprographic services.

What should the poster include?

Your poster should communicate the main research and evaluation activities initiated through *School of Ambition*. It may be useful to consider the following:

- What changes have you initiated through Schools of Ambition? *Objectives*
- Why were these changes important for your school and your pupils? *Rationale and context*
- What *methods* have you used to collect evidence on the impact of these changes?
- What does this information tell you about the impact of your interventions? *Results*
- What are you now doing differently? *Implications*
- What's next? *Subsequent cycles of enquiry*

Think about using a combination of bullet points, supporting statements, presentation of some results, photographs etc. You may wish to make available additional leaflets/briefing sheets for delegates and have examples of any questionnaires, focus group or interview guides you want to share.

How long should I display my poster?

It is a good idea to find your board and put up your poster when you arrive between 9 a.m. and 9.30 a.m. The posters should remain on display throughout the day and be removed at 3.30 p.m. There is dedicated time within the conference for delegates to visit the displays and one presenter from each school should be available to answer questions from delegates about the activities in their school at this time.

Prompts for poster presentations

- ☑ Who will be viewing the posters? What do you need to communicate to this audience?
- ☑ What are the size restrictions for the poster?
- ☑ What advice is offered on layout from the event organisers?
- ☑ What technical and reprographic support do I need to produce a professional looking poster? What do I need to do to access this support?
- ☑ Where can you laminate the poster (in advance) to protect it from damage?
- ☑ What is the total cost of producing the poster and how will this be funded?
- ☑ Where will the poster be displayed? (exhibition space at the venue)
- ☑ How will my poster stand out in the exhibition? Use of colour and attractive graphics.
- ☑ What time does the poster need to be displayed and removed (exhibition area)?
- ☑ What time and duration is the supporting oral presentation (in structured sessions)?
- ☑ When do the presenters need to be present in the exhibition area?
- ☑ How will the poster be attached securely to the display board (velcro tabs, drawing pins)?

(Continued)

(Continued)

☑ Will a table be available in the exhibition area (for an additional laptop slideshow)?
☑ Are copies of handouts prepared? How many are needed? Where will these be displayed when the presenter is not present (plastic wallet attached to the display board, table stand)?
☑ How will you transport the poster (poster tube, portable stand for banners)?
☑ Where can you display the poster after the conference?

Writing research reports: getting started – invention, voice and writing styles

Teacher researchers are often daunted by the prospect of writing formal research reports. Initial enthusiasm sustained during planning, data gathering and analysis activities, can wane if the 'reporting stage' is regarded as a final and unwelcome hurdle. This is especially true if reporting is divorced from the initial motivation to conduct the enquiry. This is most likely where the purpose of the task is seen as 'writing for grades'. We would recommend that planning for dissemination is built into the research plan from the outset as a professional obligation. University ethics committees often now require applicants to state how the findings of the proposed research will be shared with the participants and the wider education community. It is advisable to plan a dissemination strategy and consider how the impact of the enquiry can be optimised at an early stage. Opportunities for professional dialogue should arise at several points in the life cycle of an enquiry and are an important feature of the design of collaborative action research.

In the following section, we look at common components of the teacher research report and suggest strategies to help you get started and sustain your writing. Richards and Miller (2005: 65) identify five stages in the writing process from planning an outline to submission of a polished piece (Figure 14.4). It should be noted, however, that this is a recursive rather than a neat linear process. The stages are not presented as sequential steps but stages that are revisited as the manuscript is progressively refined and improved over time. *Generative writing* (invention), such as 'free writing', can be useful at several stages in the development process. A few minutes' concentrated free writing can re-energise the writing process, helping to clarify ideas and overcome writer's block. Similarly, drafting and revising can take place simultaneously. Writers can pause and revisit earlier stages as necessary in the development of a manuscript, moving back and forth or combining writing activities.

Invention strategies include:

- free writing – generation and recording of ideas on paper
- concept maps, spider diagrams and flow charts – focus on hierarchy and sequence

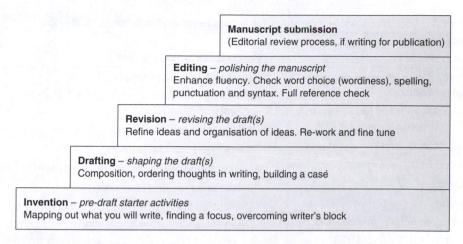

Figure 14.4 Stages in the writing process (adapted from Richardson and Miller, 2005)

- thought shower – listing all relevant ideas
- developing an index card system for ideas – cataloguing information and possibilities
- visual representations – sketch journals and drawings
- talking to others and recording ideas with a voice recorder
- creating a visual display – using Post-it notes to create a moveable ideas map
- developing a formal outline structure (see Richards and Miller, 2005: 70–99).

Drafting and revising requires considerable persistence. It is important to *write regularly* and set manageable small-scale targets to sustain momentum and maintain progress in the face of the many other demands on busy teachers' time. Teacher researchers find it useful to block out writing time and make colleagues aware of these commitments. It is important to be realistic about the time that can be protected for writing at particular pressure points in the school year, for example, within the pupil assessment calendar or school inspection cycle. Building 'writing up' into project plans and workload agreements, where possible, will enhance the quality of the final report, sustain writing at pressure points and raise awareness of the importance of this activity. Research engagement is a legitimate form of professional development and sharing research outcomes can make a valuable contribution to collegial learning.

Developing a *writing style* through which they can find their 'voice' is often a struggle for emerging researchers. Traditional academic discourse requires an objective, academic voice (see Table 14.1 below), which can appear contrived and inauthentic to practitioners (Elbow, 1998). This is particularly frustrating in the case of practitioner research, where a strong 'insider' affiliation and personal stance are key motivators to action. In all writing, and especially teacher research, it is important to connect the personal and the professional, while adopting a systematic and rigorous approach to the enquiry.

Table 14.1   Comparison of writing styles for an academic and practitioner audience

Academic audience – traditional research	Practitioner audience
Use of third-person pronouns, 'the researcher/author'	Use of first-person pronouns, 'I'
Passive voice – 'It has long been thought that ... ' 'It could be argued that ... '	Active voice – 'I concur with research that suggests ... '
Formal, objective researcher stance	First-person narratives of educators
Distanced from feelings and experiences	Stories, 'personal' or 'authentic' voice
Detached	Addresses personally meaningful questions
Past tense	Interpretation of personal experience
Authoritative voice, 'professional'	Disclosure, identifiable voice, 'expressive'
'Discoursal self' (Ivanic, 1998)	Strong focus on future implications and impact

Source: adapted from Lassonde and Israel, 2008; Pearson-Casanave and Vanrick, 2003; Richards and Miller, 2005

> Just as we cannot separate our personal selves from our teaching practices, we should not seek to separate our personal selves from our teaching stories. As teachers, we care too deeply about our students, our profession and our teaching lives to hide or deny ourselves a voice. (Lassonde and Israel, 2008, 137)

When writing practitioner research reports, it is advisable to seek clarification on expectations from course supervisors or project mentors at an early stage. Award-bearing courses may adhere to academic 'codes' that need be followed for assessment purposes. Information on submission arrangements can be found in course handbooks and assessment guides and will be a feature of dissertation preparation workshops and tutorials on taught programmes. Increasingly there is some acknowledgement of alternative practices in professional education programmes, for example, the use of e-portfolios and storying in the construction of a 'patchwork text' of different representations of professional practice (Winter et al., 1999). Where there is some flexibility, teachers are more able to negotiate a style of presentation that considers their professional identity, biography and school context – 'who you are' and 'where you are' (Fulwiler, 2002) – and which best meets the needs of the intended audience. Irrespective of the circumstances in which the project is initiated and the requirements of assessment schemes, *writing well is empowering*. Communicating clearly and adapting one's style to meet the needs of different audiences is an important and positive development for researchers and educators.

To support your writing, remember to turn on the *grammar check*, as well as the spelling check, on your word-processor and consider investing in a *style manual*. Style guides that may be helpful include *The Oxford Style Manual* or *New Hart's Rules*. Ensure accurate citation by using a reference guide such as *The Concise Rules of APA Style* or *Cite Them Right: The Essential Referencing Guide*. Consider using an electronic *reference management* system such as

EndNote or Reference Manager. Specialist software, such as StyleWriter, is available to support writers. Where possible, draw on the support of a 'writing buddy', writing group or writing mentor to review drafts and support the revision and editing processes.

Components of the practitioner research report

This section presents three examples of reporting guidelines drawn from sponsored teacher research programmes. The suggested structures are designed to report the activities of networked learning communities, lone teacher scholars and school-based teacher research teams.

Research report example 1: networked learning communities

Guidance on writing research and enquiry summaries

NETWORKED LEARNING COMMUNITIES, National College (formerly National College for School Leadership), 2006

1 **Title**
Include key words to tune the reader into the focus of your enquiry.

2 **Identification**
Include yourself, keywords, levels of learning, intended audience.

3 **Aim(s) of the research**
What problems or issues did the study tackle? What actual questions were researched?

4 **Dimensions of the study**
Concise information about the who, what, where and when aspects.

5 **Summary of main findings**
What were the headline findings? Is there any evidence of positive impact on teachers and pupils?

6 **Background and context**
Why and how did the project start? How does it build on existing knowledge? Include relevant details about the school context and the pupils and teachers involved.

7 **The intervention: processes and strategies**
What actually happened in the school or classroom? Examples of strategies and how they were implemented are useful. Mention pitfalls and how they were overcome as well as successes.

8 **The detailed findings**
Explain each of the front page findings in more depth. What evidence is there to support these findings? Use pupil or teacher quotes or examples of work to bring the summary 'alive'.

(Continued)

(Continued)

9 Research or enquiry methods
What sort of data were collected? How were they collected and analysed? Can you include a sample data collection tool in an appendix, for example, a questionnaire?

10 Conclusions
What are your thoughts about the study? How have the findings affected your school or the way you do things now? Have they raised any further questions for investigation?

11 Further reading
How was your work linked with what is already known about the issues you were researching? What literature could you recommend to teachers who want to find out more?

12 Author and contact details
Who could teachers contact if they want to find out more about your work?

Source: 'Writing research and enquiry summaries' (National College for School Leadership). Available online: http://www.nationalcollege.org.uk/docinfo?id=133211&filename=nlc-writing-research-and-enquiry-summaries.pdf.

Research report example 2: Best Practice Research Scholarships

Structure of the Best Practice Research Scholarship reports (DfES, 2000)

INDIVIDUAL AWARD HOLDERS

1 What were your original aims?
2 In what ways did you refine your aims?
3 Which research processes did you find helpful?
4 Which research processes did your pupils find helpful?
5 What were the learning points you gained from undertaking the research and what were your findings?
6 What evidence relates to this learning and your findings?
7 What are the questions for your future practice?
8 What are the questions for your school?
9 What are the questions for further research?
10 How did you disseminate your findings with others, for example, within your school, other schools, the LEA, wider?

Suggested length: 2,000 words for a level one report.

Research report example 3: Schools of Ambition

'Telling the Story' through Schools of Ambition (2006–10)

WHOLE SCHOOL TRANSFORMATION

Introduction

Outline of the school's Transformational Plan, contextualised in terms of the school's challenges.
Activities/interventions undertaken by the school during the three-year transformational period.

Reflection on interventions

How far have you come in achieving your vision?
What worked well and why?
What didn't work?
What changes were made from the original plan?
What still needs to be done?
What would you change if you were starting again, and what advice would you give to other schools?
What changes do you expect to see in the future?
What were the key learning points for the school?
Reflection on the teacher researchers' 'journeys'

Evidence of impacts and outcomes

What research questions were addressed and how do they relate to the goals in the transformational plan?
What methods were employed and why?
How was the research undertaken?
What evidence was gathered and analysed?
Were there aspects of the research that were not completed or were not successful?
What were the impacts on teachers, pupils and wider community? Presentation of evidence.

Sustaining the change

What are you doing to sustain the changes?
What will influence the sustainability of the changes?
What will you continue to do differently?
How will you know if the vision has been achieved?
Has the process promoted teachers'/others' capacity to evaluate?

External support

Input from the local authority.
Input from the university research team.
Input from the senior advisers.
Input from other sources (including partner organisations).

Writing for publication: where is teacher research published?

Opportunities for dissemination exist beyond the formal research report submitted to a funder, supporter or assessor. Journals that consider research by teachers include:

- the international journal of the Collaborative Action Research Network (CARN),[5] *Educational Action Research* (see for example Burkett, 2008; Moloney, 2009; Sproston, 2008)
- *Teacher Development*, which welcomes 'contributions from professional teachers, and those who support them, in every sector of education and training'
- *Curriculum and Instruction* a peer-reviewed, open access online journal[6] published bi-annually by East Carolina University, and contains a Practitioners' Platform section in every issue
- *Networks*,[7] an online journal for teacher research, edited by Catherine Compton-Lilly and hosted by the University of Wisconsin-Madison libraries
- *Teacher Leadership*[8] produced by the University of Cambridge, Faculty of Education, carries shorter articles (3,000–4,000 words) reporting teacher research assessed for award-bearing purposes
- the National Foundation for Educational Research extends an open call for short papers (2,000 words) in its bi-annual journal, *Practical Research for Education*.[9]

Manuscript preparation

One of the disincentives for teachers who are thinking about writing for publication is the challenge of negotiating the review process. In this section we aim to demystify the processes involved in manuscript preparation and publication. The first step in writing for publication is to identify a clear focus for a manuscript among the choices offered by the typical teacher research project. Throughout this guide to practitioner research in education we have outlined the multiple methods employed in teacher research and the importance of reflecting the complexity of education settings. A research project – or series of linked projects or cycles of enquiry – may generate a number of possible foci. Rather than attempt to report all the activity and outcomes of a completed school-based project, it may be sensible to identify the strongest area or a limited number of foci that warrant in-depth examination in different (but related) articles.

The next stage is to select an appropriate journal for submission. It is useful to conduct a literature search to see which professional journals contain articles that are relevant to your manuscript and check the references of retrieved articles for further possible sources. Check that your proposed article is a close match with the themes and scope of the journal, and is consistent with the type of contributions sought. Draw up a shortlist of possible journals. Review previous articles and establish who publishes in this journal and its readership.

Selecting a journal: different types of journal

Professional journals have a broad target audience of school-based educators, teacher educators in universities and undergraduate and graduate students. Their major focus is on improving practice and raising critical issues of theory and research as connected to practice. Instead of publishing reports of research, they publish reflections on research where the researcher discusses the findings in relation to practice in classrooms.

Research journals publish reports of original and rigorously conducted studies that advance the knowledge of a particular field and so are primarily read by other researchers. Research journals publish fewer, longer manuscripts and have a rigorous review process that makes acceptance for publication more difficult.

Many teacher researchers submit to professional journals because the voice, format and focus are accessible to classroom teachers – these journals let them speak to the audience they most want to inform.

Source: Lassonde and Israel, 2008: 151

Sample journal article guidelines

Focus and scope of the journal. This journal offers a place for sharing reports of action research, in which teachers at all levels, kindergarten to postgraduate, are reflecting on classroom practice through research ventures. It also provides space for discussion of other ways in which educational practitioners, alone or in collaboration, use enquiry as a tool to learn more about their work with the hope eventually of improving its effectiveness. We do not envisage a journal in which the contributions will necessarily be reports on studies that have already been completed; there is much to be said for reports of work in progress that can open up areas of discussion and interchange of experiences and ideas that will benefit all involved.
Source: Networks

Having made your selection, follow the author guidelines carefully and take time to check that your manuscript satisfies the stylistic and bibliographic requirements for publication. Researching previous issues will help

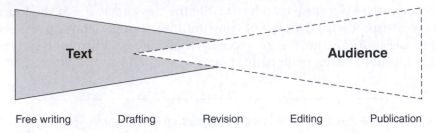

Free writing   Drafting   Revision   Editing   Publication

Figure 14.5   The influence of audience on author's writing processes
(Richards and Miller, 2005: 196)

you adapt to the style of the journal and the intended readership. Make sure you have permission for any examples you wish to include in your article, for example, direct quotations or extracts from students' work (revisit the chapter on *ethics* for a discussion of *fully informed consent* and copyright issues). Remember to consider your intended audience (Figure 14.5).

Editors of scholarly journals act as 'gatekeepers' and will not send out an article for *peer review* if the manuscript does not meet the journal aims or is not presented appropriately. Take particular care to ensure that the conventions of professional or scholarly writing are present and that the appropriate register or 'voice' is used. If the manuscript is consistent with the content and scope of the journal, it is forwarded to between one and three reviewers who hold professional expertise and interest in this area. The time between submission of your manuscript and receipt of an *editorial response* can be lengthy. Expect to wait several weeks for a response from a refereed professional journal and several months for a response from a research journal.

How do I manage the editorial review process?

There can be four possible outcomes to the peer review process, only one of which is an outright rejection.

1   Accept for publication.
2   Accept subject to minor revisions by a specified due date.
3   Major revisions needed. Revise and resubmit for a further round of reviews.
4   Reject, inappropriate for this journal.

Example of a response from a reviewer

Review for the author

Thank you for your submission. I enjoyed reading this paper and offer the following comments for your consideration.

You offer a clearly expressed *research question,* with a supporting rationale for the inquiry. The inquiry is linked to intended improvement outcomes (posed as sub-questions). Some information on the school context might be helpful at an earlier stage in the article.

In offering a *theoretical frame* for your inquiry, I wondered if it might be helpful to connect with the established professional and academic literature on XXX. Would it be appropriate to unpack some of your key concepts at this point before narrowing your focus?

A range of recent research papers is used in a *review of the literature.* The paper appears premised on a commitment to evidence-informed professional action. It may be helpful to indicate the comparability of your own teaching context and those of the studies you review, where possible.

The use of pseudonyms for the students might help the reader build a closer connection with the classroom setting. Some sense of the *timeline* for the inquiry would be helpful. You use a number of *enquiry methods* to gather a range of perspectives and the relative merits (and purpose) of the different approaches might be indicated. A justification is offered for *case selection,* but this could have greater clarity. There is some repetition in the methodology section, which could be removed with careful proofreading and further editing.

This is an interesting study and the reader is left wanting to know further information, such as the frequency of the journal entries, the focus of the observations, any time/task sampling, the focus of the questions formulated for parents. What *methods of analysis* were used in your interrogation of the data? How did you identify and test patterns?

The section on *future implications* identifies some lessons suggested by your analysis and indicates that the study will develop to include a further cycle of inquiry. I hope you find this feedback helpful and wish you every success with your future inquiries.

Preparation checklist for manuscript submission

- ☑ Close match with journal themes and scope of the journal.
- ☑ Journal has recently published an article in a related area.
- ☑ The manuscript has not been previously published or is under consideration by another journal. Submit to only one journal at a time. (Do not waste reviewers' time if you are considering publication elsewhere.)
- ☑ Cover page and author contact details are provided.
- ☑ Title and abstract offer a clear and concise description of the paper.
- ☑ The manuscript is within the recommended wordage.
- ☑ The study reported is appropriately contextualised within the field (other published work and professional knowledge).

(Continued)

(Continued)

☑ The text adheres to the stylistic and bibliographic requirements outlined in the author guidelines.

☑ You have allowed yourself ample time between initial drafting to revisit and refine the original paper through a number of iterations.

☑ Proofread the manuscript carefully. Spell- and grammar-check the manuscript.

☑ Conduct a thorough reference check. Verify all references included in the text.

☑ Recruit volunteer proof readers and 'critical friends'.

☑ Share the polished manuscript with informal mentors and more experienced writers.

☑ Author(s) name are removed from the text (and filename) if the article is being submitted for 'blind' peer review.

☑ Submission procedures are followed carefully. Check whether submission procedures are electronic and whether additional hard copies are needed.

☑ Compose a brief cover letter to the editor which introduces the subject of your article and explains why you think it will be of interest to the readers of your target journal.

Post-review checklist

☑ Interpret the journal editor's decision and reviewers' commentary.

☑ Discuss response with co-authors and experienced writers/mentors. You are not obliged to accept *all* of the revisions suggested by reviewers (and may receive seemingly contradictory suggestions).

☑ Revise the manuscript, as appropriate, if invited to re-submit.

☑ Note the turnaround time for receipt of a revised version.

☑ Compose a follow-up letter which addresses the reviewers' feedback carefully and chronologically. Specify any suggestions you do not agree with and why.

☑ Re-submit to the same journal or alternatively revise for another journal or consider other dissemination opportunities.

Summary

In this chapter, the following key points were raised:

- Teachers are under-represented as producers of knowledge about teaching.
- Writing is part of the enquiry process.
- Dissemination of teacher enquiry helps to bring teachers' voice to deliberation on policy and helps to address the lack of studies that connect strongly with classroom practice.
- Finely grained accounts that address the problems of practice help to overcome the myth of the 'super teacher' and challenge recipe knowledge of 'what works'.
- Dissemination can take the form of oral, print and digital media.

- A wide range of dissemination opportunities is presented in briefings, multimedia e-portfolios, virtual collaboration environments/online communities, Wikis, blogs, posters and presentations at professional and academic conferences, and articles in professional magazines and scholarly journals.
- Plan for dissemination at an early stage in your enquiry.

Further reading

Cochran-Smith, M. and Lytle, S.L. (eds) (2009) *Inquiry as Stance. Practitioner Research for the Next Generation*. New York: Teachers College Press.

Hatch, T., Ahmed, D., Lieberman, A., Faigenbaum, D., Eiler White, M. and Pointer Mace, D.H. (eds) (2005). *Going Public With Our Teaching. An Anthology of Practice*. New York: Teachers College Press.

Murray, R. (2005) *Writing for Academic Journals*. Maidenhead: Open University Press.

Pointer Mace, D.H. (2009) *Teachers' Practice Online. Sharing Wisdom, Opening Doors*. New York, Teachers College Press.

Useful tools and resources

British Educational Research Association (2000) 'Good practice in educational Research Writing'. Available online: http://www.bera.ac.uk/files/guidelines/goodpr1.pdf.

Inside Teaching: a collection of multimedia records of teaching. A project funded by the Carnegie Foundation for the Advancement of Teaching: http://gallery.carnegiefoundation.org/insideteaching/.

Schools of Ambition archive. Look at the 'Telling the Story' portfolios submitted by the 52 Scottish Schools of Ambition (2006–10): http://wayback.archive-it.org/1961/20100805220218/http://www.ltscotland.org.uk/schoolsofambition/about/sharingthelearning/tellingthestory.asp.

Notes

1 http://gallery.carnegiefoundation.org/.
2 http://www.teachingscotland.org.uk/.
3 The design of the project is based on the USA scheme, Teachers for a New Era, which is largely funded by the Carnegie Corporation.
4 http://www.teacherresearch.net/.
5 http://www.did.stu.mmu.ac.uk/carnnew/.
6 http://www.joci.ecu.edu/index.php/JoCI/index.
7 http://journals.library.wisc.edu/index.php/networks/index.
8 http://www.leadershiplearning.org.uk/index.php/tl-home.
9 http://www.pre-online.co.uk/index.asp.

References

American Psychological Association (APA) (2006) *The Concise Rules of APA Style*. Washington, DC: APA.

Anderson, G.L., Herr, K. and Nihlen, A.S. (1994) *Studying Your Own School: An Educator's Guide to Qualitative Practitioner Research*. Thousand Oaks, CA: Corwin Press.

Arksey, H. and Knight, P. (1999) *Interviewing for Social Scientists: An Introductory Resource with Examples*. London: Sage.

Armstrong, M. (1980) *Closely Observed Children*. London: Readers and Writers.

Badley, G. (2009) 'Academic writing as shaping and re-shaping', *Teaching in Higher Education*, 14(2): 209–19.

Bailey, R., Campbell, T., Elliot, D., Pearce, G. and Quarmby, T. (2009) 'Pupils' perspectives of new playground designs: a pilot study', report to funder.

Banks, M. (2001) *Visual Methods in Social Research*. London: Sage.

Banks, M. (2007) *Using Visual Data in Qualitative Research*. London: Sage.

Basch, C.E. (1987) 'Focus group interview: an underutilized research technique for improving theory and practice in health education', *Health Education Quarterly*, 14: 411–48.

Baumfield, V. (2009) 'Practitioner inquiry – evaluating learning and teaching', paper presented at the Professional Practice Lecture Series, University of Glasgow, 6 August.

Baumfield, V.M. and Butterworth, A.M. (2005) *Systematic Review of the Evidence for the Impact of Teaching Thinking Skills on Teachers*. London: EPPI-Centre, Social Science Research Unit, Institute of Education.

Blaxter, L., Hughes, C. and Tight, M. (2001) *How to Research*. 2nd edn. Buckingham: Open University Press.

Bryman, A. (2004) *Social Research Methods*. 2nd edn. New York: Oxford University Press.

Burkett, E. (2008) '"A new way of looking?" Reflections upon one teacher's experience of supporting learners using handheld computers', *Educational Action Research*, 16(4): 481–93.

Campbell, A., McNamara, O. and Gilroy, P. (2004) *Practitioner Research and Professional Development*. London: Sage.

Campbell, E. (2003) *The Ethical Teacher*. Buckingham: Open University Press.

Carnegie Corporation (1986) *A Nation Prepared: Teachers for the 21st Century. The Report of the Task Force on Teaching as a Profession*. Hyattsville, MD: Carnegie Forum on Education and the Economy.

Carr, D. (1999) *Professionalism and Ethics in Teaching*. London: Routledge.

Centre for Teaching Quality (2008) *Measuring What Matters: The Effects of National Board Certification on Advancing 21st Century Teaching and Learning*. Hillsborough, NC: Centre for Teaching Quality. Available online at: http://www.nbpts.org/resources/publications.

Chiseri-Strater, E. and Sunstein, B.S. (2006) *What Works? A Practical Guide for Teacher Research*. Portsmouth, NH: Heinemann.

Cicourel, A.V. (1964) *Method and Measurement in Sociology*. New York: Free Press.

Clancey, W.J. (2001) 'Field science ethnography: methods for systematic observation on an expedition', *Field Methods*, 13(3): 223–43.

Clark, A. and Moss, P. (2005) *Spaces to Play: More Listening to Young Children Using the Mosaic Approach*. London: National Children's Bureau.

Cochran-Smith, M. and Lytle, S.L. (1993) *Inside Out: Teacher Research and Knowledge*. New York: Teachers College Press.

Cochran-Smith, M. and Lytle, S.L. (2001) 'Beyond certainty: taking an inquiry stance on practice', in A. Lieberman and L. Miller (eds), *Teachers Caught in the Action: Professional Development that Matters*. New York: Teachers College Press. pp. 45–60.

Cochran-Smith, M. and Lytle, S.L. (2009) *Inquiry as Stance – Practitioner Research for the Next Generation*. New York: Teachers College Press.

Cohen, L., Manion, L. and Morrison, K. (2000) *Research Methods in Education*. 5th edn. London: Routledge.

Connell, P., McKevitt, C. and Low, N. (2004) 'Investigating ethnic differences in sexual health: focus groups with young people', *Sexually Transmitted Infections* 80: 300–5. Available online, doi:10.1136/sti.2003.005181.

Corti, L. (1993) 'Using diaries in social research', *Social Research Update*, no. 2. Available online at: http://sru.soc.surrey.ac.uk/SRU2.html.

Craig, D.V. (2009) *Action Research Essentials*. San Francisco, CA: Jossey-Bass.

Croll, P. (1986) *Systematic Classroom Observation*. London: Falmer Press

Cross, B., Hall, J., Hall, S., Hulme, M., Lewin, J. and McKinney, S. (2009) 'Pupil participation in Scottish schools: final report', report to funder.

Darling Hammond, L. (2000) 'Teacher quality and student achievement: a review of state policy evidence', *Education Policy Analysis Archives*, 8(1): 13.

Darling-Hammond, L. and Bransford, J. (2005) *Preparing Teachers for a Changing World*. San Francisco, CA: John Wiley.

Day, C. (1999) *Developing Teachers – the Challenges of Lifelong Learning*. London: Routledge/ Falmer.

Delamont, S. (2002) *Fieldwork in Educational Settings*. London: Routledge.

Denscombe, M. (1998) *The Good Research Guide for Small-scale Social Research Projects*. Buckingham: Open University Press.

Department for Education and Employment (DfEE) (2000) *Best Practice Research Scholarships. Guidance Notes for Teacher Applications*. 5 May. Nottingham: DfES Publications.

Department of Education and Skills (DfES) (2004) *Every Child Matters: Change for Children*. London: Department for Education and Skills.

Department of Health (DoH) (2007) *Trust, Assurance and Safety. The Regulation of Health Professionals in the 21st Century*. London: Her Majesty's Stationery Office.

Drever, E. (1995) *Using Semi-Structured Interviews in Small-scale Research: A Teacher's Guide*. Practitioner MiniPaper 15. Edinburgh: SCRE.

Drever, E. (2003) *Using Semi-Structured Interviews in Small-Scale Research: A Teacher's Guide*. 2nd edn. Glasgow: SCRE Centre.

Egan, D. (2009) 'Evaluation of the chartered teacher pilot in Wales. Full report', University of Wales Institute, Cardiff, Centre for Applied Education. Available online at: http://www.gtcw.org.uk/gtcw/images/stories/downloads/Chartered_Teacher_Eval_09/CT_Final_Report.pdf.

Elbow, P. (1998) *Writing Without Teachers*. Oxford: Oxford University Press.

Elliot, D.L., Gillen, A., Giannasi, S., Meeke, M. and Rothwell, N. (2008) *My Photos, My Story: An Account of College Learners' Voices*. Fife: Adam Smith College.

Elliot, J. (1991) *Action Research for Educational Change*. London: Open University Press.

Elliott, H. (1997) 'The use of diaries in sociological research on health experience', *Sociological Research Online*, 2(2). Available online at: http://www.socresonline.org.uk/2/2/7.html.

Festervand, T.A. (1984–85) 'An introduction and application of focus group research to the health care industry', *Health Marketing Quarterly*, 2(2–3): 199–209.

Fink, A. (2009) *Conducting Research Literature Reviews: From the Internet to Paper*. 3rd edn. Thousand Oaks, CA: Sage.

Folch-Lyon, E. and Trost, J.F. (1981) 'Conducting focus group sessions', *Studies in Family Planning*, 12(12): 443–9.

Franke, M.L., Carpenter, T., Fennema, E., Ansell, E. and Behrend, J. (1998) 'Understanding teachers' self-sustaining generative change in the context of professional development', *Teaching and Teaching Education*, 14(1): 67–80.

Fullan, M. (2001) *The New Meaning of Educational Change*. 3rd edn. London: Routledge/ Falmer.

Fulwiler, T. (2002) *College Writing: A Personal Approach to Academic Writing*. Portsmouth, NH: Heinemann.

Furlong, J. and Oancea, A. (2006) 'Assessing quality in applied and practice-based research in education: a framework for discussion. Review of Australian research in education: counterpoints on the quality and impact of educational research', *Australian Educational Researcher*, 6(special issue): 89–104. See also the ESRC short report online at: http://www.esrc.ac.uk/ESRCInfoCentre/Images/assessing_quality_shortreport_tcm6-8232.pdf.

Furlong, J. and Salisbury, J. (2005) 'Best practice research scholarships: an evaluation', *Research Papers in Education*, 20(1): 45–83.

General Teaching Council for England (GTCE) (2009) *Code of Conduct and Practice for Registered Teachers*. Available online at: http://www.gtce.org.uk/teachers/thecode/.

General Teaching Council for Northern Ireland (GTCNI) (2007) *Teaching: The Reflective Profession*. Available online at: http://www.gtcni.org.uk/uploads/docs/GTCNI_Comp_Bmrk%20%20Aug%2007.pdf.

General Teaching Council for Scotland (GTCS) (2002) *Standard for Chartered Teacher*. Edinburgh: GTC Scotland. Available online at: http://www.gtcs.org.uk/Publications/StandardsandRegulations/The_Standard_for_Chartered_Teacher.aspx.

General Teaching Council for Scotland (GTCS) (2006a) *Standard for Initial Teacher Education*. Edinburgh: GTCS. Available online at: http://www.gtcs.org.uk/Publications/StandardsandRegulations/StandardsandRegulations.aspx.

General Teaching Council for Scotland (GTCS) (2006b) *Standard for Full Registration*. Edinburgh: GTCS. Available online at: http://www.gtcs.org.uk/Publications/StandardsandRegulations/StandardsandRegulations.aspx.

Gillborn, D. (1995) *Racism and Antiracism in Real Schools*. Buckingham: Open University Press.

Glaser, B.G. (1978) *Theoretical Sensitivity: Advances in the Methodology of Grounded Theory*. Mill Valley, CA: Sociology Press.

Glaser, B.G. and Strauss, A.L. (1967) *The Discovery of Grounded Theory: Strategies for Qualitative Research*. Chicago, IL: Aldine.

Graziano, K. (2007) 'Photovoice', paper presented at the National Institute for Staff and Organizational Development (NISOD) Conference, Austin Convention Center, Texas, 21 May.

Greenbaum, T.L. (1990) 'Focus group spurt predicted for the '90s', *Marketing News*, 24(1): 21–2.

Griffiths, M. (1998) *Educational Research for Social Justice*. London: Open University Press.

Hannan, A. (2006) 'Observation techniques', Faculty of Education, University of Plymouth. Available online at: http://www.edu.plymouth.ac.uk/resined/observation/obshome.htm.

Hargreaves, A. and Fink, D. (2005) *Sustainable Leadership*. New York: Jossey-Bass.

Harris, A., Day, C., Hopkins, D., Hadfield, M., Hargreaves, A. and Chapman, C. (2003) *Effective Leadership for School Improvement*. London: Routledge/Falmer.

Hart, C. (1998) *Doing a Literature Review: Releasing the Social Science Research Imagination*. London: Sage.

Hatch, T., Ahmed, D., Lieberman, A., Faigenbaum, D., Eiler White, M. and Pointer Mace, D.H. (2005) *Going Public with Our Teaching. An Anthology of Practice*. New York: Teachers College Press.

Hattie, J. (2009) *Visible Learning. A Synthesis of Over 80 Meta-analyses Relating to Achievement*. London: Routledge.

Heaton, J. (2004) *Reworking Qualitative Data*. London: Sage.

Heron, G. and Murray, R. (2004) 'The place of writing in social work', *Journal of Social Work*, 4(2): 199–214.

Hinds, M. (2002) '2002 Carnegie Challenge. Teaching as a clinical profession: A new challenge for education'. Available online at: http://www.carnegie.org/pdf/teachered.pdf.

Holly, M.L. (2009) 'Writing to learn: a process for the curious', in S. Noffke and B. Somekh (eds), *The Sage Handbook of Educational Action Research*. London: Sage. pp. 267–77.

Hopkins, D. (1985) *A Teacher's Guide to Classroom Research*. Buckingham: Open University Press.

Hopkins, D. (2007) *Every School a Great School: Realising the Potential of System Leadership*. Maidenhead: Open University Press.

Hoppe, M.J., Wells, E.A., Morrison, D.M., Gilmore, M.R. and Wilsdon, A. (1995) 'Using focus groups to discuss sensitive topics with children', *Evaluation Review*, 19(1): 102–14.

Hurworth, R. (2003) 'Photo-interviewing for research', Social Research Update, no. 40, University of Surrey.

Ingvarson, L. (2008) 'Identifying and rewarding accomplished teachers: the Australian experience', paper presented at the International Symposium, European Conference for Educational Research, University of Gothenburg, 10–12 September.

Ivanic, R. (1998) *Writing and Identity: The Discoursal Construction of Identity in Academic Writing*. Philadelphia, PA: John Benjamins.

James, M., Black, P., Carmichael, P., Conner, C., Dudley, P., Fox, A., Frost, D., Honour, L., MacBeath, J., McCormick, R., Marshall, B., Pedder, D., Proctor, R., Swaffield, S. and Wiliam, D. (eds) (2006) *Learning How to Learn (Tools for Schools)*. London: Routledge.

Kiecolt, K.J. and Nathan, L.E. (1986) *Secondary Analysis of Survey Data*. Thousand Oaks, CA: Sage.

Kleinhenz, E. and Ingvarson, L. (2004) 'Teacher accountability in Australia: current policies and practices and their relation to the improvement of teaching and learning', *Research Papers in Education*, 19(1): 31–49.

Kruger, R. and Casey, M. (2000) *Focus Groups: A Practical Guide for Applied Research*. 3rd edn. Thousand Oaks, CA: Sage.

Krueger, R.A. (1994) *Focus Groups: A Practical Guide for Applied Research*. 2nd edn. Newbury Park, CA: Sage.

Kvale, S. (1996) *Interviews: An Introduction to Qualitative Research Interviewing*. London: Sage.

Lassonde, C.A. and Israel, S.E. (eds) (2008) *Teachers Taking Action*. Newark, DE: International Reading Association.

Lewis, I. and Munn, P. (1987) *So You Want to Do Research!* Glenrothes: Barr Printers.

Lewis, V., Kellett, M., Robinson, C. and Fraser, S. (2004) *The Reality of Research with Children and Young People*. London: Sage.

Lingard, B., Hayes, D., Mills, M. and Christie, P. (2003) *Leading Learning: Making Hope Practical in Schools*. Buckingham: Open University Press.

Lowden, K. and Powney, J. (1994) *Drugs, Alcohol and Sex Education: A Report on Two Innovative School-Based Programmes*. Research Report No. 59. Edinburgh: SCRE.

Lowden, K. and Powney, J. (1996) *An Evolving Sexual Health Education Programme: From Health Workers to Teachers*. Research Report No. 80. Edinburgh: SCRE.

Lowden, K. and Powney, J. (2000) *Drug Education in Scottish Schools*. Research Report 95. Edinburgh: SCRE.

MacBeath, J. (1999) *Schools Must Speak for Themselves*. London: Routledge.

MacBeath, J., Gronn, P., Opfer, V.D., Lowden, K., Forde, C., Cowie, M. and O'Brien, J. (2009) *The Recruitment and Retention of Headteachers in Scotland*. Edinburgh: Scottish Government.

MacLure, M. (1996) 'Telling transitions: boundary work in narratives of becoming an action researcher', *British Educational Research Journal*, 22(3): 273–86.

Mahony, P. (2009) 'Should "ought" be taught?', *Teaching and Teacher Education*, 25(7): 983–9.

Maimon, G. (2009) 'Practitioner inquiry as mediated emotion', in M. Cochran-Smith and S.L. Lytle (eds), *Inquiry as Stance. Practitioner Research for the Next Generation*. New York: Teachers College Press. pp. 213–28.

Mariampolski, H. (1989) 'Focus groups on sensitive topics: how to get subjects to open up and feel good about telling the truth', *Applied Marketing Research*, 29(1): 6–11.

Mason, J. (2002) *Researching Your Own Practice. The Discipline of Noticing*. London: Routledge.

McDonald, W.J. and Topper, G.E. (1989) 'Focus-group research with children: a structural approach', *Applied Marketing Research*, 28(2): 3–11.

McKinsey & Co. (2007) 'How the world's best-performing school systems come out on top'. Available online at: http://www.mckinsey.com/App_Media/Reports/SSO/Worlds_School_Systems_Final.pdf.

McLaughlin, C., Black-Hawkins, K. and McIntyre, D. (2004) *Researching Teachers Researching Schools, Researching Networks: A Review of the Literature*. Cambridge: University of Cambridge/NCSL.

McLaughlin, C., Black-Hawkins, K., Brindley, S., McIntyre, D. and Taber, K.S. (2006) *Researching Schools: Stories from a Schools–University Partnership for Educational Research*. London: Routledge.

McNally, J. (2006) 'From informal learning to identity formation: a conceptual journey in early teacher development', *Scottish Educational Review*, 37: 79–89.

Menter, I., McMahon, M., Forde, C., Hall, J., McPhee, A., Patrick, F. and Devlin, A.M. (2006) *Teacher Working Time Research*. Edinburgh: Scottish Executive.

Meyers, E. and Rust, F. (eds) (2003) *Taking Action with Teacher Research*. Portsmouth, NH: Heinemann.

Mitchell, C., O'Reilly-Scanlon, K. and Weber, S. (2005) *Just Who Do We Think We Are? Methodologies for Autobiography and Self-Study in Teaching*. London: Routledge.

Moloney, J. (2009) 'Engaging in action research: a personal and professional journey towards an inquiry into teacher morale in a senior secondary college', *Educational Action Research*, 17(2): 181–95.

Moore, G., Croxford, B., Adams, M., Refaee, M., Cox, T. and Sharples, S. (2008) 'The photo-survey research method: capturing life in the city', *Visual Studies*, 23(1): 50–62.

Munn, P. and Drever, E. (2004) *Using Questionnaires in Small-Scale Research*. Glasgow: SCRE Centre, University of Glasgow.

National Board for Professional Teaching Standards (NBPTS) (2002) *What Teachers Should Know and Be Able to Do*. Arlington, VA: NBPTS. Available online at: http://www.nbpts.org/UserFiles/File/what_teachers.pdf.

Newkirk, T. (1992) 'Silences in our teaching stories: what do we leave out and why?', in T. Newkirk (ed.), *Workshop Four: By and For teachers. The Teacher as Researcher*. Portsmouth, NH: Heinemann. pp. 21–30.

Oliver, P. (2008) *The Student's Guide to Research Ethics*. 2nd edn. Buckingham: Open University Press.

Palomba, C.A. and Banta, T.W. (1999) *Assessment Essentials: Planning, Implementing and Improving Assessment in Higher Education*. San Francisco, CA: Jossey-Bass.

Patrick, J. (1973) *A Glasgow Gang Observed*. London: Methuen.

Patton, M.Q. (1990) *Qualitative Evaluation Methods*. 2nd edn. Newbury Park, CA: Sage.

Pears, R. and Shields, G. (2008) *Cite Them Right: The Essential Referencing Guide*. Durham: Pear Tree Books.

Pearson Casanave, C. and Vandrick, S. (eds) (2003) *Writing for Scholarly Publication. Behind the Scenes in Language Education*. Mahwah, NJ: Lawrence Erlbaum Associates.

Pointer Mace, D.H. (2009) *Teachers' Practice Online. Sharing Wisdom, Opening Doors*. New York: Teachers College Press.

Pollard, A. (1984) *The Social World of the Primary School*. London: Holt, Rinehart and Winston.

Pollard, A. and Tann, S. (1993) *Reflective Teaching in the Primary School*. London: Cassell.

Prosser, J. (ed.) (1998) *Image-based Research: A Sourcebook for Qualitative Researchers*. London: RoutledgeFalmer.

Prosser, J. and Loxley, A. (2007) 'Enhancing the contribution of visual methods to inclusive education', *Journal of Research in Special Educational Needs*, 7(1): 55–68.

Pryce, K. (1979) *Endless Pressure*. Harmondsworth: Penguin.

Punch, (1998) *Implementing and Improving Assessment in Higher Education*. San Francisco, CA: Jossey-Bass.

Rabiee, F. (2004) *Proceedings of the Nutrition Society*, 63: 655–60. Available online, doi: 10.1079/PNS2004399.

Reeves, J. and Fox, A. (eds) (2008) *Practice-Based Learning. Developing Excellence in Teaching*. Edinburgh: Dunedin.

Reeves, J., McMahon, M., Hulme, M., McKie, F., McQueen, I., McSeveney, A. and Redford, M. (2010) 'Investigating the impact of accomplished teaching on pupils' learning', report submitted to the General Teaching Council for Scotland and Scottish Government.

Research to Support Schools of Ambition Annual Report (2008) Report submitted to the Scottish Government, 17 October. Available online at: http://www.scotland.gov.uk/Publications/2008/10/17105044/19.

Richards, J.C. and Miller, S.K. (2005) *Doing Academic Writing in Education. Connecting the Personal and the Professional*. New York: Lawrence Erlbaum.

Rickinson, M., Clark, A., McLeod, S., Poulton, P. and Sargent, J. (2004) 'What on earth has research got to do with me?', *Teacher Development*, 8(2): 201–20.

Ritchie, J. and Spencer, L. (1994) 'Qualitative data analysis for applied policy research', in A. Bryman and R.G. Burgess (eds), *Analysing Qualitative Data*. London: Routledge. pp. 173–94.

Ritter, R. (2003) *The Oxford Style Manual*. Oxford: Oxford University Press.

Ritter, R. (2005) *New Hart's Rules*. Oxford: Oxford University Press.

Robbins, S., Seaman, G., Blake Yancey, K. and Yow, D. (eds) (2006) *Teachers' Writing Groups: Collaborative Inquiry and Reflection for Professional Growth*. Kennesaw, GA: Kennesaw State University Press.

Robert-Holmes, G. (2005) *Doing Your Early Years Research Project: A Step-By-Step Guide*. London: Sage.

Sachs, J. (2003) *The Activist Teaching Profession*. Buckingham: Open University Press.

Salkind, N. (2008) *Statistics for People Who (Think They) Hate Statistics*. Los Angeles, CA: Sage.

Saunders, L. (2007) *Supporting Teachers' Engagement in and with Research*. London: TLRP. Available online at: http://www.bera.ac.uk/supporting-teachers-engagement-in-and-with-research/.

Scottish Education Research Association (SERA) (2005) 'Ethical guidelines for educational research'. Available online at: http://www.sera.ac.uk/docs/00current/SERA%20Ethical%20GuidelinesWeb.PDF.

Scottish Government (2009) *Schools of Ambition Leading Change*. Available online at: http://www.scotland.gov.uk/Publications/2009/04/30095118/0.

Scottish Government (2010) *Leading Change Two. Learning from Schools of Ambition*. Available online at: http://www.scotland.gov.uk/Resource/Doc/311542/0098307.pdf.

Seidel, J. (1998) *Qualitative Data Analysis. The Ethnograph v5 Manual*. Appendix E. Available online at: http://www.qualisresearch.com/.

Shulman, L. (1993) 'Teaching as community property', *Change* (November/December): 6–7.

Shulman, L. (2005) 'Foreword', in T. Hatch, *Into the Classroom: Developing the Scholarship of Teaching and Learning*. San Francisco, CA: Jossey-Bass.

Sikes, P. and Potts, A. (eds) (2008) *Researching Education from the Inside: Investigations from Within*. London: Routledge.

Simpson, M. and Tuson, J. (1995) 'Using observations in small-scale research', Scottish Council for Research in Education, University of Glasgow.

Smiles, T.L. and Short, K.G. (2006) 'Transforming teacher voice through writing for publication', *Teacher Education Quarterly*, 33(3): 133–47.

Smith, C.W., Blake, A., Curwen, K., Dodds, D., Easton, L., McNally, J., Swierczek, P. and Walker, L. (2009) 'Teachers as researchers in a major research project: experience of input and output', *Teaching and Teacher Education*, 25(7): 959–65.

Smith, E. (2008) *Using Secondary Data in Educational and Social Research*. Maidenhead: Open University Press.

Sproston, C. (2008) 'When students negotiate: an action research case study of a Year 8 English class in a secondary college in Victoria, Australia', *Educational Action Research*, 16(2): 187–208.

Stenhouse, L. (1975) *An Introduction to Curriculum Research and Development*. Oxford: Heinemann.

Stenhouse, L. (1985) *Research as a Basis for Teaching: Readings from the Work of Lawrence Stenhouse*. J. Rudduck and D. Hopkins (eds). London: Heinemann.

Stewart, D.W. and Shamdasani, P.N. (1990) *Focus Groups: Theory and Practice.* Newbury Park, CA: Sage.

Stronach, I., Corbin, B., McNamara, O., Stark, S. and Warne, T. (2002) 'Towards an uncertain politics of professionalism: teacher and nurse identities in flux', *Journal of Education Policy*, 17(1): 109–38.

Teacher Solutions National Board Certification Team (2008) *Measuring What Matters: The Effects of National Board Certification on Advancing 21st Century Teaching and Learning*. Chapel Hill, NC: Center for Teaching Quality.

Thomson, P. (ed.) (2008) *Doing Visual Research with Children and Young People*. London: Routledge.

Thomson, P. and Kamler, B. (2010) 'It's been said before and we'll say it again – research *is* writing', in P. Thomson and M. Walker (eds), *The Routledge Doctoral Student's Companion*. London: Routledge.

Tinkler, P. (2008) 'A fragmented picture: reflections on the photographic practices of young people', *Visual Studies*, 23(3): 255–66.

Training and Development Agency (TDA) (2007) *Professional Standards for Teachers*. London: TDA.

Trochim, M.K. (2006) *Research Methods Knowledge Base*. 3rd edn. Available online at: http://www.socialresearchmethods.net/kb/.

Troyna, B. and Griffiths, M. (1995) *Anti-racism, Culture and Social Justice*, Stoke-on-Trent: Trentham Books.

University of Glasgow (2009) *Research to Support Schools of Ambition Annual Report 2009*. Report submitted to the Scottish Government. 5 November. Available online at: http://www.scotland.gov.uk/Publications/2009/11/ 05160217/18.

Wallace, M. (2008) 'Towards effective management of a reformed teaching profession', in D. Johnson and R. Maclean (eds), *Teaching: Professionalization, Development and Leadership*. Dordrecht: Springer. pp. 181–98.

Wengraf, T. (2001) *Qualitative Research Interviewing: Biographic Narrative and Semi-structured Methods*. London: Sage.

Winter, R., Buck, A. and Sobiechowska, P. (1999) *Professional Experience and Investigative Imagination. The Art of Reflective Writing*. London: Routledge.

Woods, P. (1986) *Inside Schools. Ethnography in Schools*. London: Routledge.

Worden, J.K., Flynn, B.S., Geller, F.M., Chen, M., Shelton, L.G., Secker-Walker, R.H., Solomon, D.S., Solomon, L.J., Couchey, S. and Costanza, M.C. (1988) 'Development of a smoking prevention mass media program using diagnostic and formative research', *Preventive Medicine*, 17: 531–58.

Yin, R. (2003) *Case Study Research: Design and Methods*. 3rd edn. London and New York: Sage.

Zeni, J. (ed.) (2001) *Ethical Issues in Practitioner Research*. New York: Teachers College Press.

Index

Added to a page number 'f' denotes a figure and 't' denotes a table.